A Moral Creed for All Christians

Daniel C. Maguire

A Moral Creed
for All Christians

Fortress Press

Minneapolis

A MORAL CREED FOR ALL CHRISTIANS

Book design: Becky Lowe

Scripture quotations, unless otherwise noted, are from *The New English Bible,*
copyright © 1961, 1970 by the Delegates of the Oxford University Press and the
Syndics of the Cambridge University Press. Reprinted by permission.

Scripture quotations marked RSV are from the *Revised Standard Version of the Bible,*
copyright 1989 Division of Christian Education of the National Council of the
Churches of Christ in the United States of America. Used by permission.

Library of Congress Cataloging-in-Publication Data
Maguire, Daniel C.
A moral creed for all Christians / Daniel C. Maguire.
 p. cm.
ISBN 0-8006-3761-5 (alk. paper)
 1. Christian ethics—United States. 2. Christianity and politics—United States.
3. Christianity and culture—United States. I. Title.
BJ1275.M35 2005
241—dc22
 2005015201
Manufactured in the U.S.A.
09   08   07   06   05   1   2   3   4   5   6   7   8   9   1 0

CONTENTS

PREFACE

G. K. Chesterton exaggerated when he said that Christianity had not failed—that it had not even been tried. In fact, at times in history it has been tried and has led societies into new and enlivening moral vistas. This is the way with all major religions. Each of them is in its way a classic in the art of cherishing. At times their moral force is felt and history turns a moral corner. At times they fall into decadence and are even used as a cover for mean-spirited iniquity.

At this moment, confusing signals are coming forth from Christianity. "Christian moral values" are paraded in the political arena in ways that are often hard to square with the moral sensitivities of the early Jesus movement. The rich theories of justice and peace that were the hallmarks of the Christian breakthrough are only rarely visible and influential. The championing of the poor that was the test of Christian authenticity is not much in evidence. The poor can rightly wonder what it means to say that the work of Jesus and his followers is "good news to the poor" (Luke 4:18). The 1.3 billion people in "absolute poverty" (an all too abstract term for slow starvation) do not see that their plight is the prime passion of the world's Christians. Military budgets soar and poverty abounds and hunger and thirst go unrelieved. Most Christians stand passively by.

"There shall be no poor among you"(Deut. 15:4) was the prime biblical mandate, but it seems that the elimination of poverty does not rank high as a "moral value."

Easily might Jesus look at us and say: "I do not know you."

Early Christianity was a lobby for the poor and for peace. Ancient Caesars knew this and lashed out against them. Modern Caesars are all too able to co-opt the Christians, and other religious people too.

This book is an examination of Christian conscience. It builds on my *The Moral Core of Judaism and Christianity* (Fortress Press, 1993), incorporating some portions of that earlier work into this new and larger framework. It is an effort to retrieve the renewable moral energies of this great religion and apply them to a world in terrible pain. And it is an earnest attempt to discover and make our own "the mind of Christ" (1 Cor. 2:16), the goal of all Christian theology, preaching, and religious education.

The plan of the book is to draw out of the biblical traditions the essential lineaments of the Christian moral revolution. The reign of God is the *leitmotiv* of the Bible and it is a foundation-shaking challenge to human small-mindedness. That reign, a classical envisioning of "new heavens and a new earth" (Isa. 65:17), is not formless. It is fleshed out with the makings of a powerful moral creed. Heading that creed is a passionate vision of justice that turned the world around in the past and could do so again. The basic categories of life are radically rethought in this biblical *credo*, and we visit them in these pages: the stunning challenge to join in "the reign of God," a reign to be marked by justice, prophecy, hope, joy, love, peace, freedom, and truth.

From the first days of Christianity, Christians tried to reach into the heart of this religion and express it in the form of a creed. They did not all agree, and so there were many creeds and even many Christianities. Yet the effort to find, amidst all the variety, central and essential moral truths is unending, and this book is part of that effort. I dare to say that I do not know how you could be true to the Jesus movement and deny the compelling, biblically grounded themes that make up this moral creed, for they seem to be the consuming passions of Jesus and the prophets of Israel who preceded him.

And note too: this is a *moral* creed. Many creeds are heavy with dogmatic claims and light on the electrifying moral challenges that birthed the Christian movement. Perhaps that is because professing dogmas is easier than obeying the "new commandment: [to] love one another as I have loved you" (John 13:34). I take my inspiration from Paul's moral creed in 2 Corinthians 5: "God was in Christ reconciling the world to himself . . . and he has entrusted us with the message of reconciliation." The elements of the moral creed I am presenting seek to spell out just what that reconciliation entails. Again Paul: "When anyone is united to Christ . . . the old order has gone, and a new order has already begun" (2 Cor. 5:17). That "new order" is not shapeless. It is certainly not irrelevant to our economies and our politics for it is in our economies and our politics that decisions are made about the "aliens, orphans and widows" (Deut. 16:11) and the poor whose "blood [is] precious in His eyes" (Ps. 72:14). Certain values and virtues are meant to create and energize this "new order." It is the foundational values of this "new order"that the moral creed I present seeks to capture, for that is the work of moral theology . . . to go back and find the moral treasures that got lost in the chaos and sins of Christian history.

Theology and preaching are at their best when they try to resurrect the dream of a renewed Christian people loving and prophesying like Jesus, Amos, Micah, Hannah, Isaiah, and Mary. That is too precious a dream to abandon. That dream is the soul of this honest effort and of this moral creed.

A CHRISTIAN MORAL CREED

We believe in the reign of God, a God who loves us "with an everlasting love" (Jer. 31:3). We believe that we are called to join God in creating a world in which oppression gives way to justice, a world where "justice and mercy kiss" (Ps. 85:10), a world that will be like a "new heaven and a new earth" (Isa. 65:17) a world where "they shall not hurt or destroy in all my holy mountain" (Isa. 65:25), and we believe it can be done.

We believe that wholehearted biblical justice (*tsedaqah*) is the hallmark of the reign of God, a justice that sees the ending of poverty and its evils as the prime moral challenge and mission for Christian peoples. We believe that we are called to be "good news to the poor" (Luke 4:18), that making the interests of the poor our interests is the only holiness.

We believe in prophecy and that we are to be prophets, the social conscience of our society, specialists in the art of cherishing the earth and its peoples, joining with the prophetic movements of all the world's religions.

We believe that peace can be achieved by justice (Isa. 32:17), not by the horrors of war, a peace in which the hostile barriers between "Jew and Greek, slave and freeman, male and female" are dissolved for we "are all one person" in the sight of God (Gal. 3:28).

We believe that our God is a "God of Truth" (Ps. 31:5), that we are missionaries of truth in a world awash with self-serving lies where "truth stumbles in the market-place and honesty is kept out of court, so truth is lost to sight" (Isa. 59:14).

We believe that we are "called to freedom" (Rom. 5:13) and that freedom is a virtue only when it is married to justice and compassion.

We believe in hope, that "what we shall be has not yet been disclosed" (1 John 3:2), that the plan of the "God of hope" (Rom. 15:13) for us has not yet been realized. Hope drives us to dream and work for a better world where the cries of the oppressed are no longer heard and where tears are wiped from sorrowing eyes.

We believe that "the whole law is summed up in love" (Rom. 13:10), that "God is love" (1 John 4:16), and that loving like God whose "goodness knows no bound" (Matt. 5:48) is our mandate and model. That commits us to loving our enemies and persecutors for "only so can you be children of your heavenly Father, who makes his sun rise on good and bad alike, and sends the rain on the honest and the dishonest" (Matt. 5:45). We believe that love is the solvent that can end all enmity.

We believe that joy is our destiny, that the appropriate response to the promises of the reign of God is "sheer joy" (Matt. 13:44), and where joy is not present because of poverty or prejudice, our work is not done.

All of this we believe and to all of this we commit ourselves. Amen.

Chapter One

THE EMPIRE/SERVILITY SYNDROME

Reader, prepare yourself: this book will be a book of hope but it opens with a searing, even scary look at the downside of humankind. The Bible, that book of hope, does the same thing. It forces us to take a painfully honest look at how corrupt and self-destructive we can be. The same Bible that sees us as made "in the image of God," and, therefore, seemingly of infinite potential, first paints a picture of us as almost hopeless. "The Lord looks down from heaven on all humankind to see if any act wisely. . . . But all are disloyal, all are rotten to the core; no one does anything good, no, not even one" (Ps. 14:2-3). Even our best efforts seem polluted: "our righteous deeds [are] like a filthy rag" (Isa. 64:5-7). It is a desperate portrait the Bible paints. At times, any moral improvement is seen as hopeless: "Can the Nubian change his skin, or the leopard its spots? And you, can you do good, you who are schooled in evil?" (Jer. 13:23).

Apparently the Bible's view is that if we don't face our downside first, we can't build a realistic case for hope. If we don't face our capacity for total self-destruction, we may indeed self-destruct. So, before we build a case for hope, let's stare with steady gaze at our potential for evil and self-destruction. Genesis envisions the paradise that life on earth could be. We could live in harmony with one another and with our parent earth. To that hope we shall return.

But, first, let us confront head-on the possibility that humanity is a failed and short-lived species in the perspective of cosmic history. It may be that we are strapped with a fatal flaw that has already, at the peaking of our technical skills, begun our unraveling. Even in the smaller scale of Earth time, we look unlikely to match the longevity of the dinosaurs; they survived for some 200 million years. It is possible—and has been gloomily argued—that the two greatest disasters to hit this generous planet have been (1) the asteroidal pummeling of 65 million years ago that extinguished the dinosaurs and (2) the arrival of the destructive species that calls itself wise, "sapiens."

Maybe the apocalyptic voices are the realists. Georg Henrik von Wright says with chilling calmness: "One perspective, which I don't find unrealistic, is of humanity as approaching its extinction as a zoological species. The idea has often disturbed people. . . . For my part I cannot find it especially disturbing. Humanity as a species will at some time with certainty cease to exist; whether it happens after hundreds of thousands of years or after a few centuries is trifling in the cosmic perspective. When one considers how many species humans have made an end of, then such a natural nemesis can perhaps seem justified."[1] Vaclav Havel warns that if we endanger the Earth she will dispense with us in the interests of a higher value—that is, life itself. Lynn Margulis joins the grim chorus saying that the rest of Earth's life did very well without us in the past and it will do very well without us in the future. Not all religious scholars rush in with gospels of consolation. If we are the "missing link" between apes and true humanity, as Gerd Theissen puts it, our species is morally prenatal and yet armed to the teeth, with the end of our existence stored and ready in our nuclear silos and other species dropping around us like canaries in a doomed mine.[2]

Can hope, however bloodied and bruised, be salvaged? Can it be vibrant enough to bring the radical and necessary metamorphosis? That is the challenge addressed by this book. The first task is diagnosis.

EMPIRE AS ORIGINAL SIN

The Christian teaching on original sin arose from a sense that something is wrong with us. Though the theological dons played with it to the point of silliness—Augustine thought it was caused by sexual pleasure—the basic insight was correct. Something is wrong.

What's wrong? While speaking recently to a group of Ford Foundation program officers in Greece, I made reference to "the common good." As we stopped for a break, they asked me to return to "the common good" and to tell them what it is. For my break I took a walk down a dirt path toward the lovely Aegean Sea. Ahead of me I saw what looked like a black ribbon stretched across the path. As I got closer I saw that it was not a single, solid ribbon, but two columns of ants moving back and forth in single file. Each ant in one row was carrying something; the others were going back for a new load. A real estate change was in process. Every ant was committed to the project. There were no shirkers or apostates from the common effort. There were no special interest groups. All these insect citizens were bonded to the common good of that community.

How convenient for the insects! The needs of the common good are inscribed on their genes. Human genes have no such inscription. We, like the ants, have need of common good considerations, since the common good is the matrix of minimal livability necessary so individual good can be pursued. Apologies, Augustine, but biblical wisdom would point to that problem rather than sexual joy as our potential undoing. Indeed, all the moral traditions of the world religions in their distinct fashions point to this soft core in our makeup. All of them address our tilt toward moral autism. Our genetic impulse seems more directed to egoistic good in opposition to the common good, and since the common good includes the good of all of nature, this fatal flaw in our composition risks global ruin.

In a blunt indictment, anthropologist Loren Eisely says: "It is with the coming of [human beings] that a vast hole seems to open in nature, a vast black whirlpool spinning faster and faster, consuming flesh, stones, soil, minerals, sucking down the lightning, wrenching the power from the atom, until the ancient sounds of nature are drowned in the cacophony of something which is no longer nature, something instead which is loose and knocking at the world's heart, something demonic and no longer planned—escaped, it may be—spewed out of nature contending in a final giant's game against its master."[3] Tragically, we are winning that battle with the rest of nature, self-destructively failing to realize that the economy, and human life itself, is a wholly owned subsidiary of nature. Edward O. Wilson accuses *homo sapiens* of being the "serial killer of the biosphere."[4] Nature is mother and matrix, not a competitor to be subdued.

We have lost a fifth of tropical rainforests since 1950. These natural treasures provide oxygen, absorb excess carbon, and supply medicine (75 percent of our pharmaceuticals come from plants), not to mention their intrinsic value apart from our needs. We all get hurt when the global womb in which we live gets hurt. David Orr records some of the results: male sperm counts worldwide have fallen by 50 percent since 1938. Human breast milk often contains more toxins than are permissible in milk sold by dairies, signaling that some toxins have to be permitted by the dairies. At death some human bodies contain enough toxins and heavy metals to be classified as hazardous waste.[5] Newborns arrive wounded in their immune systems by the toxins that invaded their mother's womb. One report from India reports that "over 80 percent of all hospital patients are the victims of environmental pollution."[6] Human consuming is stressing the oceanic fisheries to their limits and water tables are falling as there are more of us to share this limited resource.

With us humans, this need for which our genes do not provide is met by ethics and by religion. Ethics is the expression of our natural need to discern the good and diagnose evil, and religion arises from the discovery that at the core of the good is a preciousness that we call holy.[7] A chastening look at our history shows that ethics and religion are no match for genetic inscription when it comes to the protection of our species and of our biological and terrestrial neighbors. Which brings us to:

EMPIRE

Normally we limit the word *empire* to the military and economic domination of weaker nations by stronger ones, like the Roman, Spanish, Dutch, Portuguese, and British empires of the past and the evolving United States empire of today. This exploitive imperial instinct, however, is pandemically present in all arrangements of human society. A passion for control is the engine of empire in all of its micro- and macro-configurations. Controlling others for our perceived advantage—the imperial urge—is not limited to international affairs. It powers all the vicious "isms" that make life on a good earth horrible: sexism, speciesism, racism, heterosexism, nationalism, militarism. The imperial temptation to *control-as-the-path-to-well-being* also drives patriarchy and hierarchy and the myriad forms of royalty that appear in families, corporations, professions, churches, mosques, synagogues, and governments.

The pharaohs had it right. Imperial power is aptly symbolized by a pyramid, with the privileged few at the narrow top supported by the marginalized many throughout the massive base. So insidious is the imperial lure that it can corrupt even the gentlest, most anti-imperial impulse to emerge from the Jesus movement.

JESUS, ASSASSINATED BY EMPIRE

Jesus was crucified by an empire. With all due respect for Mel Gibson's drama *The Passion of the Christ,* he was not killed so that his suffering would expiate our sins, a very bad piece of theology that turns God into a sadistic monster who tortured his son to death in order to make up for sins of other people.[8] No, Jesus was crucified as a rebel against empire. As biblical scholar Norman Gottwald says: "The clearest single piece of historical information about Jesus is that he died as a political provocateur or disturber of that 'alliance of convenience'" between the Roman occupiers and the corrupt Jewish leaders.[9] He was part of the rebellious communities of Judea and Galilee where crucifixion was the regular Roman penalty for insurgency. It is unlikely that Jesus and his family would not have known people who lost fathers or brothers to Roman crucifixion.

Around the time of Jesus' birth, the Roman general Varus scoured the hills of Judea and Galilee searching for insurgents and had two thousand of them crucified.[10]

There was a lot to rebel against. Empires, and imperial occupiers then as now, are brutal. "Tribute to Caesar" meant your grain was taken from your barn, your animals were seized by Caesar so that the people in the empire could live gloriously and well. Now, as citizens of the New Rome, consumers in the United States live gloriously and well. If you challenge this configuration, the lesson is, you get crucified. Jesus challenged the empire of his day. We are not in Jesus territory, Judea and Galilee, which were raped by Imperial Rome. Rome in Jesus' time had become the last remaining superpower in that part of the world. Jesus fought the likes of us and the lesson is that when you do that you get crucified.

The Roman Empire had to kill Jesus, not for committing any discoverable crime; he did worse. He rejected the assumptions of the Roman Empire, which was crushing him and his people. He was a subversive, a prophetic subversive, and for empires that is worse than mere capital crimes. Theologian Walter Wink describes the circumstances this way: "It is impossible to discover in the Gospels an 'adequate' cause for Jesus' execution. Every such attempt has presupposed that he must have done something punishable by death. But he did not. That is the whole point. He was innocent and yet executed. But the [imperial] Powers did not err. He had rejected their spirituality; he had shaken the invisible foundations by a series of provocative acts. He was therefore a living terror to the order of things. He had to be removed."[11]

Many Christians have lost Jesus' spirit of resistance to empire by glorifiying Jesus' suffering as salvific and atoning. This amounts to "deifying suffering."[12] This consoles the tyrants of empire because it can blunt the rebels' spirit by implying that the injustices they suffer should be borne as "our cross" in the spirit of Christ and not resisted. Suffering and self-denial take on positive meaning and can create a kind of sacral masochism. The horrors that should stir us to reform or even revolt can come to be seen as necessary sacrifices. Critics Theodor Adorno and Max Horkheimer called this the grand "deception" perpetrated by Christianity. It departed from the good sense of our Jewish forebears. "The Jews are not ascetical people as the first Christians were, they have never glorified or worshiped or sought or praised suffering but only experienced it.... According to the Jewish law men cannot become saints through suffering, as in Christianity."[13] Jesus' example is not to "suffer and bear it." If it had been, he would not have rebelled against Rome and its Jewish collaborators and would have lived a quiet, long-suffering life, avoiding crucifixion.

THE SUBVERSIVE JESUS

The tenth chapter of Mark's Gospel shows Jesus at his most subversive. The whole passage reeks of abuse by empire, the disintegration of community, the persecution of women, of children, and the poor. Scripture cannot be read by just staring at the words because texts are given meaning by the context of the reader *and* the writer. The context of Jesus' teaching is the crushing weight of Roman imperial dominance. As Richard Horsley puts it: "Jesus opposed the Roman imperial order and its effects on subject peoples...." His whole mission was directed to "communities disintegrating under the impact of imperial order."[14]

Jesus' solution was a return to the Mosaic covenant with its strong emphasis on economic justice. His conviction was that the Power that moved the stars was returning to remake society, that the reign of Caesar was going to yield to the Reign of God. This was the hope he offered. But there is nothing more subversive—or threatening to empire—than hope. Hope allows the people to imagine life without the unnecessary suffering imposed on them and reminds them that the suffering in their community is not a natural part of life to be selflessly tolerated. (Modern feminism was excoriated by the patriarchy precisely because it gave hope to the hopeless and opened doors that patriarchal controllers thought they had copper-fastened. So too for other liberation movements.)

Back to the wild, upending words of Jesus in Mark 10.[15] Jesus focused on everything that he saw the Roman Empire corrupting.

He recognized that the poisons of empire seep even into the most intimate relationships of life. He started with, of all things, marriage and divorce. Never pleasant in any time, divorce was brutal in Jesus' time. It devastated wives who could be "put away" with a mere "certificate of dismissal," and divorce and remarriage were used freely by the wealthy in their schemes to monopolize the land. Like all prophets, Jesus was alert to the scent of exploitation in economics and in politics.[16] (Religion, politics, and economics were only distinguished and separated as concepts in modern times. In Jesus' time they were of a piece and he was in the thick of it. Economics and politics were his religious business.)

Jesus turned next to children, not in the sentimentalized sense of modern affluent "childhood." In the Palestine of his time, "as in most traditional societies, children were, in effect, the persons with the lowest status in the village community."[17] They were the ultimate symbol of the weak and the vulnerable. Saying that the kingdom of God "belonged" to such as them was a radical status-challenge, promoting the rejects and downsizing the high and the mighty.

Jesus then went on to tackle greed—the natural enemy of justice—saying with peasant's irony that it would be easier to get a camel through the eye of a needle than to get those basking in unearned or purloined privilege to unite with the justice-passions of Jesus' God. Empire builders cannot indulge in compassion, much less justice. They cannot ever confess to denying justice, and so imperial intentions always wear a mischief-covering mask.

THE MASKS OF EMPIRE

Empire speak: "Wives, be subject to your husbands" as if they were divine, says Paul the Apostle. He spells it out: "So must women be [subject] to their husbands in everything." Everything! That is hard news. Better put a mask on it. *Empire mask:* "Husbands, love your wives". . . small consolation for wives who have just been defined as slaves (Eph. 5:22-25).

Nations building empires for their own economic and political advantage must always wear a mask, always attempt to put a noble face on their rapacity, whether it be "to exercise *une mission* civilatrice," to take on, in Kipling's phrase, "the white man's burden," to "make the world safe for democracy," to "promote freedom," to "promote the revolution of the proletariat," to act out "manifest destiny," or to "fight terrorism" (conveniently described to include anyone who resists the intrusions of the empire). "Rebels" and "insurgents" are names for people who resist the intrusions of the empire. Never the raw truth of exploitation—always the mask.[18]

Back to Jesus: this radical rabbi next honed in on the domination and hierarchy that are the heart and soul of empire. Even some of his followers (showing the seductive power of empire) thought he was going to set up a hierarchical kingdom, patterned after Rome, and they were politicking for better postings. They were slapped down in a hurry. Scripture scholars see sarcasm and a lack of reverence—even scorn—for Roman authority in Jesus' reference to the "seeming or so-called rulers" of Rome (*hoi docountes archein*). These people lord it over their subjects, he said, and "their great men make them feel the weight of authority" (Mark 10:42). According to Jesus, those in positions of authority should not pattern themselves after the Roman model of exploitative and privileged overlords, but after servants and slaves. But, to empire builders, this is heresy! Empire lives on enslavement. The pinnacle of the pyramid cannot survive without the slave base. Jesus, however, was pioneering a stunning reversal: the substitution of service for dominance, of community for exploitation, of a social order without a slave underpinning—an ideal no nation has even to this day fully achieved.

Small wonder that the hearers of this message about a slaveless world thought the speakers drunk (Acts 2:15). (As an Irishman I may be permitted to note that Peter offered a surprisingly weak defense: "These men are not drunk, as you imagine; for it is only nine in the morning" [Acts 2:15]. He didn't pretend that they were total abstainers.) But the shocking message from Jesus, as Peter pointed out, was actually an old and neglected one going back to the very origins of Israel. The powerful poets of Genesis wrote not of a paradise that once was—not of a golden age past—but of a golden age *possible*. They sang not about a *back then,* but a *could be.* Life on this earth could be a paradise, marked by harmony and by just, poverty-destroying modes of sharing. The Bible's opening vision of what life in this privileged corner of the universe *could be* has haunted the ages. We could be in paradise, but we're not. We're in exile with Adam. We could be clothed in the wonder of peace, but we're not. We're naked, like Adam, and exiled from our true possibilities. And yet the scent of paradise still teases our noses.

Professor Laurie Zoloth says that "Adamic exile" is a symbol of the condition of all of humankind. With poetic strength, she puts it this way: "Adamic exile is a nakedness beyond naming, a stripping of all but the scent of Paradise, carried on the animal skins of Adam and Eve, later in the skins of Esau that Jacob steals, later on the coat of Joseph, a scent that will reemerge again and again . . . as a hint of the infinite possibilities of a world healed." Knowing that we could be more, having been eloquently called to be more in our scriptures, we are stubbornly mired in less. Yet we are uneasy exiles. We have sniffed the possibilities, and so we stumble on, "bearers of the scent of Paradise and lovers of the pleasure of the desert, easily seduced by idols, losing track of the dangerous column of Fire in the night."[19]

SERVILITY, THE UNDERWRITER OF EMPIRE

Zoloth suggests that the purpose of the forty-year trek of the Israelites in the scorching desert was "to burn out the slave in the bone."[20] That ingrained slavishness is the servility syndrome.

That servility syndrome, sadly, is not yet burned out of the human bone. Slaves, not yet morally mature enough to be angry, are easily seduced into voting against their own interests, not voting at all, or not even expecting to be allowed to vote. All forms of empire, from military to corporate, depend on servile masses living under the tyranny of time-clocks. For example, the Second Vatican Council condemned military budgets as a war against the poor: "The arms race is one of the greatest curses on the human race and the harm it inflicts upon the poor is more than can be endured" (*Pastoral Constitution*, #81). Still, no indignation rises from the victims of this crime. The victims will even vote against their own interests by voting for more of the same. A passive "pay and obey" is the motto of the modern slave.

Mark's chapter 10 ends with a man who "recovered his sight," but the whole chapter is really concerned with curing the blindness that keeps victims compliantly and passively in place, whether they be soldiers led to their death by official lies, or whether they be citizens, women, poor nations, sexual minorities, religious clergy and laity, or any others subjected to the many and tangled forms of empire.

Physical and active resistance to superior power is usually futile. Attitudinal change in the victims that slowly pries loose the iron grip of control is the first stratagem of successful subversion. Empires require unquestioning servility. Slaves comply. The slave mentality leeches down into our innards. Attitudinal change is crucially needed and was actually the keynoting mandate out of Jesus' mouth as he began his mission. *Metanoia* (Mark 1:15), often lamely translated "repent," calls for a total flipping of the mind-set that is in us. "Every ravine" in our minds "must be filled in and "every mountain and hill leveled." And the purpose of this restructuring? So that "all humankind shall *see* . . . " (Luke 3:5). Sight and insight cure enslaved minds and fill them with the clarifying elixir of possibility. This is the only thing that will "prepare a way for the Lord, clear a straight path for him" (Luke 3:4).

Just looking at Jesus' talk in Mark 10 makes it clear why he did not die in his bed at a ripe old age. This was dangerous stuff he was saying, a revamping of the world's view of law and order. Of course, empires crucify those who would lift the scales from the eyes of victims and stir them to action. And so they did.

The biblical prophets were impatient with our stupid refusal to *see*. "This people's wits are dulled, their ears are deafened and their eyes blinded, so that they cannot see with their eyes nor listen with their ears, nor understand with their wits, so that they may turn and be healed" (Isa. 6:10). Peace through justice, the biblical formula, is not nuclear physics: "The effect of justice will be peace, and the result of justice, quietness and trust forever" (Isa. 32:17). Any fool should be able to see it. Peace is quite simply "the outcome of a just social order."[21] No wonder Jesus wept. He looked at Jerusalem, the symbol of us all, and said, "If only you had known . . . the way that leads to peace! But no; it is hidden from your sight. (Luke 19:41–42). And he broke down sobbing.

Let us update that text. The newly forming United States tellingly fancied itself "the new Rome."[22] Let us have Jesus say to the Roman Empire of today, "the last remaining superpower": "America, America, if only you knew the things that make for your peace, if only you could see that the answer is not in your weaponry or your economic muscle. If only I could, like a mother hen, wrap my wings around you, wings of justice and peace and compassion, if you could use your great talent and wealth to work to end world hunger, world thirst, world illiteracy, no one would hate you, you would not fear terrorism, you would know *shalom.*" That's the promise of Isaiah 32:17. Then you could burn almost all your chariots in a holy fire and you would be secure. But no. And Jesus weeps.

EMPIRE U.S.A.

Reinhold Niebuhr often and aptly spoke of "the feeble mind of a nation." If individual persons were so unaware of the facts of their lives as nations often are, we would classify them as mentally disabled. An example is at hand: it is just now dawning on the feeble mind of this American nation that we are an empire.

Is it unfair to call the United States an empire? The essence of empire is, as Chalmers Johnson says "the domination and exploitation of weaker states by stronger ones."[23] Clearly, then, Ronald Reagan spoke redundantly when he said that the Soviet Union was an "evil empire." By definition, all empires are evil and all are marked by three things: (1) an idolatrous, self-worshiping hubris, (2) hypocrisy, and (3) a malignant thrust toward self-destruction through the costs of militarism and overstretch.

All this is present in spades in the American Empire. We have 800 military installations in 130 countries and our Special Forces operate in nearly 170 nations. We spend more on the military than the next eighteen nations combined. If nations won't let us in, we invade them militarily or we tell them we'll boycott them out of our market. We take up 20 percent of Okinawa's arable land for our bases and if they protest, they are threatened with being denied access to our purchasing power. We have overthrown twenty-five governments since 1945, but would take a dim view if any nation tried to overthrow ours.[24] We flood the world with our culture and technology.

Of course the American Empire is not the same as the British Empire any more than the British Empire was the same as the Roman Empire. Economics, politics, and technology write new librettos for empire, but the main theme remains. The American Empire is set in the matrix of global capitalism. In a sense, global capitalism is the empire and the U.S. is its *charge d'affaires*. As Chandra Muzaffar says: "The Empire is Washington-helmed but it includes and incorporates elites from all over the world. The elites of Tel Aviv, London and Canberra are as much a part of it as are the elites of Saudi Arabia, the United Arab Emirates, Japan and Singapore. The British ruling class in particular with its incurable nostalgia for empire is right in the thick of this project."[25] Americans, numbly, but self-servingly, take this awesome display of power for granted.

Obvious questions do not penetrate the minds of citizens of the empire. How would we feel if Indonesia opened a naval station in Florida? Or Russia an air station in Michigan? Would that not strike us as surpassingly odd? Yet we do these things as though everyone knows that it is our birthright given us by God. What we are doing is what empires do, convinced as all empires are that their kind of might makes right. That we are overextending ourselves, starving our schools, bankrupting our state governments, weakening health care, etc., does not cool the imperial passions. The roots of this kind of reckless hubris run deep in the American story, and those roots are nourished by streams of decadent American religiosity, giving a very religious cast to our brand of imperial hypocrisy.

America began with the illusion that the founding of our country was an act of God. Our self-image was, to say the least, inflated. The Puritan experience imbued America with notions of being the promised people in the Promised Land. They were not just founding a nation but fulfilling a divine destiny. They were the new Zion. The nation said "Amen" when preacher Nathaniel W. Taylor told an audience at Yale College that this nation was the one "on which the Sun of Righteousness sheds his clearest brightest day."[26] Even the Civil War did not dispel this sanctimonious predestination complex. George Phillips of Ohio gave expression to the American myth in his literally incredible book *The American Republic and Human Liberty Foreshadowed in Scripture.* The Bible, in other words, was written to foretell our coming. Phillips proclaimed that God's Old Testament promise to found a nation fully obedient to him was fulfilled when he, God, established the United States of America. Phillips found our story in the pages of sacred scripture. With exegetical wizardry he said that Isaiah and Daniel clearly foretold the day and the hour of the Declaration of Independence. Isaiah also predicted the Boston Tea Party and even the coming of Chinese immigrants to California. Phillips roared on to this conclusion: "The United States is to fill the earth . . . so to occupy the place of government in the world, as to leave room for no other government."[27] Right-wing American scorn for the United Nations would bring applause from Mr. Phillips.

Empire is always a religious feat. "God with us" inscribed on the buckles of Hitler's soldiers. . . . manifest destiny as the writ for genocide and imperial plunder. As Walter Wink says: "Evil never feels safe unless it wears the mask of divinity."[28] At the end of the nineteenth century, Senator Albert Beveridge claimed without fear of contradiction that God had "marked" the American people to lead in "the redemption of the world." President Woodrow Wilson said that upon America "there rests nothing but the pure light of the justice of God," a light, he said, that first dawned with "the Christian Era."[29] George W. Bush, speaking in Crawford, Texas, on August 31, 2002, joined the pious chorus (even while waging two constitutionally undeclared wars against weak nations), insisting repeatedly that our nation is the greatest force for good in history.

THE ART OF SERVILITY MAINTENANCE

Empire counts on servility and has divers ways of nurturing it. The Roman Empire at its expansive peak could not maintain law and order only by violence and the threat of violence. The empire occupied everything from the Middle East to England. It did not have enough soldiers to occupy all that land and it didn't need them. Rome deployed no troops at all in the "civilized" areas of Italy, Greece, and Asia Minor.[30] The satirist Juvenal mocked the Roman people, saying that all it took to subdue them was "bread and circus."[31] Actually their formula for control involved three things: cult, bread, and circus, and the formula still works today. Bread and circus keep the people passive, but it is cult that locks the chains. It is not surprising that "blasphemy and treason are closely connected."[32] Our gods and our emperors intertwine and we call the unholy mixture "patriotism." In Rome, it was the cult of the emperor. As Richard Horsley writes: "Statues of the emperor were erected beside those of the traditional gods in many of their temples. Shrines to the emperor were placed at intermediate points between the temples in city centers, and temples were erected to Augustus at the most prominent points in those city centers. . . . The presence of the emperor thus came to pervade public space in the cities of the empire."[33]

Add to that the importation of massive amounts of grain suctioned out of the less fortunate parts of the empire and given to the peoples in Italy and the major urban centers. Add some games and festivals for distraction and *voila*, a people pacified and exploitable. Thus do military-based empires win their temporary success . . . but their success is always temporary. The worm turns.

NATIONS AS GODS

Nationalism, of course, is always full of sacral hues. Arnold Toynbee argued that it might well be that "nationalism is 90 percent of the religion of 90 percent of the people of the Western World and of the rest of the World as well."[34] He traces out how the human race moved from nature worship to state worship as communities became more organized and more impressive 5,000 years ago. Nature gods suddenly became state gods as we began to worship the power that came with collectivizing, as simple Neolithic villages gave way to places such as the towering Sumerian city-state. Nature worship was humanity's first religion. There were wind and water and sun gods and olive goddesses as well. But as we formed the first city-states, these became more impressive than nature itself and we re-directed our worship there. Suddenly Enlil the wind god becomes the deity of Nippur, Nanna the moon god becomes the deity of Ur, Athena the olive goddess becomes the deity of Athens, and the water god Poseidon becomes the deity of the state of Corinth. In Toynbee's words: "The local communities have become divinities, and these divinities that stand for collective human power have become paramount over the divinities that stand for natural forces. The injection of this amount of religious devotion into nationalism has turned nationalism into a religion, and this a fanatical one."[35]

In the United States, the new Zion, nation-worshiping patrio-tism is fully ablaze. Here the flag is as sacred as the shrines to Au-gustus. Burning that flag would be a "desecration" comparable to trashing a statue of Augustus or an effigy of Caesar, or the burning of the Qu'ran or the Catholic Eucharist. This symbolic sacraliza-tion of power fogs the optic nerve of citizens and stifles their ob-ligation to be the attentive consciences of their nation. This gives undue immunities to the powerful few in government. "The worst of madmen is a saint gone mad," said the poet Alexander Pope. And the worst of "saints" is a nation that feels itself divinely appointed to remake the world in its image.

So the American Empire does not lack for the binding power of cult, the first of the cult-bread-circus, or consumerism-pizza-football, trio. Given the wealth that accumulates at the imperial homeland, bread and circus arrive in quantity. Thus is achieved the passive base and detachment from politics that empire requires.

But this induced passivity is an illness, one that could be called ICS: Imperial Comfort Syndrome. Resting on a bed of unearned privileges, as the affluent elite in the United States do, gives a kind of inebriating comfort, not a comfort born of health.[36] Imperial Comfort Syndrome does not result in fever or in cold chills. It is symptoms are tepidity and a dull and subtle, but crippling, kind of depression. It manifests in elections where 60 percent of eligible American voters don't even show up. It manifests in an elector-ate that is contentedly ignorant of what political and corporate power-holders are doing to them and to the world. It manifests in workers blind to their own victimization and the grasping greed of their corporate oppressors. Since about 1980 in the United States the average pay for top CEOs and board chairs has soared from $479,000 to $8.1 million. Average worker pay is $26,899. If worker pay had kept pace with their CEO's, the workers would be earning $184,000 and the minimum wage would be almost $45.00 an hour.[37] Yet indignation rarely rises among the workers, sufficiently numbed by the bread and circus that comes their way and by the civil cult that says, "All is as all should be. Real changes are unthinkable." All this is ICS at work. People are numbed into passivity, sapped of any fervor for resistance.

Interestingly, Scripture saw the syndrome, in chapter 3 of Revelation, a book that shows the evils of empire and the spinelessness of servility. The author puts these biting words into the mouth of God: "I know all your ways. You are neither hot nor cold. How I wish you were either hot or cold. But because you are lukewarm, neither hot nor cold, I will spit you out of my mouth. . . . Hear, you who have ears to hear, what the Spirit says to the churches" (15–16; 22).

PONTIFFS AND AYATOLLAHS

The same ingredients are found in other forms of empire. The divine right of men to rule women, the subordination of people of color to whites, the dominance of rich over poor, of heterosexuals over homosexuals, of clergy over laity, and more. The empire temptation can corrupt all human relations, including religion. Jesus spoke of governance and the abuse of power: "You know that in the world the recognized rulers lord it over their subjects, and their great men make them feel the weight of authority. This is not the way with you; among you, whoever wants to be great must be your servant, and whoever wants to be the first must be the willing slave of all" (Mark 10:42–43). That is the very opposite of monarchy and imperial governance. Not surprisingly, the New Testament shows fidelity to that mandate. There is no pope in the early Christian community and no monarchical bishops operating as local popes as they do in the high churches today.

As church historian Walter Ullmann says, as late as the year 313, "there was, as yet, no suggestion that the Roman church possessed any legal or constitutional preeminence." Bishop Leo decided to change that. The papacy as we know it is not of Peter, but of Leo. This was Leo I, Bishop in Rome from 440 to 461, a Roman jurist who cast the Roman episcopate in terms borrowed directly from the Roman imperial court. The one who called himself *summus pontifex* (supreme pontiff), who held the *plentitudo potestatis* (the fullness of monarchical power) and the *principatus* (primacy), was the Roman Emperor. Leo grabbed all this language and applied it to himself and it has been part of the papal vocabulary ever since. As Walter Ullmann says: "This papal plentitude of power was . . . a thoroughly juristic notion, and could be understood only . . . against the Roman Law background."[38] The poison of power styled on empire had seeped into the veins of the church. Popes are not the only sinners here. Many Christian leaders embrace the monarchic claims of the papacy, exercise comparable imperial control of the laity, calling themselves shepherds and reducing the faithful to sheep.

HOPE

This book is not written as a wail of despair. It is written out of the conviction that in those flawed but powerful classics that we call "the world religions" there are renewable moral energies that can heal a dangerously sick humanity, a humanity that might have been better called *Homo insipiens,* the opposite of *sapiens.* The salt of *sapientia,* wisdom, is the cure for that. The focus will be on the wisdom that burst out of the Jewish and Christian moral traditions, though frequent reference will be made to helpful moral breakthroughs achieved in other religious traditions. There is no one true religion but the world's major religions, with all their flaws, are classics in the art of cherishing. All contain rich ore that can be mined and refined into practical visions of what life on this planet could be.

It is too much to say that biblical religion has had no successes. In heroic moments, biblical religion has been tried and applied and has helped history turn some healthy corners. It has had victories, some enduring, many lost through lack of maintenance. To discover or recover the renewable moral dynamism of the biblical tradition and apply them to a world in grim condition is the hopeful goal of the following pages.

Chapter Two

HOW TO READ THE BIBLE

It's an old saying that even the devil can use Scripture to his advantage. If the Bible is just a cafeteria where you can go to pluck whatever you want, if it is just a thesaurus you can visit to find the quote that suits your argument, its authority is not much. The peacemaker can turn to Isaiah chapter 2 and find: "Nation will not lift sword against nation, there will be no more training for war. They will hammer their swords into ploughshares, their spears into sickles." Then, the warrior can run to Joel 4:10: "Hammer your ploughshares into swords, your sickles into spears." Checkmate!

The feminist can go to Galatians 3:28: "There is no such thing as Jew and Greek, slave and freeman, male and female: for you are all one person in Christ Jesus." It could not be clearer. Women are not subordinated to men in the perspective of Christ Jesus. Sexists, however, can rush for relief to Ephesians chapter 5: "Wives, be subject to your husbands as to the Lord: for the man is head of the woman, just as Christ also is the head of the church. Christ is, indeed, the Savior of the body; but just as the church is subject to Christ, so must women be to their husbands in everything." Which is it?

In Matthew chapter 5, Jesus says if someone strikes you on the right cheek, offer the left to him, but in John 18 when Jesus is struck on the cheek, he does not offer the other cheek but protests!

On top of that, those who say the Bible is free of error should have a problem with some of its edicts. For example, the death penalty is ordered for gays and lesbians who make love (Lev. 20:13-15). Sex workers should be "burnt to death" (Lev. 21:9). God is even reported to be incensed about tattoos: "you shall not tattoo yourselves. I am the Lord" (Lev. 19:28). More drastically yet, in Numbers chapter 31, Yahweh orders the Israelites to kill everyone except the virgin daughters of their enemies and to keep these as sex slaves, concubines, and involuntary wives. Clearly the "Good Book" is not all good. What do we do about it? Is the Bible muddled and hopeless? A ship without a rudder or a compass? In a previous book, I offer criteria for finding the breakthrough message of the Bible.[1] In brief summary, here is a method for reading the Bible and getting its authentic breakthrough messages.

DESCRIPTION

The first thing is to recognize that much in the Bible is merely *descriptive* of how people lived and thought at those times, and much of that ranges from not very edifying to downright repulsive. There is darkness in the Bible, but there bursts through it a marvelous light that has had numerous benevolent effects on history and it is such light that biblical theology and social theory seek. Amid the shadows of the Bible there emerges a vision of what human life could be, were we to seek peace through justice, were we to give *tsedaqah*, the Bible's word for justice, a chance.

PRESCRIPTION

Beyond the *descriptive* parts of the Bible there unfolds in its pages a revolutionary prescription for a wholly different kind of life. The Bible works through the daring idea that the power that made the stars and the Earth is compassionate. This power, which is personalized as God, is presented as intent on seeing this recalcitrant creation turn from patterns of war, imperial domination, enslavement, and alienation to patterns of peace, reconciliation, justice, cooperative solidarity, and joy. This reimagining of life, as I will argue in this book, meets the essential criteria for truth. And it is the new truth that the Bible *prescribes*, not the evil that it *describes,* that gives the Bible its worth.

CRITERIA

No one using Scripture intelligently gives equal value to all the statements or ideas found there. Criteria for selectivity are always operating, but they should be up front and available for testing. This challenge is heightened by the fact that the Bible is not a singular classic, the product of one solitary genius. It is more of an anthology of somewhat related classics, an achievement of changing cultures unfolding in diverse communities and times. It also contains much that we could well have done without. And so we sort, select, and reject using criteria, and those criteria ought to be explicit.

The word *criterion* comes from the Greek word meaning "to judge." Truth is the business of any criterion. Criteria are the standards, the signals, the badges, and the tests of the truly true. In searching out the moral truth of the Bible, the principal criteria I use are two: *coherence* and *fruitfulness.* Pierre Teilhard de Chardin writes: "In science [and elsewhere] the greatest test of truth is coherence and productiveness."[2] He speaks of "coherence and fertility: the two inimitable touchstones, and the two irresistible attractions of truth."[3] *Coherence* points to the requirement that for something to be true, it has to cohere—that is, it has to square with our overall sense of reality, with our contemporary needs, and with other solid experiences of truth. *Fruitfulness* requires an idea to function. It has to be promising and productive.

The biblical vision described in the chapters of this book does all of that. It is a vision that is prescriptive of a new humanity with new social arrangements geared to the elimination of poverty, to ending all oppression, and to the flourishing of life on this versatile Earth. And when this vision has been given a chance, it has worked and we are all in the western world beneficiaries of its past successes. It is a vision that still rings with contemporaneity. Jesus' teaching on loving enemies has, for a long time and often, seemed hopelessly idealistic. Given today's military potential it may contain the seeds of our last, best, and most practical hope. Jesus' radical vision of response to enmity may have contained in germ the moral and political mutation required now for the survival of life on this delicate but badly bruised planet.[4] It would be a tragic loss if the energizing power of this creative vision were ignored due to the inadequacies of contemporary Christians and Jews.

SYMBOLS

There is no suggestion here that the classical biblical literature (and its various sequels) contains a systematic method to solve all of modern society's problems. Only a rationalistic and mechanistic mind-set could look for such. Where this literature excels is in poetic symbols and images that shake the foundations and challenge our small-mindedness. Culture could almost be defined as a struggle of images in which some dominate and other recede. Images, especially when undetected or even unsuspected, are imperious, and control discourse and debates as tidal currents control the waves. Literature that touches our images can change our worldview. And that inevitably changes political and economic theory, along with our notions of status, power, and possibility. Biblical literature and the classics it inspired in various traditions and cultures go to the antechambers of thought where the real power lies and critical thinking begins. If we find truth there, we can bring it with us into our modern conversations without fear of embarrassment.

RESPECT

A final rule for interpreting the Bible correctly is to respect the text and listen to those who have studied it. We can't interpret the Bible by simply staring at the words and making up what we think those words mean. In a sense, when we read the Bible, we are like voyeurs squinting to see into the visions and life of those long dead. We are never completely successful. Like archaeologists sorting in the ruined remnants of Herculaneum or Pompeii, we can reconstruct much of what living there was like, but we will never know what the dead who lived there knew. Experts who spend their lives studying those ruins are indispensable guides. So we need learned guides. We need to study if we want to read scripture well.

The guides, the biblical scholars, are not perfect and can sometimes miss the main message. Biblical scholars can be like biologists who get absorbed in analyzing tree roots but miss the grandeur of the forest. The self-serving myths of a society can often befog the mind of the best scholar.

INTERPRETATION

All who read the Bible interpret it, and interpreters can be traitors. This book seeks out the central core of the moral vision of the Bible, the canon within the canon, that opens new and truly classical envisionings of the good, the true, and the beautiful. Leaning on the best and tested insights of scholars and honest believers throughout history, comparing this classic with other religious and moral classics, one can hope to find the formative, enlivening *leitmotivs* of the Bible and give them voice in a moral creed. It is this I attempt in the following pages.

Chapter Three

RE-IMAGINING THE WORLD

In all of history or literature it is impossible to imagine a more radical or more subversive concept than the "kingdom of God," best translated actively as the *reign* of God. Repetition, rote, and listless pieties over the centuries have veiled the power of this call for revolution, this epic summons to human imagination. Caesar understood it better than many Christians then or now and he killed Jesus for talking about it and for preaching that it was already happening. Caesar saw that this reign-of-God concept undercut all his powers and pomposities, and that is the stuff of treason. The word *kingdom* (or *reign*) is "a political term." It meant "that the God of Israel would be taking over control of the country soon." "Institutional arrangements had to be changed."[1] In other words, the economic and political deals in place had to be dismantled. Caesar got it right. The folks talking reign of God were challenging his empire and challenging all of the imperial elite who basked in unearned and purloined privileges.

If Jesus had just been into private, devotional religion, he would not even have irked Caesar. According to Bruce Malina, "the most significant obstacle" blocking insight into Jesus' mission "is the widespread belief that Jesus and his program were about religion."[2] Given the self-indulgent and superficial things that religion can mean in much modern discourse, that error is fatal. Religion doesn't always reduce to mushy, unhelpful piety in modern times. Most of the revolutionary movements that transformed, shaped, and reshaped the American nation grew out of religious circles.[3] The idea of religion as private piety blocks access to the Bible. "The Kingdom of God proclaimed by Jesus was a political institution in which religion and economics were embedded."[4]

The separation of religion from politics and economics is a modern trick. In the ancient world, as Morton Smith writes, there wasn't even a "general term for *religion*." If you want to express what Judaism was about, "the one Hellenistic word which came closest was 'philosophy.'" To the surrounding peoples who admired Israel, it was "the cult of wisdom."[5] This was Deuteronomy's self-portrait: "You will display your wisdom and understanding to other peoples. When they hear about these statutes, they will say, 'What a wise and understanding people this great nation is!'" (4:6). The cocky Israelites were on to something big and they were sure the world would come to appreciate it. To an extent, their confidence was fulfilled. This little movement became "the seedbed of the subsequent religious history of the Western world."[6] And, one could add, a major force in the political history in the West. The echoes of early Israel resonate still in the American Bill of Rights and in the Charter of the United Nations.

JESUS: REALIST OR DREAMY IDEALIST?

As Jesus watched the chariots of Rome rumble through his streets, and the heavily armed soldiers stampede over his people, did he actually think he could overthrow this Leviathan and do what well armed enemies of Rome could not do? Hardly. There is no indication he was stupid. His response to Roman imperial oppression was more radical. It targeted all the assumptions of the status quo. As Mary Hobgood says, he pioneered a "new vision" and "a confrontational lifestyle," doing what he could with what he had in the villages where he worked. He dared to have "open table fellowship with outcasts, touching and healing outsiders, calling religious and political leaders to task, and treating women and slaves as equal. More than annoyance to dominant groups, these behaviors and practices were in fundamental opposition to the religious, cultural, political, and economic hierarchies of the time. They challenged the very foundation of the social order."[7]

This is far more radical than modern American liberals who feel that unless they can have a president of their choosing and leanings, they are impotent. Not so. His form of subversion was "change from the bottom up."[8] Leaders of today's "religious right" know this better than most progressive Christians. They gave up the idea that mere conversions of individuals, one by one, was the answer and saw the need for efficient grass roots organizing. Liberals seem to feel that the very force and righteousness of their ideas and ideals is enough. Ralph Nader is a pure example of this naïveté.

An ancient, now anonymous, seer once said that if you want change, do two things: clarify your ideas and get friends. The getting friends part means working within the groups, however small, that are now within your reach. You cannot dismantle the congressional arrangements that put the same co-opted congresspersons back in no matter what they do. Once elected, a president is not easily dislodged. Once in a lifetime is the most any of us will see that. But subversive organizing done with the confidence that we can reach people with good sense and better instincts is the heart of any successful moral revolution. A defeatist sense of inevitability and unchangeability is the servility foundation of unjust leadership. It is the blatant opposite of creative reign-of-God thinking.

SMASHING CONTENTMENT

In a classic of discontent, Judaism and early Christianity looked at the world and found it wanting. In disrespect for the status quo, this tradition has few peers in all of history. The immodest goal of reign-of-God thinking was to turn the world on end. The biblical peoples measured reality by their richly value-laden conception of God, and concluded that reality failed the test in all of its particulars. They judged no value, no relationship, and no social arrangement to be worthy of their exalted notion of the divine Exemplar.

They saw the society around them as a collection of petty idols worshiped by the unimaginative. God was obviously not yet "all in all" (1 Cor. 15:28); creation was unfinished. But something could be done about it.

The strength of these revolutions lay in the simple belief that radical, upending social change is necessary and possible. The reign of God was their principal code name for that revolutionary conviction.

It would be easy to brand this belief naïve, but there are two reasons that stay the charge. First, both Judaism and Christianity, in their origins and intermittently afterward, have displayed genuine revolutionary power. At significant times, they have passed the results test with distinction. Second, their blazing hope of reversing perversity is coupled with a stunning pessimism about human moral character. If Descartes were right about clarity and noncontradiction being the marks of truth, Judaism and Christianity are false. They offer a clashing mix of depressing pessimism and exuberant hope. If, however, paradox is the mark of all profound experience of truth—and I urge that it is—their case remains before us.

SPOTTED LEOPARDS

Gerd Theissen has suggested that we can call off the search for the "missing link" between apes and true humanity. We are that missing link.[9] The species that is capable of genocide through hunger or holocaust, that budgets more for kill-power than for life-power, and that treats its own environment barbarically is not yet true humanity. Such moral pessimism is thoroughly biblical.

The self-portrait of modern western civilization is unduly flattering. At root, we think we are a goodly people. The evils that fill our recent history are seen as deviations from the norm. The Nazi Holocaust, the killing fields of Cambodia and El Salvador, the wars and rumors of wars, environmental destruction, the corruption of political power, the proliferating murders and rapes that fill our cities, and the crimes of the corner office—all these are seen as atypical and if they are newsworthy it is only because they are exceptional. They are not us.

Again, the biblical view of humankind is less gentle, even dismal: "The Lord looks down from heaven on all humankind to see if any act wisely. . . . But all are disloyal, all are rotten to the core; not one does anything good, no, not even one" (Ps. 14:2-3). Even when we have done our best, we are "servants and deserve no credit" (Luke 17:10). "We have done evil from of old, we all became like a man who is unclean and all our righteous deeds like a filthy rag" (Isa. 64:5-7). It is a desperate portrait. At times, any moral improvement is seen as hopeless: "Can the Nubian change his skin, or the leopard its spots? And you, can you do good, you who are schooled in evil?" (Jer. 13:23). It is not God but evil that reigns over us (Rom. 5:21). In this view, the evil that fills our headlines reflects us perfectly.

For those of us who have managed to be economically secure, buoyed by the perquisites of empire, the diagnosis is even more dire. It would be easier to get a camel through the eye of a needle than for the well-off to understand justice (Mark 10:25). It is not surprising that we are killers in our economics and politics—we are, after all, the children of Cain. The prophets of Israel did not come to compliment us. They look at us and weep (Luke 19:41).

Such drastic pessimism is not the soil from which naïveté grows. And yet this very soil did yield hope, wrapped in the symbol of the reign of God. From a totally unromantic view of human moral potential rises a rich utopianism, hedged, but stirring and subversive and always practical.

THE STORY OF A SYMBOL

Great symbols and myths have complex origins and are never univocal. Their roots run deep because, as Alan Watts put it, people regard them "as demonstrations of the inner meaning of the universe and human life."[10] In the ancient Near East, the symbol of the kingship of God often expressed the hope that life, with all its tragedies, is good and full of promise. The Israelites had taken the symbol from the Canaanites and its roots have been traced all the way back to ancient Sumerian times.[11] Only the name of the king-god changed: in Babylonia, Marduk; in Assyria, Ashur; in Ammon, Milcom; in Tyre, Melkart; in Israel, Yahweh.

Kingship was often associated with the triumph of springtime life over winter death. The god that pulled this off proved that hope was stronger than fear. The renewal of spring was the creation miracle recapitulated. The ancient Israelites joined their neighbors in this common celebration of hope, but they added to the symbol. They saw God as reigning not just over nature, but over history. The reign of God, with all of its political and economic content, became the overarching theme of their morality and their religion.

Reign-of-God imagery had "an appreciable range of meaning."[12] It embraces present and future, and the various authors of biblical literature use it with poetic freedom. Still, it houses a core belief that a wholly new economic and political system can replace all of our current arrangements. The reign of God contemplates "nothing less than the renewal of the world on the lines of God's original purpose."[13] The image of the reign of God is a tour de force of creative imagination, and talk about it should be about a doable, massive overhaul of all of human life.

It is widely recognized that the reign of God was pivotal to the Jesus movement. "'The Kingdom of God' is the central theme of the teaching of Jesus, and it involves his whole understanding of his own person and work."[14] Biblical scholar Rudolph Schnackenburg calls it "the principal subject of Jesus' preaching" and also "the most powerful of motives" operating in the Jesus movement.[15] Stephen Charles Mott calls it "central in Jesus' teaching."[16] Richard Horsley joins the dunning: "It is clear that the dominant theme running through the Gospel is the kingdom of God."[17] What is less acknowledged, as Jorge Pixley points out, is that "Yahweh's kingdom is the seminal idea of the Old Testament. . . . Jesus was not preaching something new, but announcing a hope with a long history in Israel."[18] As Mott says, the "reign of God may be called the center of the whole Old Testament promise."[19] T. W. Manson cites it as "fact" that "the ethic of the Bible, from the beginning to end, is the ethic of the Kingdom of God."[20]

Too many barrels of ink, however, have been spent discussing whether Jesus and the early Jesus movement considered the kingdom present or future. Much of this derived from attempts by Christian theologians and biblicists to use high Christologies to show the superiority of Christianity over Judaism. These struggles over timing seem misplaced. From the start, the early Yahwist movement believed that God was trying to get a grip on history, to reign by leading us on the path of justice as the only route to peace. The accent was often on the future because the realistic Israelites could see that the job was not done. Jesus, in the text much labored by exegetes, Luke 17:21-22, could hardly have been saying that the hopes for the kingdom were fulfilled in himself or his times. If he said that at all, and if he meant it, subsequent history proves him wrong. He did not usher in the age foreseen by the prophets. The lion and the lamb were still at odds when Jesus finished.

No matter how multivalent the image of the reign of God is, the presence of this central and unifying theme and symbol grounds all the other moral themes of these rich religious moral traditions and gives a foundation for a core. The other themes that will be developed in subsequent chapters of this book are specifications of this master, anti-empire theme of biblical morality.

Again, in Israel, religion and politics were born as twins. The early Yahwists met Yahweh in their liberation from slavery, and that experience marked Yahweh's personality and theirs ever after. In their experience, the God who got them out of slavery was still on the job. As a people they were born of dramatic change—a marvelous escape from tyranny. They credited God with this feat and expected more of the same. Their Yahweh was a can-do God, and they were made in his image. Israel's neighbors saw God as king of the heavens. Israel saw God as ruling over not just the heavens, but over politics and providing a new vision not just for Israel but for all the recalcitrant and stupid nations of the world.[21]

Symbols are always biography. The kingship of God for the Israelites reflected their history and their hopes. Israel was born of defiance. It was a "contrast society," a community of rebellion.[22] The very word *Hebrew* seems to come from *apiru,* the name for rebel bands that threatened the stability of the states of Canaan. "'Apiru' were any group that placed itself outside the law and sought its interest by means which were not acceptable to the constituted authorities."[23] It was no slight irony that this group took over the idea of a kingly God—they hated kingship and were pioneering a radical, tendentially "democratic" social organization that was immediately seen as a major threat by all the surrounding royal states. Israel's use of the king-God was more than ironic—its clear purpose was subversion.

Kings were not good news to the Hebrews. Kings were slavers and they had had enough of that. Samuel was horrified when the people started asking for a king at a point when the "contrast society" of Israel was weakening in its social revolution. In the story Samuel speaks to God, who tells him that the offense was not against Samuel but against God. God sends Samuel to warn the people about what a king will mean:

> He will take your sons and make them serve in his chariots and with his cavalry, and will make them run before his chariot. Some he will appoint officers over units of a thousand and units of fifty. Others will plough his fields and reap his harvest; others again will make weapons of war and equipment for mounted troops. He will take your daughters for perfumers, cooks, and confectioners, and will seize the best of your cornfields, vineyards, and oliveyards, and give them to his lackeys. He will take a tenth of your grain and your vintage to give to his eunuchs and lackeys. . . . You yourselves will become his slaves. (1 Sam. 8:11-17)

In modern terms the Hebrews sensed that kings import a class system and a military establishment to preserve themselves. Militarism is essential to kingship and to empire. Domination for the benefit of a few requires slaves, weapons of war, and mounted troops.

Judges 9:8-15 contains a sarcastic fable told to belittle kingship. The trees decide on having a king and so they go to the worthy olive tree and ask it to be king. It refuses to leave its "rich oil by which gods and human beings are honored" just to hold sway over the other trees. The fig tree also refuses, as does the noble vine. Finally the trees betake themselves to an old, brambly thorn bush, and it accedes to their wishes, with ominous threats of what will happen if they do not indeed come under the protection of its shadow. Despotic royalism, even in the modern democratic forms it takes, would get no blessing from the literature of Israel.

If kings are so scorned and ignoble, then why make the good Yahweh one of them? The reason was the denigration of all royal power except that of Yahweh. The Israelites' project was to rethink the very meaning of authority, and, indeed, to rethink all the rules of life that other peoples took as eternally valid. To bring this about, they hoped for the end of political despotism in a new society without oppression, poverty, or violence. Israel's king-God was not a tribal or nationalistic god. Yahweh was more the champion of justice than the champion of Israel.[24]

God's kingship involves a "great reversal."[25] This reversal is to be a transformation of all "the basic conditions of human life."[26] The result will be a new kind of humanity. Early Israel was nothing less than a workshop on human possibility. And talk of the reign of God was a blast of possibility-thinking.

Isaiah put into the mouth of God many extravagant promises like this: "For behold, I create new heavens and a new earth. Former things shall no more be remembered nor shall they be called to mind. . . . Weeping and cries for help shall never again be heard. . . . Men shall build houses and live to inhabit them, plant vineyards and eat their fruit. . . . They shall not toil in vain or raise children for misfortune. . . . The wolf and the lamb shall feed together and the lion shall eat straw like cattle. They shall not hurt or destroy in all my holy mountain, says the Lord" (65:17-25).

"Gladness and joy" will be the escort of all, "and suffering and weariness shall flee away" (35:10). Isaiah anticipated nothing less than peace and the end of militarism. "All the boots of trampling soldiers and the garments fouled with blood shall become a burning mass, fuel for fire" (9:5). Amid the unrestrained imagery, the practicality of Hebrew morality endures. The symbols point to a new, demilitarized politics and a new economics and they insist that nothing else works. The end result of their plan will be a peace sustained by justice, a peace that will last "from now and for evermore" (9:7).

The "holy mountain" that will be saved and the "parched desert" that will "flower with fields of asphodel [and] rejoice and shout for joy" (35:2)—these do not refer just to Israel, but to the whole of the earth. This vision is presented as something that everyone wants and needs and senses to be a human possibility. It will be as welcome as water in a parched land (35:7). Israel is to be "a light to the nations, . . . [shining all the way] to earth's farthest bounds" (49:6). This is a message meant for "all nations" and for "people everywhere" (Matt. 28:19). It is not the vision of sectarians or separatists. It is not just for Jews and Christians. It is to be taken to all the peoples of the world who need it "to open their eyes and turn them from darkness to light" (Acts 26:18).

The Jesus movement continued Israel's radical utopianism. If Adam is the symbolic name of original humanity, the symbol of the reign of God envisions "a new Adam," a qualitatively new humanity (Rom. 5:12-21; 1 Cor. 15:45). "A new world," "a new order," "a new creation" are seen as possible and are expected (2 Cor. 5:16-17). Nothing will be left untouched by this grand reversal. Everything is relativized. The reign of God undermines "all absolute claims of sex, marriage, and family as well as society, culture, and religion, the profane and the sacred."[27] Jesus' preaching of the reign of God "condemned all the political and social structures of the world as it was in his day."[28] None of it was worthy of God's original plan, and none of it needed to stay in its present paltry or noxious form. Never was a utopianism so drastically hopeful or so sweeping.

EARTH VERSUS US

Perhaps the most radical and damning text in reign-of-God theology is Genesis 1:31: "And God saw all that he had made, and it was very good." The radical heart of this revolutionary viewpoint is in the insistent belief of Israel that the world the good God made is "very good" indeed. If hunger and starvation exist, if children are dying for lack of basic necessities, and if fruitful fields are rendered sterile, it is not God's fault. God's contribution was "very good"— the failure is ours.

In the biblical view, the earth is good, history is the problem, and it is there that God meets the most intractable of challenges: us. It is in history that God is trying to reign, to get us to reimagine everything, to make everything new. God's purpose is to try to rescue the potential and beauty of this Earth from the mess we are bent on making of it. The enthusiasm for the Earth in these poetic texts is extraordinary and recapturable.

For theists, reign-of-God imagery means that God exists and is active on our behalf, calling us into active consort with the divine efforts to renew the Earth. For nontheists, the metaphor of a continually active God expresses a dynamic perception of the ongoing possibility of change. In this imagery, God-talk means hope. It means that the project is feasible. God-talk senses possibilities and clashes with apathy and despair. For theist and for nontheist, however, this proposes a piercing challenge to our underdeveloped creativity.[29] It is a vision alive with a sense of what might yet be. "What we shall be has not yet been disclosed" (1 John 3:2). The current state of things is an insult to the moral imagination that lies latent within us. That is the central, liberative message of reign-of-God symbolism.[30]

UTOPIA WITH DETAILS

Utopianism often repairs to protective generality marked by fuzzy, impressionistic, or surrealistic landscapes. Such a tactic is not dishonorable, since we need some escape from the tyranny of pragmatism and what passes for "realism" if we are to glimpse a new horizon. Hebrew utopians, however, were too practical and impatient for that approach. The passion of their vision was too fiery. They sought no haven on the safe side of generality. Instead, they precisely spelled out where improvements were needed. These practical dreamers touched on a remarkable number of the details of social organization. Here are some of their specifics:

- History is malleable. Lost alternatives can be realistically pursued. The actual does not outweigh the possible.
- Radical change is necessary for survival. We are in terminal danger unless we undergo in-depth *metanoia (conversion), transvaluation, and reorientation.*
- Humanity is a shared treasure that accrues also to foreigners and strangers. We must rethink enmity and to acknowledge the humanity of every person.
- Wealth and poverty are correlative terms. Because the under-class is created by the over-class, the burden of proof for poverty is placed on the rich and on their arrangements.

- All manifestations of authority must be re-evaluated. In the spirit of Daniel 7, the harsh ruling power suitable to animals can be replaced by political authority suitable to persons.
- A basic social status must be assumed for all people. Women, children, and slaves of every sort must be re-enfranchised with the perquisites of full humanity.
- Hope should implicitly and constantly be recognized as the most practical of political emotions.
- Power must be redefined in nonmilitary terms.
- Justice is the specific cause of peace.
- Among other targets: legalism; the meaning of property; reverence for the earth; the arrogance of waste; the permanent human temptation to royalty; motives and reasons for altruism.

As is the way with classics, there is nothing in these writings that does not tug at modern political and economic theories with the special power of ideas whose time comes again and again.

Happily, these ideas found expression in extraordinary literature. Israel "showed astonishing creativity" in its literary production, and its writers developed "multiple forms and styles of expression that were put to the service of egalitarian communal needs."[31] Ancient Israel was a literary as well as a religious moral event. The reign-of-God utopianism of Israel and subsequently of Christianity found eloquent—indeed, classical—voice and so enjoys an enduring audibility.

PRESENT AND FUTURE

The reign of God is a symbol in two tenses. Its vibrant sense of possibility causes it to crash against the inadequate present and to struggle toward a fantastically different yet plausible future. In the present tense it calls for a totally new mind-set, for new habits of the heart and mind.

When the Bible is going to propose something drastic, it gives fair warning. Major changes are needed if this revolutionary message is to be received and understood. Jeremiah asks his readers to "remove the foreskin of [their] hearts" and to "wash" their hearts from wrongdoing (4:4, 14 RSV). All the customary ways of thinking must be jettisoned. A highway must be built through the desert of our minds. The mountains must be made into valleys and the valleys into mountains (Isa. 40:3-5; Luke 3:4-6). The opening cry of the Christian Scriptures is for *metanoia* (Mark 1:14). This Greek word, etymologically, means only change of mind, but in the Semitic cast of biblical literature, it takes on stronger emotive content. It calls for a shift in feeling, sensitivity, and seeing, and represents a divorce from previous attitudes.[32] The Scriptures fully recognize that this will not be easy. The early hearers of this new vision are berated for their obtuseness: "Have you no inkling yet? . . . Are your minds closed? You have eyes: can you not see? You have ears: can you not hear?" (Mark 8:17-18). Our own security blinds us to the possibility of a society reformed and reimagined. "It is easier for a camel to pass through the eye of a needle than for a rich man to enter the kingdom of God" (Mark 10:25).

The axe must be laid to the roots of our old mental habits (Luke 3:9). The transition to a higher level of consciousness and entering into this new vision of life can even be compared to going back into the womb and being reborn (John 3:4). Clearly this literature does not underestimate its own radicality.

Herbert Marcuse expresses this mind-set when he says with pregnant enigma: "That which is cannot be true."[33] The now is heavy with the not yet. Here Marcuse is at one with John's "what we shall be has not yet been disclosed" (1 John 3:2). Our present, debased existence is not definitive. The call is to radical openness to an alternative future. The reign of God is a summons to adventure and to a destabilization of the status quo. Bonding with the given state of things is seen as adulterous. Present structures, perceptions, and pieties cannot lock us in and stifle us, for the reign of God is movement that brooks no atrophy.

The theology of the spirit , or breath, of Yahweh expresses the confidence that impregnates reign-of-God imagery.[34] The Israelites were keenly aware of the human resistance to the new state of affairs they were imagining. Their pessimistic views on human iniquity are stark. Still, their sense of possibility was expressed in terms of God's life-giving breath. This spirit could move over the chaos of the forming earth and bring order and beauty and life

(Genesis 1). Genesis is prologue to exodus.[35] Creation is prehistory to the main event of liberation of the oppressed from Egypt. In this light, the same Yahweh whose breath turned chaos into beauty and order is also the Lord of the exodus and of human history. That same powerful spirit is available to us. Ours is also the can-do spirit of Yahweh. "I will put my spirit into you" (Ezek. 36:27). As a result, the nations will know God's plan for human life by seeing it in action in the people of Yahweh (Ezek. 36:23). Israel was convinced that good ideas are communicable.

In this way, the Hebrews expressed their profound hope in the malleability of their society and of all the nations of the world. In spite of the obstacles, in spite of the stupidity and arrogance of humankind, it can happen. Maybe even soon, many naïvely thought. The Kaddish, the prayer at the end of synagogue services, is full of hope: "May he let his kingdom rule in your lifetime and in your days in the lifetime of the whole house of Israel, speedily and soon."[36] The same sentiment is in Jesus' beautiful prayer: "Thy kingdom come" (Luke 11:2).

Hope is the matrix of all powerful ideology.[37] A decadent culture is one where false absolutes, or idols, reign. Reign-of-God symbolism accosts all idols. It dethrones all our divinized arrangements. Eric Voegelin writes of Christianity what he also could have written of Israel: "The Christians were persecuted for a good reason; there was a revolutionary substance in Christianity that made it incompatible with paganism. . . . What made Christianity so dangerous was its uncompromising, radical de-divinization of the world."[38] In the third century CE, the power of this seditious group was enough that the Emperor Decius said he was less concerned about the revolt of a rival emperor than he was about the election of a new bishop in Rome.[39] The Kaddish's "Let his kingdom rule" and Jesus' "Thy kingdom come" may have become hackneyed and harmless pieties by thoughtless repetition. But in their origins, they represented aspirations that were politically, economically, and personally revolutionary. They invite reapplication in our times.

Chapter Four

JUSTICE BIBLE-STYLE

The English word *justice* is thin broth compared to the favored Hebrew word for justice, *tsedaqah*. I experienced its emotive strength one time when I traveled from New York to Washington on a train with a charming old rabbi. We had a lively conversation about all the goods and evils of the world and I sensed in him a strong moral passion for justice, a passion seasoned with a very gentle spirit. As we parted, I said, "Sir, you have in your heart the true *tsedaqah*." And he winced. I wondered about that wince for a long time. But the more I studied *tsedaqah* the better I knew that what I said to him was, "Sir, you have beating in your chest the very heart of God." And his humble wince said, "Too much, too much." That's the power of the word.

In the preceding chapter we saw that the reign of God evokes an image of a topsy-turviness in which the first will be last and the last will be first (Matt. 19:30). It says we can break free of the stranglehold of the status quo, no longer adapting ourselves "to the patterns of the present world order," but, in a root-level transformation, letting our "minds" be "remade" and our very "nature" be "transformed" (Rom. 12:2). All the stodgy economic and political absolutes of the old world are melted in the heat of this imagery.

Genesis pictured us as patterned on nothing less than the "image" of God (Gen. 1:26). That, however, was a challenge, not a fact. It was an imperative, not an indicative. The project of establishing the reign of God by making ourselves over into "the likeness of God" (Eph. 4:23-24), as imaged in these traditions, may be the tallest order in the history of moral symbols.

The reign of God, however, is not odorless, colorless, or shapeless. The great reversal is not from something to an unspecified otherness, but from one set of moral, economic, and political assumptions to others at the antipodes. Beyond any doubt, *justice* is the primary distinguishing theme and hallmark of the new order envisioned by the reign. If reign-of-God symbolism is the defining inspiration of the biblical symphony, justice is its *leitmotiv.* The form that justice takes in these traditions is unique and countercultural to modern western theories of justice. This innovative, biblical justice, this *tsedaqah*, is the foundation of the reign of God, the secret of the humanity that could have been and could yet be. Biblical literature drums incessantly on this central category.

Every viable society knows, as Aristotle did, that justice "holds the city together."[1] Israel knew it and fashioned a theory of justice that would create an entirely new kind of city. For Aristotle, justice was to sustain people in their place in the community. Current status was an absolute, and justice involved not transgressing the current arrangements.[2] In this kind of justice "marginal people remain marginal *after* justice is finished."[3] Israel's concept of justice was more creative than Aristotle's. It would put an end to marginality.

This metamorphic theory of justice emerged insistently over centuries in the remarkable assortment of biblical writings. In spite of the variety of authors and times that produced this literature, it remains surprisingly true that "there is a unified picture of justice which appears throughout the canon and in a great variety of literary forms."[4] To accentuate this grand theme and stress its core status, the Bible does two things: it identifies justice with God, which is the highest compliment available in the imagination of this society, and it predicts total social, political, and economic collapse if this kind of justice is not realized. The biblical writers do not feign modesty about the importance of their discovery. Justice, *tsedaqah,* defines life's latent possibilities and its essential needs.

THE PRIMACY OF JUSTICE

The gods in ancient religions were not always tied to morality, and, often enough, were a fairly scandalous bunch of rascals. Not so in the morality-centered religion of Israel. Though the pictures of God that Israel paints are at times puzzling and contradictory, there is a strong thrust toward seeing God as not only committed to justice, but actually defined by it, at times in extravagant language. God is a "God of justice" (Isa. 30:18) whose heart is set on justice (Jer. 9:24). God "loves justice" (Ps. 99:4). It is the foundation of God's throne and the grounding of divine majesty (Ps. 97:3). God's reign will be established and sustained by justice (Isa. 9:7). If you ask in what sense God is holy, the answer is that it is only by justice that "the holy God shows himself holy" (Isa. 5:16). Holiness is thus *morally* defined, and justice is the ultimate moral expression. Justice is the sacrament of encounter with God because the act of justice "belongs to God" (Deut. 1:17). Being just is being "in the likeness of God." If God is committed to this form of justice, so, too, must we be, since God is the pattern of our reality. This God of justice "secures justice for widows and orphans, and loves the alien who lives among you, giving him food and clothing." The moral corollary of this is spelled out: "You too must love the alien . . ." (Deut. 10:17-19). (Notice how justice-talk blends into love-talk.) To practice *tsedaqah,* you must *love* the alien. Justice, indeed, is the primary love-language of the Bible. Quite typical of his tradition, Jesus "seems to have been sparing in his use of the word 'love'" as a noun or a verb.[5]

Abraham Heschel puts it this way: justice is nothing less than "God's stake in history." If life is clay, justice is "the mold in which God wants history to be shaped."[6] Justice is "the way of the Lord." The greatness of Abraham was that he was commissioned to teach it to "all nations on earth" (Gen. 18:17-19). In Martin Buber's phrasing, justice constitutes the completion of creation "by human activity."[7]

PEACE AS THE PAYLOAD OF JUSTICE

It is stunning and even depressing to see the frivolous things that usually win Nobel Prizes in economics. The Nobel Committee should redeem itself by awarding a posthumous prize to Isaiah for these seven words alone:"The effect of justice will be peace" (32:17). If you plant justice, you reap peace. Only when justice in all of its unique biblical meaning is established will people "live in a tranquil country" with all their cities "peaceful" and their "houses full of ease" (32:19). No other scheme, political, economic, or military, will achieve this effect. You may, like the United States, have 800 military installations around the world and pour 400 billion dollars a year into enough weaponry to destroy all life dozens of times, but "the effect of this" will not be peace. You may, like the modern state of Israel, store up hundreds of nuclear weapons and have one of the strongest military forces in the world, but the effect of this will not be peace. This reliance on kill-power is not *tsedaqah*.

Isaiah's clear message: *tsedaqah,* and only *tsedaqah,* will bring peace and economic security. "Justice, and justice alone, you shall pursue, so that you may live" (Deut. 16:20). "Justice shall redeem Zion" and nothing else. (Isa. 1:27).

Justice, then, is not at odds with well-being. In fact it's the only way to get there and stay there. Hegel reversed the old axiom "Let justice be done should the world perish" *(Fiat justitia, pereat mundus)*. Hegal rephrased this in a way that harmonizes with biblical justice:"Let justice be done or the world will perish"[8] *(Fiat justitia ne pereat mundus)*. Justice is a creative life force.

The Israelites were sure they had discovered something of universal validity. Israel was the emissary of justice to the world. "I, Yahweh, have called you to serve the cause of justice" (Isa. 42:6).[9] By living and teaching this kind of justice, Israel could be "a light to all peoples, a beacon for the nations, to open eyes that are blind" (Isa. 42:6-7). The surrounding mighty nations did not impress the Israelites. As far as they were concerned these titans were blind giants bumbling around and settling for half a life. They needed instruction on *tsedaqah* or they would die without knowing peace.

The prophets, spurred by the absence of *tsedaqah* in their nation, were obsessed with justice. "Amos, Hosea, Isaiah, and Micah know only one decisive theme: justice."[10] Nothing else counts and nothing else works. The alternative to justice is social chaos and violence. That was their message, and the history of the world since then lends credibility to their convictions. Winston Churchill is alleged to have said that people will always do the right thing after having exhausted all possible alternatives. Because we seem to have exhausted all alternatives, this classical envisioning of justice may be ripe for a revolutionary new reading.

SO WHAT IS THIS *TSEDAQAH*? TRANSLATING THE UNTRANSLATABLE

The Bible is not a textbook in economics or politics. It does, however, contain the ingredients for a major critique of both modern capitalism and socialism. The poetic and allegorical dress of these classics should not blind modern readers to the profound social theory implicit in this pregnant literature.

Fundamental concepts like justice always embody a worldview and indicate the scope of a culture's imagination. When we speak of biblical justice, however, we are often at the mercy of translators. Our pale, cold word *justice* does not express the expansiveness of biblical *tsedaqah*. The translators play the traitor even more mischievously when *tsedaqah* is translated "righteousness." When you choose a word, you cannot avoid all of its relatives, and *righteousness* brings with it some messy unsavory ones, like its cousin *self-righteous.*

AN EXERCISE IN CONTRAST

Just as the overall utopianism of Hebrew and Christian literature did not hide in blurred generality, so too justice, the prime mark of the new order, is spelled out in rich detail. An outline of its principal contrasts with the dominant western notions of justice offers an illuminating exercise in countercultural analysis.[11] Schematically, western and biblical justice diverge in the following fashion.

Western Justice	Biblical Justice
Avowedly impartial	Biased in favor of the poor and critical of the rich, i.e., the economically secure
Private definition of property	Social definition of property
Rights defined in terms of sovereign individuality	Rights defined in terms of social solidarity and need
Static and conservative	Evolutionary and revolutionary

BIAS VERSUS BIAS

Most modern western conceptions of justice stress its essential impartiality. Judges, who are supposed to symbolize justice (Aristotle called judges "living justice"), cannot be considered proper judges if they are biased, prejudiced, or partial.[12] All bias is incompatible with our abstract concept of justice. Biblical justice will have none of this. It is forthrightly biased, prejudiced, and partial. More accurately, it recognizes that *all* systems of justice are biased, covertly or overtly, and it opts for overt discovery of the bias. Biblical justice theory introduces its own bias and is up front with it.

Its bias is two-edged: it is unequivocally partial to the poor and suspicious of the rich. This meaning is etymologically grounded in the very word for justice, since the biblical root for *tsedaqah* "has from the first a bias towards the poor and needy."[13] The related Aramaic *tsidqah* meant "showing mercy to the poor."[14] Our modern tendency is to think of justice in terms of criminality or litigation. Our justice is concerned with trouble. The biblical preoccupation is wholly other. Justice is "good news," especially "to the poor" (Luke 4:18).

"So positive (versus punitive) is the terminology used for justice that according to Exodus 23:7 God says (literally), 'I will *not* do justice . . . to the wicked.' Justice applies to the innocent."[15] Justice is not reacting to evil, but responding to need. Woe to those who "deprive the poor of justice" (Isa. 10:2). The prime focus of this justice is not on the guilty, but on victims and the dispossessed.

Deuteronomy says: "You shall not deprive aliens and orphans of justice." What justice requires is spelled out in detail: never "take a widow's cloak in pledge" or a poor man's cloak if he needs it to be warm—even if it is owed to you by a mathematically strict standard of justice. "When you reap the harvest in your field and forget a swathe, do not go back to pick it up; it shall be left for the alien, the orphan, and the widow" (24:10-22). This early and often-repeated formulation of justice primarily involves not contracts and torts, but compassion, benevolence, and redistribution.[16] Augustine summed up the tradition simply when he said: "Justice consists in helping the needy and the poor."[17] The poor, quite simply, are God's children and they are marked out for special handling (Ecclus. 34:20). That special handling is the prime work of justice.[18] All this is counterintuitive to those of us bred on paler and wizened theories of justice.

Because of its overarching concern for the poor, biblical justice is not quibbling legalism. It is large-hearted and magnanimous. It does descend to the picky details of legality, but its heart is not there. For example, a text in the Mishna prescribes that if purchased goods have not yet been delivered to the purchaser, the latter may legally renege on the whole deal. That seems straightforward enough, but it does not end there. It goes on to say that if people do what the letter of the very Mishnah has just permitted, a terrifying curse will fall upon their heads: "He who punished the generation of the flood and the generation of the dispersion will take vengeance on him who does not stand by his word."[19] That does not make legalistic sense, but it does emphatically show a different mind-set that condemns petty and self-protective righteousness. Marvin Fox calls this example "extreme," and so it is. Symbols, like caricature, are permitted some extremity. The large point they are making indulges that. And the point here is that biblical justice calls for a heart larger than the small print.

There is, to be sure, lots of small print in the justice of Israel. Life will not go on without it. "You shall not pervert justice in measurement of length, weight, or quantity. You shall have true scales, true weights, true measures dry and liquid" (Lev. 19:35). "You shall not keep back a hired man's wages till next morning" (Lev. 19:13).

There is plenty of that sort of thing, common to all systems of justice. The distinctive feature of Jewish justice is the stress on *redistributive sharing and remedial systemic changes that favor the poor.* Its distinguishing accent is on what we call today social and distributive justice, not on inter-individual, or commutative, justice.

IDENTIFYING THE POOR

The Scriptures meticulously spell out who the prime targets of justice, the poor, are. Isaiah lambasts the temptation to substitute ritual and rite for justice-doing, saying that this would miss religion entirely. Real religion means doing real justice and that means helping the overworked, freeing the slaves and oppressed peoples, sharing food with the hungry, providing housing for the homeless, clothing the naked, and satisfying the needs of the wretched (Isaiah 58) with the ultimate goal of seeing that there are absolutely "no poor among you" (Deut. 15:4). *In a word, real religion dismantles empire by taking away its base of slaves.*

Psalm 146 says that there will be no happiness unless we "deal out justice to the oppressed, . . . feed the hungry, . . . set the prisoner free, . . . straighten backs that are bent," and, of course, using the usual mantra, care for the aliens, the widows, and the orphans. Jeremiah adds the victims of crime to this list (21:12). The God who is called a "God of justice" (Isa. 30:18) is also called a "God of the humble, . . . the poor, . . . the weak, . . . the desperate, . . . and the hopeless" (Jud. 9:11). Talk about weird credentials!

When Job defended his virtue, he went right to the tradition of *tsedaqah* to do it. He had been "eyes to the blind, feet to the lame, a father to the needy"; he saved the orphan, the widow, and "the poor man when he called for help." He took up the cause of persons whom he did not even know (29:12-20). It would not have fit this Hebraic tradition for Job to say simply that he had not harmed anyone, had paid his debts, and had honored all contracts. Such minimalism would have been no defense at all within the framework of biblical justice. As you can see, biblical justice transforms the whole idea of citizenship. You're not a respectable citizen if the cause of the poor is not yours. When voting, an American Christian who is faithful to this tradition would ask if the *poor* are better off than they were four years ago.

THE JESUS MOVEMENT AND THE POOR

When it comes to the poor, Jesus was "an Israelite worthy of the name."[20] In the salutatory address of his prophetic rabbinate, Jesus emphasized that what he would be about would be "good news to the poor" (Luke 4:18). According to Luke, he practiced what he preached (Luke 7:22-23). The hungry, the thirsty, the abandoned children, the widows, and all the poor were the center of his concern. And there was nothing grudging about this. In fact, the Jesus movement had a festive tone, even when it was immersed in the care of the poor. The approach to the poor was not incompatible with partying. "When you give a party, ask the poor, the crippled, the lame, and the blind; and so find happiness" (Luke 14:13). Jesus, in fact, apparently practiced what he preached in this regard and was criticized as "a drunkard and a glutton" who, unlike John the Baptist, was more for feasting than for fasting (Luke 7:31-34; Mark 2:18-20).

The reason for the festivity was the great reversal, the new moral, political, and economic order that was its goal. Once the schemes that maintained poverty had been undone, then all could really party and feast. Exploitation and poverty were to be attacked directly and generously with all possible ingenuity. The Good Samaritan is the model. He found a victim of violence, bathed and bandaged his wounds, took him to an inn, and stayed overnight to help him out. Then he left money for him and told the innkeeper that if it were necessary to spend even more on the victim, he would repay it all on his return. This active solidarity with victims was the norm for the Jesus movement. "Go and do likewise" (Luke 10:29-37).

The norm was as old as Israel. "Open wide your hand to the poor and the distressed" (Deut. 15:11). The Scriptures of the Jesus movement, like the Scriptures of ancient Israel, see the main goal of justice as the utter elimination of poverty. The essence of morality is found in our response to anyone in need (Matt. 25:31-46). Both sets of Scriptures are realistic about how poorly received this ideal is likely to be, but the ideal is pressed relentlessly.

At times, the message is extreme: "Sell everything you have, and give to the poor" (Mark 10:21). The book of Acts suggests that a strict communism, with no private property, was practiced in the Jesus movement with drastic penalties for nonconformism (Acts 4:32-35; 5:1-12). This was probably more symbol than historical fact, but again, the symbol was the message and a literal reading of this literary genre can miss the point.[21] The enduring nub of it all was this: *poverty must be eliminated by appropriate modes of sharing, and the burden of ending poverty falls on the economically secure.* No particular form of government was prescribed, but modes of societal sharing that would eliminate poverty were essential and feasible. On this, the Jewish and Christian Scriptures are at one.[22]

THE SACRAMENTAL STATUS OF THE POOR

In the most soaring metaphors imaginable, these writers gave the poor the highest standing in society, virtually identifying the poor with God: "He who oppresses the poor insults his Maker" (Prov. 14:31). When David abused poor Uriah and Bathsheba, his crime, so massively punished, was to have "despised" God (2 Sam. 12:9-10). Anyone who acts unjustly against people "commits a grievous fault against the Lord" (Lev. 6:2). According to Matthew's Gospel, whatever you do for the most demeaned of persons you have done for the Lord. Similarly, to neglect any of the dispossessed is to turn your back on God (Matt. 25:31-46). Thus does this literature draw upon its most sublime superlative, divinity itself, to champion the humanity and rights of poor people.

Holiness is closeness to God, the source of life and hope, and thus holiness is the goal of all biblical morality. Justice is the only way to achieve it. Often, holiness is expressed in terms of *knowledge* of God: "He dispensed justice to the lowly and poor; did not this show he knew me? says the Lord" (Jer. 22:16). And to the contrary, if you treat your fellow unjustly it means "you have forgotten me" (Exod. 22:12). Knowledge of God in biblical language means affective bonding with God. Without care for the poor, the linkage to

God is ruptured. The alternative to active and proactive concern for the poor is moral, religious, and spiritual bankruptcy.

THE POOR RICH

The same Luke who said "blessed are you poor" added with equal bluntness: "Woe to you rich" (Luke 6:20, 24). There are wealthy people who are paupers in the sight of God (Luke 12:21). In all of this, Jesus was not original, but was the heir of an ancient Hebraic suspicion. Deuteronomy had set the tone: wealth can make its possessors unfeeling and cold. Take care "when you have plenty to eat and live in fine houses, . . . when your herds and flocks increase, and your silver and gold and all your possessions increase too." All too easily these things can lead to "haughtiness of heart" and forgetfulness of justice (Deut. 8:11-18). Jeremiah sounded the warning. He presented God as condemning those who "grow rich and grand, bloated and rancorous; their thoughts are all of evil and they refuse to do justice [to the] orphans [and to] the poor" (Jer. 5:25-28). Empire builders, take heed! "Money has been the ruin of many and has misled the minds of kings," says Ecclesiasticus (8:2). "He who hopes to be rich, must be ruthless. A peg will stick in the joint between two stones, and sin will wedge itself between selling and buying" (Ecclus. 27:1-2).[23] The distinguished rabbi Hillel had a similar cynicism regarding those involved in what we would call "business and high finance." "He that engages overmuch in trade cannot become wise."[24]

The prophets showed the same suspicion of excessive wealth. They railed at the rich who are accused of "building Zion in bloodshed" (Mic. 3:10). "The spoils of the poor are in your houses" (Isa. 3:14). Habakkuk looked at the homes of the rich and said that they had "built a town with bloodshed" (Hab. 2:12). Amos lashed at those who "hoard in their palaces the gains of crime and violence" (3:10). The accumulation of wealth was seen as potentially or even probably violent because of its relationship to the poverty of the poor.[25] "Bread is life to the destitute, and it is murder to deprive them of it" (Ecclus. 34:21). The logic of all of this led inexorably to redistribution, and Judaism did not flag before this demanding implication.

The Torah calls for specific modes of redistribution through such historic innovations as the sabbatical and jubilee years, as we shall see shortly.

Jesus was one of the toughest of the prophets when it came to the powerful rich. When Jesus made his sarcastic comment about a camel passing through the eye of a needle the apostles were "astonished" and thought he had overstated the case. Rather than backing down, he went on to say it would take a miracle for a rich man to understand and join the reign of God and its justice. For us, "it is impossible, but not for God; everything is possible for God" (Mark 10:25-27).

Jesus was obviously raised this way by his mother. Luke pictures Mary echoing the sentiments of Hannah, the mother of Samuel—sentiments that were by then the warp and the woof of the tradition (see Ps. 107:39-41). Both women, in their short, great reversal soliloquies, plunge into criticism of the rich and call for redistribution of wealth to the poor. Hannah rejoiced in the God who distinctively and typically would "lift the weak out of the dust and raise the poor from the dunghill." The first again are last for Hannah—a mark of the reign of God—because "those who had plenty sell themselves for a crust and the hungry grow strong again" (1 Sam. 2:8).

Mary also rejoiced in the redistributive predilections of God. Her short Magnificat has been called "one of the most revolutionary documents in all literature, containing three separate revolutions," moral, political, and economic.[26] "The hungry he has satisfied with good things, the rich sent empty away." The "arrogant of heart" and the "monarchs" are routed and the "humble" are lifted high (Luke 1:46-55).

Mary was a clever subversive. She began on a pious, totally nonthreatening note: "My soul magnifies the Lord and my spirit rejoices in God my savior." Power-holding bystanders would say: "That's fine, dear, you magnify away there: it won't disturb us." But having put them at ease, she roared into her blistering attack on the assumptions of the arrogant rich. There is nothing balanced about the message of these two Jewish women. Indeed, the rhetoric is overstated, and it almost looks like the goal is to make the rich poor, and the poor rich. Such is not the case. The aim of Torah is that "there will never be any poor among you" (Deut. 15:4). The point, poetically and prophetically made, is that the burden of proof for poverty must be shifted from the poor to the rich, to those who have the power to make change. This is what the scriptural bias for the poor means. If people are poor, the arrangements of the powerful rich are primarily responsible. The burden of proof rests with the power-holders of the society. That is the crucial foundation of biblical economic theory. If your brother is weak, it is your problem to go find him and make him strong (Lev. 25:35). You do not huddle in security with kith and kin, but must make "the stranger's cause" your own. If there are feeble arms out there, it is for the strong to strengthen them; if there are tottering knees, the well established should steady them (Isa. 35:3-4).

This is pointedly countercultural to western ideas, and particularly to American attitudes. We put the burden of proof firmly on the deprived. Wealth and possessions are their own vindication. They are, in fact, the sacramental badge of virtue. The philosophy of John Hay is quintessentially American. Hay looked disdainfully on the labor riots of 1877, seeing in them society's propertyless dregs rising up against law and order. His view, according to his biographer, was this: "That you have property is proof of industry and foresight on your part or your father's; that you have nothing is a judgment on your laziness and vices or on your improvidence. The world is a moral world: which it would not be if virtue and vice received the same rewards."[27]

Herbert Spencer was clearer yet: "Each adult gets benefits in proportion to merit, reward in proportion to desert."[28] If you've got it, you deserve it. Bishop Lawrence of Massachusetts joined this merry chorus of the elite: "In the long run, it is only to the man of morality that wealth comes. . . . Godliness is in league with riches."[29] Those who have, deserve, and on the nether side, those who do not have, do not deserve. This is not gospel, good news, for the poor, but glad gospel for the rich. The widows, orphans, and the homeless must fend for themselves. God and the godly are not in league with them. The worthy haves need not concern themselves for the unworthy have-nots. Notice again how God-talk is always ethics. It always embodies a moral worldview.

This dour philosophy of self-righteousness did not die with Hay and Spencer. Robert Nozick displays the same insular egoism in 1974: "There is no justified sacrifice of some of us for others."[30] His resistance to sharing and his absolutizing of the right to property go the full limit: "Taxation of earnings from labor is on a par with forced labor."[31] There is no good news for the poor in this cold American gospel.

The biblical perspective, on the contrary, lifts the burden of proof from the stooped shoulders of the dispossessed and powerless and assigns it firmly to the well-off and secure. This makes good sense. It puts the burden where the power is.[32] And it recognizes, with Aristotle, that "the greatest crimes are caused by excess and not by necessity."[33] People do not become tyrants, said Aristotle, just to keep warm, but in the pursuit of the honor that comes from wealth and power. It is the pursuit of this hostile passion—which, absent morality, has no brakes—that the just society must restrain.[34]

Again, Christianity was not original in all of this. Judaism led the way in indicting "the scandals of priests," "the callousness of the rich," and "the corruption of the judges."[35] It recognized early on that power—sacral, economic, and political—can corrupt, and prescribed its special form of justice as the antidote. That antidote would call for some specific modes of redistribution, and the traditions also attended ingeniously to that social need.

REDISTRIBUTION:
THE SABBATH AND THE JUBILEE

Israel was convinced that if we allow unlimited, laissez-faire plunder and accumulation, both the poor and the earth will suffer and there will be no peace. Israel responded to this reality through such inventions as the sabbath and the jubilee. The civilizing concept of the sabbath—bequeathed to modernity by ancient Israel—was based on the insight that life is not just work. It is also play, joy, celebration, relief from burdens, and "sacred rest" (Lev. 25:5). This clearly had social justice implications since it would be hard for the poor to play and dance and take their rest while weighed down with the ruinous burden of poverty. There is also a marked ecological aspect to the sabbath and to *tsedaqah*. What is good for the human goose is good for the terrestrial gander. Every seventh year, the land is to be left in untilled peace. There shall be a sabbath of the land; "the land shall keep a sabbath of sacred rest." It will, of course, keep producing during this year of rest, and what it produces should be shared with strangers and kin, and with animals, domestic and wild (Lev. 25:5-7). Not to do this would be to risk forgetting the status of the earth as a gift to be shared (Deut. 8:11-19).

In every seventh, sabbatical year, the inevitable encumbrances that afflict the earth and its dwellers should be relaxed. Debts—even honest and fair debts—should be cancelled and all slaves should be released (Deut. 15:12-18). Narrow legalisms must yield to a more generous disposition. But even the sabbatical was not enough in this theory of economic justice. The Israelites believed that wealth and poverty both tend to become excessive. This is a structural defect that can only be structurally corrected. Hence, every fiftieth year would be the jubilee year. If people had lost their land through legitimate bankruptcy, it was to be restored to them. The persons who had added this land to their own by means fair and legal must now yield it. (It is God's property, anyhow.) It is only right that "each man shall dwell under his own vine, under his own fig-tree undisturbed" (Mic. 4:4). The reason for this radical redistribution? "There shall be no poor among you" (Deut. 15:4) because "poverty is the undoing of the helpless" (Prov. 10:15). And "precious" in the eyes of God is the blood of the poor (Ps. 72:14).

One might wonder if all these ideals were realized. Of course they were not, and the biblical literature was not naïve about sin. After stipulating the elimination of poverty as the goal of both justice and religion (Deut. 15:4), it is impatiently admitted a few verses later that "the poor will always be with you" (v. 11). The Gospel of Mark says the same: "You have the poor among you always" (Mark 14:7). If the United States disappeared and all that subsequent ages found was our Declaration of Independence and other foundational documents, those texts would hardly tell them how life was lived here. They would, however, tell of our ideals and might intimate that we tried to live up to them.

What is striking in early Israel is that these onerous and unique demands–such as the massive redistribution demanded by jubilee legislation—were actually ensconced into the solemnity of Torah. They were the sacred law of the land. And we do know that they were not always ignored. Even in Deuteronomy there are signs of nervousness about the remission of debts (Deut. 15:7-11). Leviticus recognized that these rules were not always well received (25:20-21). To keep credit from drying up, efforts were made to circumvent the rigidities of the law. The necessity to do this shows that the ideals were there and that there were efforts to enforce them, efforts that continued into the time of Jesus.[36] Indeed, the spirit of the jubilee was "not marginal, but central to the teaching of Jesus."[37]

Aside from jubilee and sabbatical, other laws pervade the Torah. Farmers are told never to reap all of the harvest in their fields; neither should they strip their vineyards or glean all the fallen grapes. "You shall leave them for the poor and the alien" (Lev. 19:10). Every third year, a tenth of all the year's produce was to be laid up in the towns so that the poor could "come and eat their fill" (Deut. 14:29). The Pentateuch also set stringent limits on taking interest on loans. "If you advance money to any poor man amongst my people, you shall not act like a money-lender: you must not exact interest in advance from him" (Exod. 22:25). These writers recognized the common human imperial temptation to use "accumulated wealth" as "leverage over poor and powerless people."[38] But the goal of Israel's social justice system was a "living unity of the many and the diverse." Torah worked for this "by means of a reviewed leveling of the ownership of the soil."[39] The right to ownership was tempered by social needs. Every society tempers ownership, but in Israel the goal was spelled out. Absolute property rights were modified by the need for the absolute elimination of poverty. You can "own" but you cannot ignore how you got what you "own" and what impact it had on others. Jesus' injunction to give to the poor is "not rooted in self-satisfying charity, but in God-ordained socially required restitution."[40]

The core idea behind all of this does not dissolve with the economic simplicities of ancient Israel. The ideal of the jubilee was to restore the productive capacities of the able poor. The need for such redistributive empowerment endures. The problems of poor nations strapped by debt to rich nations and of starving people existing alongside sybaritic wealth are quite contemporary and are still just as antithetical to peace.

Though studies of influences on modern policies are always tentative the redistributive principles of justice born in ancient Israel are a probable influence on western humanitarian theories of progressive taxation and social-welfare policy.[41] It is fair and even wise to reappropriate them when an old human problem exists in a new form. Thus, Trude Weiss-Rosmarin, writing in the *Jewish Spectator,* says of the sabbatical and the jubilee: "Obviously this was *expropriation.* But it was considered necessary so as to restore socioeconomic equity and equilibrium."[42] Structural injustice requires structural relief and a relativizing of private claims by setting them into their social context. She goes on to apply this ancient insight to a justification of affirmative action. The principle of the jubilee alone would not provide a full case for anything as specific as affirmative action, but it does add perspective to the enduring problem of unfair monopoly and the need for redistributive relief. Our problems are not entirely new, and conversation with past solutions illumines dimensions and sharpens our analyses.

That we owe prime attention to the poor and that if we ignore them we will not know peace are hard-nosed biblical ideas whose time has never passed. These ideas are the economic and political linchpins of the original Jewish, Christian, and Islamic movements. Take note: the option for the poor is not only a sublime moral choice; it is also in our enlightened self-interest. That insight has not lost its potency or applicability.

THE SYMBOLS OF JUSTICE

Symbols clash when cultures meet. It is instructive to see the contrasting symbols of justice chosen by the modern United States and by ancient Israel. The preferred symbol of justice in the U.S. is a blindfolded woman holding a scale that balances perfectly. There is our dream of justice: neat, mathematically balanced, and blindfolded! We must suspect that this effort would bring smiles to the face of an Amos, a Micah, or a Jesus. For the prophets of Israel justice is not found "blindfoldedly holding the scales in just equality."[43] The sin-conscious advice of biblical realism to the lady in question would be to remove the blindfold and see who is tampering with the scales. With the blindfold gone, she will quickly see that the scales never do balance. The actual administration of justice is affected by factors of status, gender, class, and race. And so, for biblical justice theory, the image of the gentle lady with the balanced scales is sweet in its optimistic idealism, but hopelessly naïve.[44]

Biblical justice, eschewing scales and blindfolds, offers in their stead the symbol of a mighty mountain stream, roaring down a ravine with enormous power, taking with it all it touches (Amos 5:23). My understanding of this text grew when I spent a week speaking to a group of Lutheran pastors in the high mountains of Colorado. It was my first experience of the summer Rockies. As you approach one of these torrents that feed on ancient glaciers and winter snows, you hear an ominous and awesome roar. When you come closer, you see spume rising up, as tons of water smash against the resisting rocks, gradually defeating them. One instinctively draws back, for it could be fatal to fall into this surging rapid. Indeed, one of the pastors, attempting to take a picture of a scene close to this mighty stream, lost his footing and fell in. Fortunately, he was immediately thrown against a large rock. Had no one been there, he would never have been able to move, pinned as he was by the force of the water. With the help of ropes and the strong arms of friends, he was tugged to safety.

So here was Amos's symbol of justice. Obviously, it is worlds away from our placid statue of the unseeing lady. But what does it mean, this massive rush of water, stampeding down the side of the mountain, gobbling up everything in its path—Lutheran pastors included?

Water, of course, even in its stillness, is the richest of symbols. It nourishes, gives life, cleanses, and restores. Unless the Earth is baptized in water it fades into death. But when the waters of justice roll down, like Amos's mighty river, their purpose is the absolute elimination of poverty and the sweeping away of all of its causes.

Justice is active and relentless, wearing down the rocks of resistance, effacing poverty and washing away all its pernicious causes. This is the poetic imagery Israel chose when it spoke of justice.

OWNING, NEEDING, AND RIGHTS

No theory of justice can claim profundity if it does not accost the concept of property and ownership. Biblical justice theory wrestles with this subject relentlessly and honestly. It sets a good example for all social theorists because, most often, law, economics, and politics operate out of hidden philosophical assumptions. What Justice Benjamin Cardozo said of law has broader application: implicit in all the judgments of law is some particular philosophy of values, "a philosophy which, however veiled, is in truth the final arbiter. It accepts one set of arguments, modifies another, rejects a third, standing ever in reserve as a court of ultimate appeal," pressing constantly "to the front or to the rear."[45]

Modern economic theories are usually self-servingly naïve about their philosophical and historical underpinnings. They are unaware of the motors that drive them. Modern capitalism, particularly, knows little of its moral lineage. It neither senses nor acknowledges the value assumptions that push it "to the front or to the rear." Acknowledged or not, capitalism has "a court of ultimate appeal" that exercises hidden controls over how it functions and responds to new crises. It assumes that its current notion of private property is the obvious and untainted law of nature and that any other view is heretical. George Bernard Shaw said that a barbarian was one who thought that the customs of the tribe were the laws of nature. His irony stingingly applies to modern capitalists with their unquestioned and contradictory notions of property. History does not smile on such confusion.

THE PRIVACY OF PROPERTY

Recent adoption of some capitalist ideas in Eastern Europe and in parts of the former Soviet Union is understandable. This does not mean, however, that the sinner has been saved by the saint. European, American, and Latin American capitalisms are not victimless success stories, nor are they all the same. And the crowing over the fall of bungled communist systems shows adolescent bravado, not a sense of reality. Considerable offense was taken in 1981 when the conservative Pope John Paul II did a moral assessment of communism and capitalism and pronounced a pox on both their houses.[46] The pope's biblically based critique, though unpopular, raised questions that are rarely asked, much less answered. Capitalism is too cocksure of itself to dare a perestroika with all the profound self-questioning it necessarily involves.

First, then, to the two cardinal principles regarding private property that are controlling in most forms of modern capitalism; then to the sharp and telling criticism of those notions available in the biblical classics. The two cardinal principles are (1) property is sacred, and (2) the individual is prior to and superior to the community.

Rome's Lasting Empire: Property as Sacred

Rome's military imperium failed, but its law did not. The majority of law students in the world are still fed with it. It dominates the legal systems of most of western Europe, the United States, and beyond. "The law of places so diverse as Louisiana and Ceylon, Quebec and Japan, Abyssinia and South Africa is based firmly on Roman law."[47] And it was Roman law that pioneered and enshrined the concept of private property, which dominates many cultures.

This notion of unlimited property rights was a historical novelty. Even in Rome, for millennia before the Caesars, tribal and nomadic peoples held much more in common than they claimed individually.[48] "All tribes and peoples, in all countries and continents of the globe, originally viewed the right to land as a common right." The main natural resources that are essential to survival could not be monopolized by anyone. They did uphold "the individual's exclusive right to the produce of his or her labor."[49] But this primeval ethics obviously insisted on a considerable amount of sharing and common ownership, and it resisted the idea that one person could lay absolute claim to the product of someone else's labor. All of this changed in Rome, which conceived new predatory economic practices while ethical theory and law trailed along uncritically.

Through the appropriation of public lands and the takeover of small holdings, the huge Roman estates created a dominant aristocracy. Sharing yielded to a new kind of owning and to the idea that you could absolutely own the fruit of other people's labor. The owner was deemed to have the right to use, enjoy, or abuse whatever he owned—*ius utendi, fruendi, abutendi.*[50] Any social dimension is removed by this absolutizing of individual possessive right. The needs of others—or of the environment—did not factor in to this theoretic of ownership.

One of the first fruits of this imperial ownership arrangement was slavery. When you acquired much more land than you and yours could work, you developed a need for free or cheap labor, and so a new class of slaves and indentured tenants was created. Homelessness also ensued, as more lands were gobbled up. "The great estates," said Pliny, "ruined Italy," and Tiberius Gracchus lamented that the animals had their lairs and holes in which to rest, but the people of Italy were "without house and home."[51]

The assumptions behind this new system were widely unexplored, as they are often in our day. Those who own a plant have a right to close it with no regard (and possibly with no advance notice) for those whose labor enriched its owners. Roman law would raise no questions. *Res fructificat dominum*—property enriches the *owner*. Others have no rights beyond negotiated salaries. Third-world debt is repaid by gouging the poor through "austerity measures" imposed by the International Monetary Fund.[52] "It is the poorest people who suffer most from the "austerity measures required when a country seeks the IMF 'seal of approval.'"[53] The philosophy we inherited from Rome allows us to sacrifice the rights, and even the lives, of the third-world poor to our property rights. The sanctity of property trumps the sanctity of life.

Ravenous executive bonuses raise no questions for those with a Roman sense of absolute ownership.[54] Since the top executives function as the owners, they have *dominum,* a Latin word for private property. (The Greek is *despoteia,* which is the root, tellingly, of the English word *despotic.)* There is no assumed limit to their right to use, enjoy, and abuse. The workers have no more natural right to protest this than did the serfs and tenant farmers.

The reason given for these huge remunerations of executives is often "incentive." Clearly this is specious since those who need that amount of money to be motivated should find work in which they are more interested. In simple honesty, this greedy grab is a purely logical extension of the absolute right to private property that has been willed to us by the patricians of Rome. So deeply is this concept of private property imprinted on our social consciousness that few can even recognize the mischief it begets. As executives in pursuit of "incentives" gobble up corporate profits, funds are diverted from research, from plant and technology improvements, and from alternate investments. This adds to the prices of products, thus hurting competition, and it hardly inspires workers or stockholders. Were we not so convinced of the unlimited right to own, these costly, productivity-damaging considerations would impress us—and would offend at least our business sense. But there is nothing so powerful as an idea whose hegemony is unsuspected for generations.

Private property is not an evil. We cannot imagine a society without some of it.[55] The failure of most modern capitalism is making it absolute. When we absolutize something it becomes a dominant power, an idol. This theoretical absolutism can, of course, never be realized in practice. Taxation and other modes of sharing are inevitably enacted out of practical necessity. Many, however, see these essential sharings as intrusions to be minimized. Politicians imbued with this mean-spirited philosophy run "against government" and "against taxes" because government enforces the essential sharing processes.

By its own inner logic, the absolutized notion of private property is unrelated to the common good or the environment. It has no solidarity with the needs of others, to whom it relates out of perceived advantage only by a "social contract." It can no longer speak the language of Thomas Jefferson, who said that when there are unemployed poor, "it is clear that the laws of property have been so far extended as to violate natural right."[56] Absolute ownership has no natural relationship with justice or with love. It cannot be the foundation of a just or fair society because it is a form of hostile ideological egoism.

In the expression "the absolute right to private property," two words tell it all. *Private* means "to take away from or deprive," and denotes separation. *Absolute* means "to loosen or separate from," and denotes that a right called "absolute" is not limited by any other claims.[57] When the terms are wed, they imply radical isolation and a simplistic innocence of the social dimension of both being and *having.* This brings us to the second principle of modern western ownership: *individualism.*

Of Hobbes and Horatio Alger: Individualism

No socially ensconced concept, such as "property is sacred," is traceable to only one source. Roman law does not get all the blame. Douglas Meeks, for example, argues that the attributes of God such as absolute autonomy that were developed in ancient Greece infected Christian theology and crept from there into the modern notion of property. Plato's "maker and father of the universe"[58] was self-sufficient and unrelated to other beings. Such a god could do whatever he pleased. Freedom implied unfettered mastery. He could, in effect, use, enjoy, or abuse whatever was his. This gave divine blessing to autonomous, absolute ownership and provided potent symbols for western political economy. The mind feeds on symbols, and these religious symbols were partially noxious. The ancient attributes of God "are at the heart of many modern and contemporary notions of property."[59] Secular society had no trouble moving from "the earth is the Lord's" to "the earth is ours," and it is ours on the same absolute terms. (Knowing how we know is the beginning of all wisdom, and yet we rarely do.)

Add to this the seventeenth-century stress on the primacy of the individual. Thomas Hobbes was a major actor in this cultural shift and there was a cruel isolationism at the heart of his thought. As C. B. MacPherson wrote: "Discarding traditional concepts of society, justice, and natural law, [Hobbes] deduced political rights and obligation from the interest and will of dissociated individuals."[60] Maggie Thatcher lived this out as she transferred wealth from the bottom to the top. She could not have a social conscience since she did not admit the existence of society. "There is no such thing as Society. There are individual men and women and there are families."[61]

Discarding the concepts of society and justice is the very definition of radical mischief. The utilitarian theories of the eighteenth and nineteenth centuries enlarged this mischief and successfully infused "possessive individualism" into the modern western mind. Again MacPherson: "Its possessive quality is found in its conception of the individual as essentially the proprietor of his [or her] own person or capacities, owing nothing to society for them."[62] Society came to be seen as a collection of proprietors, and politics was for the protection of property and the maintenance of an orderly system of exchange.[63] For those who were not in the retinue of the wheeler-dealers, the outlook was bleak.

The shift here is from seeing property as a *means to an end,* to seeing the accumulation of property as an *end in itself.* The instrumental view of property pointed toward the end of justice, security, and peace. When property is viewed solipsistically as an end, it points to nothing but itself. It is divorced from conscience. During the development of liberal utilitarianism from John Locke to Jeremy Bentham, the accumulation of property became an ethical end in itself.[64] Those who had plenty of it could call themselves noble and *gentle*men. Wealth, in and of itself, had a sacramental value. This "liberal" tradition survives and pounds at us, in varying versions, from the seemingly gentle John Rawls to the overtly un-gentle Milton Friedman. It offers us "a murky theoretical prospect" at best.[65] How could it offer more? Its individualistic definition of rights takes too little account of needs and is deficient in its sense of human solidarity.[66] Essential needs are important because persons are important. To ignore the essential needs of others is an implicit denial of their stature as persons. It is barbaric.

Small wonder the firstborn child of such theory is scarcity. "There is scarcity because *need is not [treated as] an economic category.*"[67] The right to acquisition would be limited if it gave moral standing to the needs of others. Property could not be so sacred if need, too, had sacred claims.

The place of property is the key to one's social theory. It reveals either a noxious egoism or a sense of human solidarity. The dominant property view of western capitalism is suspect in its origins and, not rarely, lethal in its effects.

INCONSISTENCY AS SAVING GRACE

Of course, no person or theory is consistent. Even where capitalism is the national creed, private property is limited by way of taxes, tariffs, eminent domain, environmental-impact laws, land preserves, and so on. In the United States some account of the needs of others is expressed in programs like Medicaid, Medicare, and affirmative action. Such programs, however, are stinting and halfhearted, not to mention constantly controversial because they have no natural home in our reigning theory. They are ultimately anomalous to our possessive individualism and anomalies rarely thrive. Efficiency is valued highly, but in a system of competitive acquisition, it is not the efficient meeting of *needs,* but of *wants,* that rules. Hence the estimates of very poor people run as high as 60 million in the United States, a nation that prides itself on being the richest nation in the world.

Also missing in possessive individualism is any coherent sense of the common good so there is no theoretical space for either distributive or social justice, which are concerned with how the to-and-fro dealings of all individuals influence the common good. *Individual,* or *commutative, justice* is concerned only with dealings between two individual persons or entities. This form of justice provides most of the work for lawyers and courts. *Social justice* is what individuals owe to the common good, taxes, service on juries, surrendering of property to "eminent domain," obedience to just laws, and so forth. *Distributive justice* relates to the fair distribution by the various social powers of the goods and burdens of the society, as in providing a tax system that does not privilege the rich, breakup of hostile monopolies, and so forth. Government is the main, but not the only, agent of distributive justice.[68] Political or economic theory that operates without explicit theories of social and distributive justice acts out of a blind faith in the beneficence of chance. Possessive individualism, sometimes called conservatism today, does just that.

This abortive theory also lacks a sense of internationalism. Tribalism, nationalism, and empire are examples of extended egoism. It is logical for an individualistic nation to want to become an empire. Otherwise it has to recognize the essential needs of others and work cooperatively and fairly with them.

John Chrysostom, a dynamic fourth-century Christian, wrote that words like *mine* and *thine* are "chilly words that introduce innumerable wars into the world."[69] These chilly words are unavoidable and can have positive moral content, but they are also open windows to the soul. The word *mine* always harbors a philosophy of society. It reveals our attitudes toward other people. "Ownership is a relation, but not so much a relation between a person and the thing owned as between the owning person and other people, whom the owner excludes from, or to whom the owner concedes, possession."[70] The sense of ownership in modern capitalism is neither intellectually nor ethically complete. In place of a theory of social justice it offers a naïve faith in the "ideology of beneficent cupidity" and in a utopia powered by self-interest.[71] It is a faith system that believes, in the teeth of inveterate contrary evidence, that greed will erect a cornucopia from which goods will trickle out to one and all. But there is no empirical base for the bland and blind optimism that grounds social Darwinism and laissez-faire conservatism. Raw capitalism doesn't work. Economist Paul Samuelson says: "We have eaten of the Fruit of the Tree of Knowledge and, for better or worse, there is no returning to *laissez-faire* capitalism."[72] To mature morally and to find an intellectually coherent sense of property, obsolescent modern capitalism needs constructive moral critics and, if it can borrow a bit of humility, it will find help in the brilliant revolution that began in ancient Israel.

PROPERTY WITH A CONSCIENCE

When the Torah set down rules for ownership, the overarching theme was God's proclamation that "the land is mine" (Lev. 25:23). "The Israelites could no more lay ultimate claim to the land than they could to their own life breath; it came as a constantly renewed gift."[73] Because the land was God's, God's ways should control its use. But God's ways are *tsedaqah*. If the divine owner of the land is obsessively concerned that "there be no poor among you" (Deut. 15:4) and that the land flourish and bear "fresh fruit" (Gen. 1:11–

12), then individualistic accumulation of wealth is not the norm. Indeed, if such greedy accumulation blunts the Earth's fruitfulness or contributes to poverty, it is condemned as both murderous and sacrilegious. In this biblical worldview we see a remarkable blend of passion for social justice, concern for ecology, and a definition of private property that is seasoned with a consciousness of human solidarity and sociality.

The five main elements of this grand vision of property are these:

1. Israel's sociable and sharing God is the absolute owner of everything; we are only managers.
2. A relative right to private property exists.
3. We must define property or it will become an idol and define us.
4. The dominant economic paradigm is not the possessing individual, but the terrestrial *household* of humanity.
5. Given the problem of self-interest, there is a permanent need for systematic criticism and redistributive change. This is rich cuisine, compared to which—I dare to say—our conservative, possessive individualism is meager fare.

1. God Is the Absolute Owner

"The earth is the Lord's and all that is in it, the world and those who dwell therein. For it was he who founded it upon the seas and planted it firm upon the waters beneath" (Ps. 24:1-2; see Ps. 95:4-5; Rom. 14:8; Heb. 11:3; Lev. 25:23). The sense of giftedness should condition all claims of ownership. "What do you possess that was not given to you? If then you really received it all as a gift, why take the credit to yourself?" (1 Cor. 4:7). In the biblical tradition "one senses owingness rather than ownership." To be truly human requires a "consciousness of indebtedness."[74] While the legal right to property exists, we are repeatedly told that God is the owner of everything there is, since we are but "tenants for a day" who hold everything in trust.[75]

This is the controlling assumption of Jewish and Christian economics. Property is relativized. All property is subject to justice because it belongs to God, whose economic *nom de plume* is Justice.

Therefore, no human claim to property is absolute and property as an end in itself is philosophically excluded. It is always a means to the clement purposes of the reign of God.

The ethical claim here survives disbelief in a personal God. The biblical moral position is this: property is subordinated to the good of persons and to the good of the earth. Its accumulation without reference to these ends is irrational and inhumane, and will ultimately lead to the defeat of peace. One need not be a theist to see the sense of that.

2. Relative Property Rights

There are hints of communism in early Christianity. The book of Acts says that "all who had property in land or houses sold it, brought the proceeds of the sale, and laid the money at the feet of the apostles; it was then distributed to any who stood in need" (4:34–35). The result was that the mandate of Deut. 15:4 that "there shall be no poor among you" was fulfilled. "They never had a needy person among them" (Acts 4:34). This seems to be an idealized account that did not become common practice, but it was a recurrent dream in early Christianity.[76] Since the earth was "very good" and poverty could and should be eliminated, the thought of a kind of communistic sharing to end want appeared as an intermittent strategy. Chrysostom saw the maldistribution of property as the cause of poverty and wondered if the solution did not lie in "all giving all that they have into a common fund."[77] Justin claimed they were already doing this: "We who valued the acquiring of money and possessions above everything else, now bring what we have into common ownership, and share with those in need."[78]

Though such texts may not portray the common practice, they illustrate the primacy of *need* as an economic category in this philosophy. Although the early Christians were ready to consider any economic scheme to achieve this, they did allow ownership. Ezekiel, while in exile, engaged in economic planning for the return. The people were to have land and were not to be separated from their holdings (Ezek. 45:8-9; 46:18). Ownership had its place: "Each man shall dwell under his own vine, under his own fig-tree, undisturbed" (Mic. 4:4; see Zech. 3:10). No one was to rob anyone of their home or steal their inheritance (Mic. 2:2; Isa. 5:7-8). Jeremiah promised that "houses, fields, and vineyards will again be bought and sold in this land" and "deeds of purchase" would be written and preserved (32:14-15). Proverbs called for "neither poverty nor wealth" since wealth corrupts and poverty turns people to desperate criminality (30:8-9).

There is copious evidence of early Christians owning property. They broke bread "in their own homes" (Acts 2:46), and Peter had access to a home when he left prison (Acts 12:12). Also, they had money for almsgiving. Zacchaeus was described as a "very rich" man. He was impressed by Jesus' message and responded generously, giving half of his possessions to the poor and repaying fourfold anyone he had ever cheated. He was still, presumably, somewhat well off after this largesse, but Jesus was more than satisfied. "Salvation has come to this house today!" (Luke 19:1-10). Second-century Jewish apocalyptic literature optimistically predicted that "even wealth shall be righteous among the people for this is the judgment and the rule of the mighty God."[79] It would take a "mighty God" to pull it off, but wealth, too, could be just.

Therefore, within the absolute mandate to devise modes of sharing to eliminate all poverty, the right to own property was approved of in Judaism and Christianity. This endorsement of property, however, was heftily hedged.

3. Avoiding Idolizing Property

Biblical literature was as cynical as it was subtle. It shows a deep-rooted conviction that "ownership holds a secret malice in store."[80] Indeed, avarice was seen as more obscene than lechery "because it feeds on self-centeredness."[81] Scripture is blunt: "Money is the root of all evil" (1 Tim. 6:10). When Jesus spoke of "unjust wealth" (Luke 16:9) and said, "You cannot serve God and money" (Luke 16:13), he was echoing a thoroughly Jewish refrain. In the Pseudepigrapha, *1 Enoch* used the expression "riches [mammon] of iniquity" (63:10). Other ancient texts spoke of the "wealth of dishonesty," of the "riches of violence," and of "the unclean riches of wickedness."[82] The "false glamour of wealth," we are told, chokes the growth of wisdom (Mark 4:19).

Money is power, and the Scriptures viewed all power with a sage wariness. Money was seen as mesmerizing. It was a demon that could possess it possessor. Chrysostom and Augustine were the heirs of these biblical suspicions. Chrysostom said, "Possessions are so called that we may possess them, and not they possess us. Why do you invert the order?"[83] Augustine said that the person who buries his gold to avoid sharing has also buried his heart: "The man belongs to his riches, not the riches to the man."[84]

In biblical perspective, money had religious overtones. It was an idol—"ruthless greed which is nothing less than idolatry" (Col. 3:4). This "greed which makes an idol of gain" (Eph. 5:5) alienates people from the goals of the reign of God. The psychology of the idol can be lost on modern seculars who fail to see that idolatry is not "a harmless quirk of ancient peoples but an endemic disease of the human spirit."[85] We absolutize things that are not absolute; we are natural idolizers. The Wisdom of Solomon railed against idols as "the root of immorality; they are a contrivance that has blighted human life" (14:11–14).

Moneytheism   Money still has religious status. As William Greider writes: "*Moneta*, the Latin root for 'money,' was an epithet applied to the goddess Juno, in whose temple the first Roman coins were made. . . . Greeks, Babylonians, Egyptians—virtually every early society conferred sacred qualities on its currency."[86] This extends into modern times, sometimes with the religiosity not at all concealed. Conservatives argued that the United States had offended God when it abandoned the gold standard. Money, with its bewitching power, is serious business for any serious theology. The prophets of Israel were onto this.

David Loy, a Buddhist, has said that "market capitalism" has become a religion and, indeed, "the most successful religion of all time, winning more converts more quickly than any previous belief system or value system in human history."[87] If you define religion functionally as that which grounds us, telling us what our world is and what our role in that world is, then market capitalism is now doing that. With the collapse of Communism, market capitalism has become "the first truly world religion, binding all corners of the globe into a worldview and set of values whose religious roles we overlook only because we insist on seeing them as 'secular.'" Economics is less a science than "the theology of that religion, and its god, the Market, has become a vicious circle of ever-increasing production and consumption by pretending to offer a secular salvation." The major religions, though not moribund, are failing to mount a challenge to this new, domineering religious value system. "On those few occasions when they are not in bed with the economic and political powers that be, they tend to be so preoccupied with past problems and outmoded perspectives (e.g., pronatalism) that they are increasingly irrelevant (e.g., fundamentalism) or trivialized (e.g., television evangelism)."[88]

Money as Identity   The essence of its blight is the power of money to define our being. *Owning* is not a univocal term. The farmer's farm and the playboy's Ferrari represent two different moral experiences of owning. The owning does not isolate the farmer, but rather bonds him or her to nature and to other people. The farm is a creative, hopeful, and redemptive property. It extends the farmer's being without splitting her or his personal and social reality. (The huge corporate megafarm may do little or none of this and may be more of a Ferrari.)

The playboy's Ferrari is not socially bonding. This owning is hostile, competitive, and separative. Its main purpose is not transportation, but prestige: "I have, therefore I am." This, however, is backwards. In reality, being precedes having: "I am, therefore I can have." If the having enhances my being personally and socially, if it is a good means to the ends that befit my being, then the having and owning are moral and good. In the case of the Ferrarist, the property is an end in itself, not a means to some humane end. That makes it an idol. An idol, in Paul's words, "stifles the truth" (Rom.

1:18). The truth is that our owning should not define our being in ways that contradict our personal and social reality.

Taking this example one step further, imagine what would happen to the opulent Ferrarist who lost his wealth but had all he needed in shelter, security, and food. He would presumably be miserable, because his god and source of meaning would be dead. He would stand, hollow and empty, in the dust of his demolished idol.

The biblical tradition saw this outcome. Owning that is not set in a framework of sharing and solidarity is a form of falsity that will prove its own undoing. Because our being is marked essentially by privacy and sociality, owning that offends either dimension "stifles the truth." "Property is too important to be left to those who covet it."[89] There are moral limits to owning on the earth that we share with all who now exist—and with all who ever shall. To be moral, private property must have a social conscience and be marked by a sense of human and ecological solidarity.

4. Human Household as Economic Paradigm

Possessive individualism is a flaccid economic theory that offers no paradigms of social coherence. The prime biblical economic paradigm is the household, the *oikos* (the Greek root of the word *economics*). The powerful household metaphor for life on earth conditions all understanding of human biological life. Creation is God's fragile household, and so the prime concern in Judaism, Christianity, and Islam is this: "Will everyone in the household get what it takes to live?" As Douglas Meeks says, this is "the first and last question of economics" from the biblical perspective.[90] This question does not proceed from unsophisticated piety, but relativizes all claims in the direction of a common good in which no one is excluded from consideration. It leaves private property intact, but crucially seasoned by the civilizing force of social conscience.

A cartoonist captured the simple wisdom of this metaphor. The cartoon pictured a family of five seated around the kitchen table, with bills and checkbook before them. The father says: "I've called

you all together to let you know that because of inflation, I'm going to have to let two of you go."[91] The corporate metaphor provides the humor when applied to a household. We do not dump
people in a household. We rearrange, do more sharing than we
have done before, without sacrificing some to others. The idea of
a parent accumulating excessively while children starve is highly
offensive within the family paradigm. Beneficent cupidity does not
a household make.

Isaiah heaps scorn on greedy accumulators who imperiously
pretend that they "dwell alone in the land." The result of this
is "ruin" (5:8-9). Possessive individualism—which is not only a
modern but a permanent human temptation—offers a hostile
Darwinian and draconian wilderness, not a household. And it
does not work. Try it and "down go nobility and common people" alike (Isa. 5:14).

The 1992 United Nations Development Report offers the
graph in Figure 1 to show the horrors of current income distribution on planet Earth, something that is achieved by greed, by
accumulators who think that they "dwell alone in the land." This
income distribution causes discontent, anger, and hatred and provides a breeding ground of the protest now called "terrorism." The
model is also a potent portrayal of the dynamics of empire, the glut-
ted at the top and the starved below—including 250,000 children
who die of malnutrition every week while hundreds of millions
more languish in hunger and deteriorating health.

In December 2004 the London-based relief agency Oxfam said
that some 45 million children around the world will die in the next
decade because rich countries have failed to meet their aid promise
of 1970—to give 0.7 percent of their gross national income in aid.
According to the report the United States was giving just 0.14 percent of gross national income in aid—one-tenth of what it spent
on invading Iraq—and that the aid budgets of rich countries were
half of what they were in 1960.[92]

Global Income Distribution

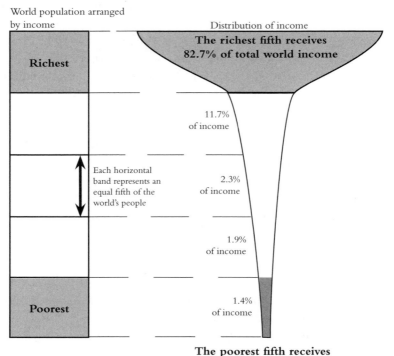

World population arranged by income

Distribution of income

Richest

The richest fifth receives
82.7% of total world income

11.7%
of income

Each horizontal
band represents an
equal fifth of the
world's people

2.3%
of income

1.9%
of income

Poorest

1.4%
of income

The poorest fifth receives
1.4% of total world income

Figure 1. Source: United Nations Development Programme, *Human Development Report 1992* (New York: Oxford University Press, 1992).

5. Possessive Individualism versus Redistributive Change

Conservative individualists are convinced that poverty is a personal achievement. The poor wreak poverty on themselves. This is a remarkable position since the largest group of the poor are children who have neither the desire for poverty nor the power to bring it about.[93] Oblivious of contrary data, individualists self-servingly insist that the poor do not want to work.[94] Individualists also believe fervently that poverty is unavoidable and its elimination unthinkable. Conservative Jews and Christians have rushed to those texts in Scripture that seem to normalize poverty: "You have the poor among you always" (Matt. 26:11; Deut. 15:11). But such texts are stinging indictments of our weaknesses, not blessings of the status quo. Finally, individualists fervently believe in a god called Chance. Here is one ardent expression of this creed: "The most dire and fatal hubris for any leader is to cut off his people from providence, from the miraculous prodigality of chance, by substituting a closed system of human planning. Success is always unpredictable and thus an effect of faith and freedom."[95] Note the telltale words: *providence, miraculous, faith*. An amateurish theology is displayed here. Any interference with current patterns of ownership would be an impiety. This is the gospel of the rich and bad news for the poor.

This illustrates that individualism, or economic conservatism, is also an epistemology, a method of seeing reality. It comprehends only of individual, discrete, unrelated instances, reducing poverty to a series of atomistic happenings susceptible only to individual, voluntary solutions. This voluntary innocence of systemic causation appeals to people who profit from current distributive arrangements.

Centuries before the development of disciplines like sociology and political economics ancient Israel rejected such views as simplistic and self-serving. As Elisabeth Schüssler Fiorenza says, "In Israel poverty was understood as injustice."[96] Guilt was assigned to the system, not to the poor. The temple of economic arrangements had to be attacked, and the prophets from Jeremiah to Jesus did just that. The "temple" for Jeremiah was close to what we would call "the system." Jeremiah scorned the very word *temple*: "This catchword of yours is a lie; put no trust in it" (Jer. 7:4). It had come to embody a number of socially blessed "ways" and "doings" that oppressed the poor and led to bloodshed and injustice (7:5-15).[97]

The temple for Jesus also was "the basis of both economic and religious power," and when he "symbolically seized that control, the Jerusalem aristocracy sought his death."[98] He messed with the system, and scholars now think he may have been killed within hours of his attack on the temple.[99] Jesus was attacking the law and order that preserves unjust privileges and exploitative social arrangements. Had he and Jeremiah contented themselves with urging private charity and a depoliticized piety, they would not have been so publicly punished. But they were prophets of Israel and agents of the subversive reign of God. For them, the great reversal was necessary because the current *kosmos,* the social ordering of things, was wrong.[100] In the Johannine writings the term *kosmos* came to mean "human society insofar as it is organized on wrong principles."[101] Israel felt a critical need not for a lot of congenial do-gooders, but for "new heavens and a new earth" (Isa. 66:22). The system, the arrangements, had to be replaced.

Public or Private?   The biblical literature had a sophisticated sense of social power. It divined that the circumstances matter more than the one-to-one deals. Only when "the old *order* has passed away" will tears be wiped from the eyes of the poor; only in a new order will an end come "to mourning and crying and pain" (Rev. 21:4). The purpose of justice (and therefore of just government) was the elimination of poverty (Deut. 15:4). To offer the poor hope in the miraculous prodigality of chance or in beneficent cupidity would be denounced as cynical, even idolatrous, because it would give sacred status to greed and whim. Only when "the tallest are hewn down, the lofty laid low, the heart of the forest is felled with the axe, and Lebanon with its noble trees has fallen," only then shall a new shoot "grow from the stock of Jesse" (Isa. 10:33-34). Only in a power and status shift where "many who are first will be last and the last first" (Mark 10:31) will we know the possibilities envisioned in the symbol of the reign of God. Small wonder that the religious right, corrupted by the god *Moneta,* has perverted this noble biblical vision.

Biblical economic thinking radiates the sense that the problem of poverty is systemic. It is in the current *kosmos,* the old heavens and old earth fashioned by the self-serving power-holders that need to be redone. This is perennial and practical truth. Private benevolence will not relieve world poverty, ease third-world debt, promote full employment, stop the mangling of the environment, mitigate obscene excesses of wealth, or negate all the damaging alienation that exists between groupings of people such as "Jew and Greek, slave and free, male and female" (Gal. 3:28). Poverty is a complex form of disempowerment. It will not be solved by chance or by unleashing of greed, but only by the intelligence, compassion, and restructuring of *tsedaqah* and by recognizing the whole human family as a sharing "household." That may seem hopelessly idealistic until you see that nothing else will bring peace to this earth.

JUSTICE, GOVERNMENT, AND PLANNING

There is no such thing as an unplanned economy or a free market. The postwar recovery and ascendancy of Japan were models and marvels of planning. In the United States planning of some sort makes the economic world go round. The Federal Reserve plans the amount of money available in the system and does not leave this to the invisible hand of the market. Price subsidies, acreage allotments, tax incentives, Social Security, regulation of trade, environmental and defense budgets, zoning laws, bailing out corporations, and joint ventures with foreign firms—all of this is planning. *Homo economicus* is a planner.

Aside from the sheer necessity of planning to avoid chaos, the disciplines of economics and political science were born as planning enterprises, and their foundational purpose was to achieve a just society. That preoccupation dried up in the intellectual drought of positivism. It has been succeeded by a fear of planning and the naïve illusion of value-free objectivity.

The authors of the Bible did not have enough faith in humankind to believe that unrestrained pursuit of self-interest would promote common welfare. They did not believe that there was an invisible hand guiding society inexorably toward equity. Instead the authors of this literature believed—or, rather, knew from empirical evidence—that there were multiple visible and invisible hands stacking up wealth at the expense of the powerless. When economic power is turned loose, the economically powerful do well. Needed is a balance of power. Government is the only power of the poor. It is not an intruder on the happy campers on the economic field. *Government is the overseer of the common good.* It is the prime agency of the common good, and the protector of the weak from the powerful by ensuring justice. The poetry of the psalmist expresses this theory of government: "O God, endow the king with thy own

justice, . . . that he may . . . deal out justice to the poor and suffering," bringing "peace and prosperity." Everyone benefits from just
governance. Where there is justice, there will also be "abundance
of corn in the land" and "sheaves as numberless as blades of grass."
A just society increases in productivity and everyone gains. Poverty
is the cancer that gnaws at peace, but it is curable. Hence the ruler
must "rescue the needy from their rich oppressors, the distressed
who have no protector." It is up to the good ruler to redeem the
powerless from "oppression and violence," for "their blood is precious in his eyes" (Psalm 72).

The powerful can largely take care of themselves. The main
duty of the ruler is to "*know* justice" (Mic. 3:1) and to do it. Government that knows justice and does it is no menace to enterprise
but rather is a guarantor of well-being and creativity. The modern American tendency to belittle government efficiency is a lie.
Government can put people on the moon when we wish it to.
(Corporate America is the prime source of government critique. Its
criticisms should be filed under G, for gall, since American business
stands embarrassed by the business efficiency of Japan, a nation the
size of California, full of mountains, and devoid of oil.)

Government is a good and even holy work in the biblical view.
As the Israelites saw it, all "kingly power" and "dominion" "belong
to the Lord" (Ps. 22:28). Human governors merely share in this
governance, and their authority is limited to promoting justice and,
through justice, prosperity and peace. Such a conception of government threatens no one. It guarantees both political and economic
rights. In the American tradition, however, economic rights have
been slighted. We have been more impressed with the need to be
free of all limitation than with the need to be sufficiently fed. The
contemporary call for an economic Bill of Rights to complement
our political Bill of Rights coheres with a more holistic, biblical
view of human need.[102]

Does all of this translate into a call for "central planning," bloated
bureaucracies, and interference with entrepreneurial creativity? No.
The biblical insight does not require government to do everything. It
is not a "statist" vision. It would be true to this view of government
as the prime agency and overseer of the common good to establish a

principle such as this: *government* should do nothing unless it is essential and will not otherwise be done. Such a principle cannot be glibly branded as liberal or conservative, in the modern use of these terms, but it does make sure that the good of all will be protected.

By way of examples of roles that require governmental action, here are three concerns that no agency but government could or would address: (1) In all of history, unjust monopolies of power have never voluntarily disbanded. (2) Never in history have the needs of the weak been the preoccupation of the strong. (3) More specifically, corporations, with an eye to quarterly reports, are not likely to take a long-term or environmentally benign view. Understandably, their dominant passions are for immediate growth and profit. According to economist Theodore Levitt, "Organized business has been chronically hostile to every humane and popular reform in the history of American capitalism."[103] All of these concerns must be addressed for the sake of justice, which creates peace and therefore the well-being of society, and the duty falls to government.

A second biblically grounded principle of justice is this: government should work toward the elimination of all poverty. Since, as Aristotle said, "poverty is the parent of revolution and crime," this goal of government should be congenial to conservatives and liberals alike.[104] You cannot be tough on crime unless you are tough on poverty. Morally speaking, there is no acceptable level of unemployment.

In the biblical view we are made in the image of the Creator, and the opportunity to express ourselves in work is essential to our being.[105] Contrary to self-serving, upper-class myths, studies show that an overwhelming majority of the poor want to work, and their lack of access to it is the painful center of their poverty.[106] To eliminate poverty government policy should promote and reward job creation. Alice Rivlin, former Congressional Budget Office director, directly refuted the idea that this is impossible: "It does not seem, for an analytical point of view, that there is any magic number below which we cannot push unemployment. It is a question of the will and of choosing the right mix of politics."[107]

One could add a third principle founded on the Bible's sense of justice and its preoccupation with the least of them: what is good for children is good; what is bad for children is ungodly. That principle, guiding every governmental decision and legislative act, would transform politics.

In a more detailed chart than that given above, the differences between modern western and biblical theories of economics and economic justice are as shown below.

Western Justice	Biblical Justice
Avowedly impartial	Biased in favor of the poor and critical of the rich
Poverty caused by poor	Poverty caused systemically by the powerful
Accepts poverty as a given	Sees poverty as a product of injustice
Reactive	Proactive
Primarily punitive	Primarily benevolent
Individualistic	Social
Stressing merit and individual social rights	Stressing need and the social dimension of rights
Sacred property rights	Redistribute empowerment of the poor
Ecologically insensitive	Stresses stewardship of the earth
Conservative	Revolutionizing, calling for creative systemic corrections
Nationalistic	Universalist, solidaristic
Minimalist	Effusive
Seeks end of litigation	Seeks shalom
Pessimistic	Guardedly hopeful

Chapter Five

PROPHETS: THE CONNOISSEURS OF *TSEDAQAH*

Albrecht Haushofer was imprisoned and executed by the Nazis for joining plots against Hitler. While in prison he reflected on how the Nazi court had found him "guilty." In his poem "Schuld" ("Guilt"), written while in shackles in prison, he admitted to a different kind of guilt, the guilt of not protesting early enough and loudly and clearly enough against the evils of his government. "I should have known my duty earlier, and called evil by its name more sharply—My judgment I kept flexible far too long." This man, as J. Glenn Gray said, "had already atoned more than is required of most of us" and went to his death convinced that his protest had been "nicht hart genug und klar!" (not strong enough and clear).[1] *His "guilt" indicts us all, numbed and complacent as we are while our governments wreak havoc in our name.*

Every society is paralyzed to some degree by the tyranny of the usual and mesmerized by the seduction of the status quo. We mistake the customary for the good; what is convenient for us we see as decent, or even noble. In fact, we instinctively defend the "deals" our comfort depends upon. The prophets have a message for us as we craftily wallow in our contentments, never crying out *hart und klar,* averting our eyes from the injustices our silence endorses, preferring our mostly unearned privileges to justice and fairness.

PROPHETIC MIDWIFERY

Enter the prophets, the midwives of a new consciousness, the heralds of suppressed or previously unsuspected human possibility. They are the enemies of normalcy as commonly and meanly defined by small minds. They are the purveyors of "a permanent cultural revolution."[2] Prophecy, in Walter Brueggemann's words, is the attempt to "evoke a consciousness and perception alternative to the consciousness and perception of the dominant culture around us."[3] Our culture gets into us like DNA with encoded messages to make our unearned or stolen advantages seem natural and normal. No wonder prophets who challenge this ingrained web of lies get killed.[4] Every age needs prophecy and every age resists it. Like fish swimming in rancid waters, we bite the hand that would lift us into unpolluted streams of newness.

False, self-serving, privilege-concealing orthodoxies continue to grip our social theories. Prophecy is a solvent for these orthodoxies, and we shrink from its discomfort. We poison our prophets with hemlock, exile them, crucify them, shoot them at their motel doors, and banish their work from our literary canon. Israel is distinct in history because it dared to "sing a new song" (Isa. 42:10) in the face of imperious oldness. This talent, this boldness, like genius, is rare. Israel's theory of prophecy has no known parallel in literary history. The prophets of Israel were the poetic sculptors of a new humanity. Martin Buber saw them as the iron chisel of Israel, reshaping this workshop of a nation so that its pioneering form of justice "might go forth as the light."[5]

PROPHECY AS ANTIDOTE

As a species we are more cunning than gentle. The civilizing advance of compassion is slow: what we call normal, we should often call cruel. What is statistically normal is for the imperial over-class to inure itself to the pain of the under-class and to enjoy the perquisites of unfair societal arrangements. The norm for antiquity's gods, if we use the *Iliad* as an example, was indifference to the injustice inflicted on others.[6] Through most of our history, as anthropologist Ralph

Linton observes, moral concern was limited to those near and dear. Members of other tribes were even seen as a legitimate source of meat![7] In ancient Greece, even murder did not always conflict with social respectability. We find there that "outside the circle of the dead man's kinsmen and friends, there is no indication of any popular sentiment against ordinary homicide."[8] Known murderers became honored members of the community. However we may have progressed, this moral primitivity did not pass with antiquity. Even today, as economist Robert Heilbroner writes, there is "a barbarism hidden behind the superficial amenities of life."[9] We bear hunger, death, and the destruction of our environment with an eerie equanimity. Responses to these crises are pallid and sporadic. The dominant culture, which modern prophecy is pitted against, is marked by callousness and a deadening pessimism. With Moses we could wish that "all the Lord's people were prophets" (Num. 11:29).

Old Israel's urgent prophetic warnings ring with alarming contemporaneity. The nations are sinking into a pit that they themselves have dug and are tumbling into their own traps (Ps. 9:15). Hosea could have been looking at our ecological and economic disasters when he said, "They have sown the wind, and they shall reap the whirlwind" (Hos. 8:7 RSV). And Ezekiel could add: "Throw off the load of your past misdeeds; get yourselves a new heart and a new spirit. Why should you die?" (Ezek. 18:31). In the striking view of Israel's prophets, the Earth's problems are solvable. What's missing is the moral integrity and political will, and this is what the prophets lament.

Israel's concept of prophecy is housed in its God-talk, though it is translatable into other moral idioms. God-talk expresses a culture's view of ultimate reality. One's theory of God (or ultimacy, however conceived) is one's theory of life. Indifferent gods are the creation of an indifferent and unfeeling culture. In prophetism, we see the full power of imaginative God-talk. The Israelite portrait of God reveals the Hebrew soul. To be filled with a passion for justice and to grieve with all who grieve is to be "theomorphous," that is, identifying with the grief of God.[10]

Israel's God was a moved mover, the very personification of compassion for the Earth and all its denizens. This God loved his

people and his Earth with a parental "everlasting love" (Jer. 31:3
RSV) and ached for all that caused us pain. Prophecy amounted to
"solidarity with the pain of God," a symbiotic communion with
the compassion of God.[11] God's benign and creative breath (*ruach*)
brooded over the primeval chaos and brought forth order and life.
Then, in Martin Buber's words, that same caring power "storms
into the midst of the historical world" and becomes the spirit of the
prophet.[12] In this sense, "the vast bulk of biblical record is produced
by prophets or at least reflects an unmistakably prophetic understanding of history."[13] Prophecy is the key to understanding the
moral history of Israel and the story of Jesus and the Jesus movement. As Bruce Malina says, Jesus was "a recognized prophet."[14]

Specifically, prophecy refers to the signal figures of the eighth,
seventh, and later centuries BCE, to some of their predecessors, as
well as to their Christian successors.[15] The prophets of Israel were,
as Abraham Heschel puts it, "some of the most disturbing people
who have ever lived."[16] Their moral rage was monumental. They
reacted fiercely to "the secret obscenity" and to "the unnoticed malignancy of established patterns of indifference."[17] They were particularly attuned to that kind of moral callousness that is in league
with economic power and political and religious authority. Their
ears were sensitive to the cries and the sighs of the plundered poor
and the helpless of the Earth. They were convinced that justice is
essential to real prosperity, and that injustice is ultimately murderous and destructive of peace. The prophets of Israel make a historic
and resounding roar in the long cold night of apathy. They are the
specific antidote to the cruel passions of empire.

A REVOLUTION IN AFFECT

What is a prophet? A prophet is one who stands at the piercing
point of evolving social conscience. Prophets crash through the en-
velope of indifference that imprisons our moral potential. They are
not just interested in an exchange of ideas. They didn't arrive with
flow charts and data banks. Their goal was to take stony hearts and
turn them into feeling flesh, pulsing with hunger for justice. Their
goal, ultimately, is a revolution in our affections, in what we feel and

value. Naked reason will not effect social reform. Reasoning and information can help if they penetrate into our affective awareness, but, until they do, they are sterile and peripheral to effective moral and political action. If we do not bring change to how people feel about justice toward other human beings and toward the earth, then we will continue to career toward Armageddon. Underlying all brilliant arguments in law, economics, and politics are felt values. These controlling commitments are the tides, the arguments are the waves. If we do not change the affective tides that govern human behavior, our arguments will perish with us. A Supreme Court justice who does not grieve over the plight of African Americans will consistently find ingenious reasons not to support efforts to relieve their pain. Economists and social theorists who are not affectively moved by poverty will offer dazzling rationalizations for the very conditions that create and sustain poverty. Prize-winning brilliance that is not "grieved at the ruin of Joseph" (Amos 6:6) does not advance civilization or bring relief to "Joseph."

The root causes that threaten us with disaster are in the heart, not the head. More precisely, the problem is a disembodied, technological intelligence that is devoid of an affective awareness of our actual environment and its value. Affective necrosis blunts intelligence. It impairs our reality contact. Value-free rationalism will not meet our problems. Should we continue to destroy the earth and rob posterity of the basics of life? As Heilbroner says: "There is no rational answer to that terrible question."[18] If we do not care enough about people born and not yet born, if we do not prize the Earth enough to preserve its miracle, there is no hope for it or us. If the affections are not engaged, there is no movement and no hope.

The prophets were convinced of this perennial feature of human nature. They were champions of grief and anger. They damned the tearlessness that is the undoing of human good. They knew that their message must get "into the heart" (Isa. 51:7) or it would be dead seed. Unless "our eyes . . . run with tears and our eyelids be wet with weeping," we will come to a fearful ruin (Jer. 9:18-19). Their purpose was not to win arguments with people, but to write the law of *tsedaqah* "on their hearts" (Jer. 31:33). The imagery used to make this point is relentless and extravagant. We are told to cut the foreskin off our hearts (Jer. 3:4); to wash the wrongness out of our heart (Jer. 4:14); to disjoin ourselves from those who have goodness "on their lips," but do not have its values "in their hearts" (Jer. 12:2).

Even their central word for knowing, *yada,* embodies an epistemology that makes affect central to moral cognition. The word is so rich that its meaning is never adequately translated by "know." It always means more than the possession of information or abstract concepts. It is the word used for sexual union: "Adam knew his wife Eve and she conceived" (Gen. 4:1 RSV). It implies sympathy and feeling for what is known: "You know the heart of a stranger, for you were strangers in the land of Egypt" (Exod. 23:9 RSV). As Abraham Heschel says, "The correct meaning is: you have sympathy, or a feeling for the heart of a stranger."[19] The Revised Standard Version's "they know not the Lord" is better translated by the New English Bible as "they care nothing for the Lord" (Hos. 5:4). When the prophets bewail the absence of "knowledge of the lord," they are not citing the lack of abstract ideas about divinity. Indeed, the people they are attacking are full of theology and piety but they do not "know" God because they do not love and do justice (see Hos. 6:6). Israel's moralcentric religion involves not just skills in the subtleties of ethics, but baptism by immersion in the feelings that ground ethics. If love of justice has not entered into the cordial regions of the affections and is not exploding out in action, then all talk of morality and liturgical sacrifices to God is noxious vacuity. Passionate, lived justice is the only conduit to the holy.

The prophet of Israel was, in Henri Bergson's words, a "genius of the will" who knew that moral discourse that does not reach the heart is noise.[20] The experience that drew the prophets into prophecy was a revolution in affect, not an overlay of new concepts. Jeremiah described his own conversion in terms of seduction and even, unhappily, of rape: "O Lord, Thou has seduced me, and I am seduced; Thou has raped me, and I am overcome" (Jer. 20:7).[21] Even if the prophets tried, they could not be silent. In Jeremiah's words, what he felt was "like a fire blazing in my heart, and I was weary with holding it under, and could endure no more" (Jer. 20:9). The prophet Jesus said that if prophetic voices were silenced, the very "stones will shout aloud" (Luke 19:40).

A HOPELESS TASK?

It would be easy if the world could be saved by logic or mathematics. Converts could be made simply by efficient organization. The future prospects for civilization, however, lie in the affective core of conscience. Militarists, racists, and sexists have defects not so much in logic as in feeling. Is there any hope for reaching them? Is prophecy any more than a hopeless lament?

At times and slowly, there has been movement from coldness to caring. Logic is often an ally of the heart, and the need for change can penetrate our obtuseness. Recent history gives some hope: The prophetic "green" movements have had some unpredicted success. Warriors have been put somewhat more on the defensive. The middle and upper classes do not line up at recruiting offices, and the military must work to recruit the lower classes. Ten million people around the world marched in unprecedented protest as the American empire planned to thwart the United Nations and invade Iraq. Conscientious objector status is gaining on the traditional prestige of the warrior. Superpower power is being embarrassed as insurgents with the military advantages of *invisibility, versatility, and patience* on their side drag the imperial military into pathetic quagmires. The species is turning some moral corners.

Dag Hammarskjöld looks for hope in the successes of Jesus' mission to resistant audiences. He asks: "Was his humanity rich and deep enough to make contact, even in them, with that in human nature which is common to all [human beings], indestructible, and upon which the future has to be built?"[22] There is something in prophecy that reaches for a center of sensitivity that exists even in the worst of us. We have to hope that felt truth that is well defended is communicable. The prophets reached hearts with some success: heart speaks to heart. The affective core of people's convictions can be touched. Therein lies the hope of prophecy and the future of civilization.[23]

Walter Wink speaks of the execution of the early Christians rebelling against Rome's empire. These unarmed Christians could not challenge the kill-power of Rome, and yet, even in dying, they embarrassed the muscles of empire. "When Christians knelt in the Colosseum to pray as lions bore down on them, something sullied the audience's thirst for revenge. . . . What happens when a state executes those who are praying for it? . . . These Christians were demonstrating the emperor's powerlessness to impose his will even by death. The final sanction has been publicly robbed of its power. . . . It was a contest of all the brute force of Rome against a small sect that merely prayed. Who could have predicted that the tiny sect would win?"[24]

PROPHETIC ANGER

Anger has a bad name in much of our modernity. It is a disorder requiring therapy and sedation. Some anger is, of course, sick and in need of care. But the prejudice against all anger is politically conservative and paralyzing. Anger threatens the status quo. It withdraws consent and does so with a vengeance. In the biblical vision, well-targeted anger is a virtue. It is the appropriate response to injustice. Domination requires a base of compliance. Anger threatens the powers that be, the keepers of the unjust arrangements. A sexist society will have ugly words for angry women. A racist society will praise the passivity of its victims.

Prophetic writing is full of angry speech that sensible people would label intemperate. Jeremiah confesses that he is filled with "indignation" (Jer. 15:17). Political leaders were called "stupid" (Jer. 10:21). Kings were told that dogs would lick up their blood (1 Kings 21:19). With literary boldness, even God is portrayed as filled with fierce, volcano-like anger (Isa. 13:13). "Who can stand before his wrath? Who can resist his fury? His anger pours out like a stream of fire and the rocks melt before him" (Nah. 1:6). Jeremiah saw God's anger as a "blazing fire" that "shall burn for ever" (17:4).

Our anger-shy culture would say these writers had a problem with anger. The prophets would say that we have a problem with heartlessness, because anger is the voice of frustrated love that will always be needed in an imperfect world. Thomas Aquinas understood this biblical message. With approval he cites John Chrysostom: "Whoever is not angry when there is cause for anger, sins."[25] (That deserves a banner in every church and mosque and temple.) Thomas, like the biblical writers, insisted that anger could be a virtue and that patience can be "irrational" in the face of some evils.[26] He found it telling that in Latin there was a word for too much anger (*iracundia*), but no word for the virtue of anger or for the lack of appropriate anger. Following the Pythagorean notion that "virtue stands in the middle," between excess and deficiency, he noted that, for anger, we name only the excess.[27] Regarding courage, for example, the virtue is called courage, and there are words for the two vices, one of excess, foolhardiness, and one of deficiency, cowardice. When it comes to anger, we condemn only the excess. The virtue, says Thomas, is *innominata;* the virtue stands unnamed, as does the vice of too little anger.

What was true in Thomas's Latin remains true in our cultural idiom. Prophecy is an angry corrective for this age-old fetishism of the status quo. We do not believe, with Thomas and the prophets, that appropriate anger is concerned with "the good of justice." When we are not angry in the face of injustice, we love justice too little. Anger as a virtue is rooted in the love of justice. If men are not angry over the suppression of women, if whites are not ablaze over the degradation of blacks, if humans are not outraged over the abuse of the earth, if heterosexuals are not offended by the demeaning of sexual minorities, it points to affective stunting, a lack of love for the good of persons and their preciousness. It is necessary to call these failings by their ugly names. Again, domination rests on indifference and servility, but its natural enemies are feeling, anger, and hope. Genuine prophecy specializes in all three.

THE EIGHT MARKS OF PROPHECY

Hebraic prophecy has eight special markings. It is marked by a stress on (1) the condition of poverty; (2) politics; (3) healthy guilt; (4) eccentricity; (5) courage as a civic virtue; (6) the loneliness of truth-telling; (7) the seduction of bad-faith piety; and (8) fidelity to the best in the tradition.

1. The Primacy of the Poor

As the agents of *tsedaqah,* the prophets had a preferential option for the poor. Their animating genius was a sensitivity to the *anawim,* the benighted poor—the powerless, exploited base of society. The prophets excoriated those "who grind the destitute and plunder the humble" (Amos 8:4). In many ways, Nathan was the quintessential Hebrew prophet. His advocacy for the poor in the court of David is classic. David, after a regal rape of the beautiful Bathsheba, arranged a hopeless military mission for her husband, Uriah, the Hittite. On news of his predictable death, David took the pregnant Bathsheba as a wife. Enter the prophet Nathan. He engaged David with the story of a poor man who owned nothing but a little ewe lamb. It was the joy of his life. It slept in the old man's arms, ate from his bowl, and was his constant companion. "It was like a daughter to him" (2 Sam. 12:3). Then a rich man came, seized the lamb, killed it, and served it to a guest for dinner. David was outraged at this rich man who had "shown no pity" (v. 6). At this, the prophet ended the subterfuge and spoke truth to power. Nathan blasted the king: "You are the man! . . . Uriah you have murdered . . . and stolen his wife" (vv. 7, 9).

Prophecy catches the scent of exploitation. It finds the Uriahs and the Bathshebas. It knows that the essence of poverty is not the absence of money, but the lack of power along with exploitation by those who have power. Prophecy's instinctive reach is for the have-nots who are being had by the haves. "Pursue justice and champion the oppressed" (Isa. 1:17). That is the creed of the prophet. And, again, the pragmatic payload of this approach is peace. Without attention to oppression, we will never know *shalom.* Without concern for the dispossessed, we will never flourish. This kind of "justice dawns like morning light. . . . It will come to us like a shower, like spring rains that water the earth" (Hos. 6:3). In spite of *tsedaqah's* apparent difficulty, nothing else will work and nothing else will "water our earth" and bring verdure and hope to our fields.

Being preoccupied with the poor, of course, is an assault on the usual definitions of status. It is the root of that precocious Hebraic egalitarianism that has inspired liberal social policies in the West into our day. It is notable that in that time this high moral calling of prophecy was not to be denied to women or even to slaves. There is Miriam, "the prophetess" (Exod. 15:20), and Deborah, "a prophetess [who] was [a] judge in Israel, . . . and the Israelites went up to her for justice" (Judg. 4:4). Joel promised that the spirit *(ruach)* of God would be poured out on all of humankind: "Your sons and your daughters shall prophesy. . . . I will pour out my spirit in those days even upon slaves and slave-girls" (Joel 2:28-29). In the early Christian movement, prophecy was highly esteemed and seen to be a characteristic of the whole community, including, of course, women.[28]

The new humanity envisioned in prophetic Israel and in the Jesus movement would not be built on dominative status claims. The poor and social outcasts will be mainstreamed. The poor will be part of us, not a foreign "them." In the main, poverty is socially caused and socially curable. Rich and poor are correlative terms. Poverty and wealth are organically linked. The under-class is organically tied to the over-class. The privileges of the over-class are not innocent. Thus spoke the prophets of Israel.

Whose Poor Are They?   Prophetic class analysis rarely finds a hearty welcome. It clashes, on the American scene, with the idea that poverty is a condition created by the shiftless poor. Ralph Waldo Emerson was an all too successful teacher when he canonized the haughty sense of "self-reliance," in a way that Robert Bellah says "has been the common coin of moral life for millions of Americans ever since."[29] Emerson says we deserve only the property we work for. The logical conclusion is that if you don't have a job you deserve nothing. Emerson posed the question bluntly: "Then again, do not tell me, as a good man did today, of my obligation to put all poor men in good situations. Are they my poor?"[30] This gospel of the secure was preached also by Herbert Spencer, who said that poverty was the direct consequence of sloth and sinfulness. Even feeding the poor was seen as encouraging them in their laziness and so it was said that next to alcohol the most pernicious fluid is indiscriminate soup. Preacher Cotton Mather said that if people indulge themselves in idleness, it is the command of God that we let them starve. Such ideas, so comforting to the well-off and the secure, do not stay unapplied, in this rich American land or in a world where many starve while the few live in glut.[31]

2. Politics

The birth of Judaism was a political act, a critique of empire. Moses founded a new kind of non-imperial society, not a church. The prophets of Israel were, therefore, political to the core—politics was their vocation. They knew that poverty could not be eliminated by private magnanimity, but only by rewriting the script for "the whole of public life."[32] Judaism and Christianity are political religions, not mystery cults for the solace of the pious. Because the prophets' religion was intrinsically moral and their morality was thoroughly political, the prophets could never stay out of the courts of power.

Israel was born of rebellion against empire. It was the "underclass Canaanites who became Israelites."[33] They became an identifiable people (eventually to be called Jews) by reason of their refusal to submit to the states and empires around them. "They refused allegiance to the states that taxed and conscripted their subjects, and they themselves strove not to extract tribute from one another." Simply expressed, earliest Israel was in rebellion against internal and external empire-builders "and the political and religious arrangements that legitimated and enforced" these systems. "They emerged bit by bit as a new people whose ethnic identity was formed in the midst of their struggle to establish themselves firmly in the hill country of western Palestine."[34]

When, two hundred years into their experiment, Israel succumbed to the temptation of royalty, it was the prophets who tried to recall it to its antiroyal, anti-imperial beginnings and to its foundational concern for the poor.

Nathan the prophet is typical. He appears three times in the books of Samuel and Kings and each time he is engaging the king.[35]

The prophets could never accept the dangerous modern distinction between morality and politics (or between the moral and the military, or the moral and the economic, or the moral and the cultural, etc.). They recognized such dichotomizing visions as vicious nonsense. The lifeblood of the poor and the good of the society are in politics, in economics, and in the operative values of a culture. It is here that decisions are made about who will live and who will die, who will thrive and who will starve for lack of power and food. It was precisely in these areas that the prophets' moralcentric religious vision was to be tested. Prophets work where power lives.

Jeremiah claimed as his credentials prophetic "authority over nations and over kingdoms, to pull down and to uproot, to destroy and to demolish, to build and to plant" (Jer. 1:10). Notice that the mission is not just to Israel—a big enough task—but to the whole world. Small wonder Jeremiah tried to decline the invitation to prophecy! (see Jer. 1:6). The prophet Isaiah had confidence that if Israel would hear his message, "the nations shall march towards your light, and their kings to your sunrise" (Isa. 60:3). It must have amused the courts of surrounding powers to hear that this ragtag bunch of rebels thought it had a sunrise toward which they and all of history should march!

Notice sharply: the prophets did not think that "a thousand points of light" in private charity would solve the problem of poverty and systemic exploitation. That's why they spoke to "kings," to governmental power. Systemic problems require systemic cures. Only governmentally enforced systemic affirmative action would have given white women closer-to-equal standing with men in the legal and medical professions. (For people of color, the prime concern of affirmative action programs, success has been sluggish.) The scandal of world poverty needs systemic cures like the tax proposed by James Tobin, winner of the 1981 Nobel Prize for economics. Billions of dollars whisk around the globe in speculative international finance. A mere 0.5 percent tax collected on all transactions in foreign exchange would produce funds to cancel the impossible debts of the poor nations, to bring water and education and literacy to the desperate, and to fund the underfunded humanitarian missions of the United Nations.[36] It is only arrogant kings who would piously hope that "a thousand points of light" would do the job of government, the prime caretaker of the common good, and, in biblical terms, the prime champion of the poor.

Dethroning Royalty The prophets did not arrive before the kings in a posture of fawning obeisance. Israel was founded, in Julius Wellhausen's phrase, as "a commonwealth without authorities," and the prophets were congenitally undaunted by royalty.[37] Unlike most of its neighbors, as Roland de Vaux observes, "Israel never had, never could have had, any idea of a king who was a god."[38] For the prophets, as the spokespersons of Torah, kings could not be gods since only God was king in Israel. Only God was "judge, law-giver, and king" (Isa. 33:22). With that theology, all royalty is relativized.

Israel delivered a double whammy on royalty. First, since only Yahweh was King, all "kings" were subordinates. There was always a higher court to which the prophets and the people could appeal. The kings had no divine right. That would be sacrilege. This radical critique of power extended also to priests and judges, and even to purported prophets. No human authority was beyond appeal. Second, just as Yahweh was beyond all kings, so *tsedaqah* was beyond all laws. Israel escaped the eternal temptation of juridical positivism. The Israelites were ethical realists. They realized that an unjust law was no law at all—*lex mala, lex nulla*. A law is not good because it is commanded by authority (juridical positivism)—it can be commanded only if it is good. Justice is primary. Law, at its best, is only its imperfect reflection.

The king who did not become the embodiment of *tsedaqah* was an imposter. Far from believing that "the king can do no wrong," as English jurisprudence would put it, the Israelites were convinced of the opposite. They were so cynical about the moral reliability of royalty that they banished it entirely for the first two centuries of their existence. Even after they succumbed and returned to kingship, the prophets gave the kings no peace. They were convinced that royal power in all its forms corrupts.

Hosea reminded kings that the whole institution of royalty could be discontinued. Israel could entirely "abandon this setting up of kings and princes" (Hos. 8:10). Wholly other modes of gov-

ernance were conceivable as early Israel had already proved. No
system of government can be absolutized in this view. The king's
power, when conceded at all, was conditional. Jeremiah's words
to those who "sit on David's throne" were these: "Deal justly and
fairly, rescue the victim from his oppressor." Care for "the alien,
the orphan [and] the widow." Protect "innocent blood." With these
rules spelled out, the king was told: "If you obey, and only if you
obey," the royal rule will be blessed. This text goes to the heart of
governance. "If your cedar is more splendid, does that prove you a
king?" No. The mark of the true king is that he "dispensed justice
to the lowly and poor" (Jer. 22:1-4, 15-17; see 1 Kings 10:9-10).
If government does not do this, it has abdicated its own rights.
Martin Buber cites these words from Jeremiah 22 as "unparalleled
in the literature of the ancient Orient for their liberty of spirit."[39]
If the king rules with *tsedaqah,* the result will be "boundless peace."
One who governs with justice will be "God-like, a Father," and a
"Prince of peace" (Isa. 9:6-7). Justice and justice alone gives legiti-
macy to power.

Applying these ideas to our time, if a government becomes
only a collection of lobbies, bought and subdued by corporate interests and the wealthy, it cannot make a moral claim to legitimacy.
It may be resisted by all feasible means and it should be. That is the
bite in the prophetic message. That is the bite that is missing in
much of what modern Christianity has become.

Speaking Hard Truth to Power   The prophets were rarely satisfied with kingly performance. A "vulture" is over the house of the
Lord, warned Hosea (8:1). This radical prophet felt that all kingship
was self-sacralizing, a form of idolatry, and idols, said Hosea, "stink"
(8:4-5). The prophets perceived an ageless failing of political power
holders—the tendency to sacralize their office—and that sacraliz-
ing has hardly waned in modern societies. Because they preside so
powerfully over the sanctity of life, they come to see themselves as
sacred and beyond the law. But to treat ourselves as beyond the law
is to make of ourselves an idol, and, following Hosea, it means that
we "stink." Rather than deriving their authority legitimately from
their service of the common good and the consent of the governed,

these power holders claim executive privilege (*olim,* a divine right) to dominate. Illusions of divinity stubbornly continue to attach to modern forms of political power.

Many deceptive terms hide the claims of divine right to kingly dominance in modern parlance. "Common good," "revolution of the proletariat," "law and order," "will of the people," "national security," "military secrecy," "war on terrorism," and so on—these may all disguise the grasp for absolute power. Fear is the favored tool of those who want to rule like monarchs. The fear of Communism, "the evil empire," allowed for the building of an imperial presidency in the United States. Communism's striking-fear-into-the-heart successor is the amorphous enemy "terrorism." Modern governments like the United States, Israel, and Russia use this slippery term to describe rebellions against their imperialism and unjust occupations of other people's land and resources.

Like Olympian gods, political leaders have always tried to inure themselves to criticism and to the claims of justice. In an older idiom, they idolize themselves. That is why the need for prophecy is eternal. Ezekiel saw all this in the prince of Tyre and he mocked him roundly: "In your arrogance you say, 'I am a god'; . . . because you try to think the thoughts of a god I will . . . lay your pride in the dust" (28:1-10). The amount of God-language used by modern political leaders is revealing, especially as it often increases in proportion to the mischief afoot. King Uzziah is the enduring paradigm of the regal thirst for priesthood. "When he grew powerful his pride led to his own undoing: . . . he offended against the Lord his God by entering the temple of the Lord to burn incense on the altar." A group of priests, described as "courageous men," confronted him, and the king with his priestly pretensions was rudely banished (2 Chron. 26:16-23).

Jeremiah did not flatter kings. The shepherds (kings) are "stupid" (10:21 RSV) and "mere brutes" (10:21). Ezekiel agrees: "I am against the shepherds," he says bluntly (34:10). Isaiah continues the scathing chorus: "Israel's watchmen are blind, all of them unaware. They are all dumb dogs who cannot bark, . . . lovers of sleep, greedy dogs that can never have enough. They are shepherds who understand nothing" (56:10-11). Zephaniah promises punishment for "the royal house and its chief officers," because they are nothing but "roaring lions" and "wolves of the plain" (1:8; 3:3). This harsh appraisal is even woven into the Psalms: "Put no faith in princes" (Ps. 146:3). These prophetic voices make modern pundits sound timid and bland.

Jesus the prophet was in this same vein when he attacked the powerful religious leadership of his time as "hypocrites, blind guides, blind fools, snakes, vipers" who were guilty of spilling "innocent blood" (Matthew 23). Even when he appears to be conservative in advising people to "pay to Caesar what is due to Caesar, and pay God what is due to God," he was being subversive. Religious power and political power were noxiously blended in his day and he was dividing them in a way that was novel, desacralizing, and freeing.[40] Jesus' activities "had indeed led to the estrangement of the people from their leaders."[41] When Jesus heard that Herod wanted to kill him, he sent him a defiant message beginning with "Go and tell that fox . . ." (Luke 13:32). (Calling King Herod a fox sounds mild to modern urban ears. However, in a pastoral and agricultural setting, the fox was a vicious menace. Calling someone a fox was more like saying "Go tell that murderer. . . .") "The Bible, more than any other ancient document, exposes government as frequently acting in disobedience to God."[42] This does not mean that it is a literature of anarchy. It is, rather, a demand that government fulfill its destiny as the prime servant of the common good. The Israelites were not resisting government as modern conservatives do—because government interferes with their greed and exploitative deals. They were resisting government that did not interfere with greed and exploitation, and they were demanding good government because that is the best hope of the powerless and the poor. One cannot imagine the prophets being invited to the White House for a prayer breakfast.

3. Good Guilt

Tsedaqah, in its fullness, is the function of and justification for government. The king's justice should mirror that of God, with all God's compassion for the dispossessed. "Oh God," sings the psalmist, "endow the king with thy own justice, and give thy righteousness to a king's son, that he may . . . deal out justice to the poor and suffering."[43] He was not writing about the guilt that requires a therapist, but the guilt that springs from the conscience and requires reform. Guilt is the experience of moral pathology. If that pathology is real and lethal, the denial of the appropriate symptom (guilt) leaves the malady without remedy. We and the planet can die for lack of guilt. Guilt is primal, remedial pain. It is a form of affective knowing. It is both feeling and recognition that we are not responding properly to the value of persons or their environment. It rises from being conscious of a split between our being and our doing, between our *is* and our *ought*. It is a nuisance, and we resist it. And yet we need it to survive.

There are many ways of resisting it: we blot it out by denial, we misname it as illness in need of therapy, or we blame the evil on forces or persons outside our control. Frances Moore Lappé, writing about world hunger, says: "Historically, people have tried to deny their own culpability for mass human suffering by assigning responsibility to external forces beyond their control."[44] The Black Death of the Middle Ages was attributed to divine intervention, whereas it was undoubtedly related to society's indifference to the sanitation and nutritional needs of the poor masses. Lappé says that today world hunger is similarly blamed on causes beyond our control—climate, lack of resources, and the thoughtlessness of the reproducing poor. This country-club logic anesthetizes guilt. It also opens the door to Garrett Hardin's popular "lifeboat ethics," which concludes, with gesticulations of pained innocence, that the death of the disadvantaged is the sensible and unavoidable solution.[45] The well-known commentator Paul Harvey is one herald of this deadly conclusion. He intones: "You don't waste limited resources on those who are inevitably doomed."[46] With guilt thus dismissed, there is no felt need to indict our military allocations of research monies or the economic and political arrangements, or the penury of our real foreign aid. The United States is the richest and the stingiest in per capita foreign aid of the twenty-two richest nations, a fact most pious, nationalistic Americans are ignorant of. [47]

The prophets of Israel had remarkable insight into this natively human trickery. They saw the summoning of guilt as a supreme challenge: "Acknowledge your guilt!" (Jer. 3:12 RSV). "It is your own wickedness that will punish you, your own apostasy that will condemn you. . . . The stain of your sin is still there and I see it, though you wash with soda and do not stint the soap" (Jer. 2:19, 22). Micah saw the proclamation of guilt as his mission: "I am full of strength, of justice and power, to denounce his crime to Jacob and his sin to Israel" (Mic. 3:8). The good life is possible, says Jeremiah, but it will not come if we do not turn from our "wicked ways and evil courses." There is no hiding from the effects of our guilt and neglect: "Do you think that you can be exempt? No, you cannot be exempt" (Jer. 25:5, 29).

Can we sit now in our first-world comfort at a table with a view of the golf course and ignore starvation in the third world and joblessness and homelessness in our own cities? The prophets answer, "No, you cannot be exempt." Injustice will come home to roost, whether in wars over maldistribution of wealth (the most likely military threat of the future), or in crime and "terrorism," or in far-reaching economic shock waves. The planet will not forever endure our insults. If the prophets' law is correct—and the facts of history endorse it—we will not be exempt.

The opposite of evil for the prophets is grateful reverence for people and the earth. Those who lack that reverence "are like a troubled sea, a sea that cannot rest, whose troubled waters cast up mud and filth. There is no peace for the wicked" (Isa. 57:20-21). Instead there are terror alerts.

The Guilt of Apathy   In the biblical tradition, sin is at root a failure of sensitivity. It is not just the practitioners of cruelty who are condemned but those who simply do not respond. "Show compassion to one another" (Zech. 7:9). Even King David recognized that to show "no pity" is to sin "against the Lord" and to have "contempt for the Lord" (1 Sam. 12:6, 13-14). Caring is the essence of religion.

Omission, the absence of caring, is the commonest form of sin. A capital biblical text puts it this way: "When I was hungry you gave me nothing to eat, when thirsty nothing to drink; when I was a stranger you gave me no home, when naked you did not clothe

me; when I was ill and in prison you did not come to my help"
(Matt. 25:42-44). When a man is mugged and left near death, the
condemnation centers not on the cruel muggers but on those who
did not respond to the victim's plight. The priest and the Levite
(both professionally religious people) are faulted because they saw
the victim but "went past on the other side." The hero of the story
was the Samaritan who "was moved to pity" and reacted with generosity (Luke 10:29-37). The absence of pity is the root of all evil.
Solidarity with victims is the goal of prophecy and the only cure
for societal brokenness.

Caring and pity are antidotal to anger run amuck. Violent anger
is a fearsome vice and implicitly murderous (Matt. 5:21-22). If it
dominates a personality or a public policy, it diminishes reason and
obstructs community. Hosea, in a remarkable passage, explores the
dialectic of compassion and anger by showing the tension as part of
the anguish of God. The passage begins in love: "When Israel was a
child, I loved him." But then the child grew up and turned bad and
God is consumed with anger and is ready to destroy or abandon
this errant "son." But then the tug of compassion begins to pull:
"How can I give you up, O Ephraim! How can I hand you over, O
Israel! My heart recoils within me, my compassion grows warm and
tender. I will not execute my fierce anger, . . . for I am God and not
man, the Holy One in your midst, and I will not come to destroy"
(Hos. 11:1-9 RSV).

Caring and anger are basic components of the moral self, essential to the design of healthy conscience. They interrelate and
clash, but their tension must never be lost.

4. Eccentricity

The prophets, even the classical ones, often behaved weirdly. Their
conduct was eccentric and even bizarre. If, as I am proposing, the
prophets of Israel represent a paradigm for social criticism, this pecu-
liar trait must be analyzed along with the rest. First, to the not slightly
embarrassing exploits that fill their literature. And then to the question of how, in this respect, the prophets are in any sense imitable.

It is shocking but clear that the prophets had a marked penchant for nudity. Isaiah wandered about for three full years "na-

ked and barefoot." He wanted to demonstrate to the people that if current trends continued, they too would be "naked and barefoot, their buttocks shamefully exposed, young and old alike" (Isa. 20:2-4). Undoubtedly, it was a remarkable way to make a point. Isaiah preached the nudity he practiced. He told the complacent women: "Strip yourselves bare!" (32:11). And he predicted for all of Zion that "she shall sit on the ground stripped bare" (3:26).

Micah also had a penchant for nudity and added some exceptional flourishes: "Therefore I must howl and wail, go naked and distraught; I must howl like a wolf, mourn like a desert-owl" (1:8).[48] Indeed, nudity seems to have been almost institutionalized as the mark of the prophet. When Saul stripped himself naked "all that day and all that night," the people questioned pointedly: "Is Saul also among the prophets?" (1 Sam. 19:24).

The bizarre activities of Jeremiah took another form. When he was going to appear before a group of foreign statesmen, he first harnessed a wooden yoke to his neck with cords and bars used to harness oxen for plowing. Thus accoutered, he presented himself to these shocked gentlemen (27:2-3). Again, to make a point, Jeremiah renounced marriage and parenting, a curiosity in his day (16:1). Small wonder Jeremiah was censured as a "madman" who should have been put "into the stocks and the pillory" (29:26). Hosea married an unfaithful wife and then dismissed her as the law prescribed. However, in an unusual gesture, Hosea bought her back "for fifteen pieces of silver, a homer of barley and a measure of wine," and entered into a celibate marriage with her (3:2-3)! Here again, characteristically, the prophet was "made a fool and the inspired seer a madman" (Hos. 9:7). When the commander of the army of the Northern Kingdom was visited by a prophet, his servants asked: "What did this crazy fellow want with you?" (2 Kings 9:11).

The prophet Ezekiel also did strange things. In one demonstration, he acted out going into exile. Dressed like one in mourning with his face covered, he worked all night, breaking through "the wall" with his hands (12:1-7). On another occasion, this same Ezekiel seems to have cut off his beard and hair in an allegorical gesture. He burned a third of that hair in a fire in the center of the city; another third he cut with a sword and distributed it "all round the city"; and he scattered the rest in the wind (5:1–2).

John the Baptist and Jesus were also in the train of prophets, and they too were marked by eccentricity. John lived in the Judean wilderness. His "clothing was a rough coat of camel's hair, with a leather belt around his waist, and his food was locusts and wild honey" (Matt. 3:4). He called the people who were nice enough to come out to hear him a "vipers' brood" (Luke 3:7) and attacked the powers of his day with intemperate language. He was beheaded for his efforts. Jesus too was seen as "a prophet like one of the old prophets" (Mark 6:15). He stirred up the people "all through Judea." It was said at his trial that his trouble-making "started from Galilee and has spread as far as this city [Jerusalem]" (Luke 23:5). Jesus' behavior was a scandal because he violated "propriety, reason, and good public order."[49] He was executed for sedition against the empire and treason with "the priestly aristocracy as the prime movers."[50]

What relevance can all of the above have to modern social criticism? Are we to go naked, are we to wear yokes, or go about burning our hair to relate to this tradition? No. Bizarre activity does not a prophet make. After all, even those described as false prophets did weird things. (Zedekiah made iron horns for himself in making his case [1 Kings 22:11–12].) What is imitable is eccentricity in the strict sense. At root the term means "out of or away from the center." Prophecy is a centrifugal force. It knocks the cozy beneficiaries of the status quo out of their artificial balance. The status quo is filled with those for whom comfort and security are sacred, not with those who hear the "groaning" (Exod. 2:24) of the poor. Prophecy hears the marginalized and speaks and acts for them.

Why the flamboyant extremities of expression and symbol? Sometimes only outrage speaks to outrage. The effete center does not hear well. If you would speak an unpalatable message, if you would speak of insensitivity and exploitation to the insensitive exploiters, you must elevate the intensity of your language from persuasion to poetry. The prophets were outrageous poets, and they proved the old Irish saying that kings have more to fear from bards than from warriors. Poetic prophecy unmasks imperial royalty so that its "nakedness may be plain to see" (Isa. 47:1–3). White American royalty was shocked at the African American civil rights movements and offended by the piercing poetry of Martin Luther King Jr., but its "buttocks" were "shamefully exposed," in Isaiah's words, and the social order was shaken.

Isaiah, in his nakedness, was saying to the people: "It is not I who am ashamed. It is you who have been stripped of that vision that gave birth to the glorious revolution of Israel." Jeremiah was saying that it was not he who was demeaningly yoked in ox harness. It was Israel that was strapping itself to meanness and to lesser expectations of life. Hosea was indicting the whoring people for infidelity to the justice that is the very aura of God.

Eccentricity, at the very least, means tension, tension with the policies and institutions of the overbearing, with the keepers of unjust arrangements. Those who purr softly to power, who find new reasons to blame the victim and dignify the vices of the status quo, are the false prophets. They are ubiquitous, and eccentric prophecy is the antidote to their syrupy poison.

5. Courage and Conscience

Courage and its opposite, cowardice, are key factors in the epistemology of morals. They condition whether and how we know the most basic truths of our existence. Fear dims this optic nerve. What we dare not see, we do not see. Such is the controlling power of affect in the phenomenon of insight. For that reason, it is a real debit that courage is so little addressed in modern philosophy, theology, and social theory.[51] The ancients did not neglect it.

Courage unto death   Early Greek thinking assigned courage to the aristocracy and the military. Peasants were deemed cowardly and "servile" by nature.[52] The concept was broadened slightly by later Greek philosophy, which made it the mark of the philosophical life. Hebrew and Christian notions of courage radically democratized the concept. It became a moral ideal within the reach of all. Revelation lists the cowardly with "the faithless, and the vile, murderers, . . . and liars of every kind" (21:8). Their cowardice will not spare them death—instead, the imaginative author says, they will endure a "second death." John's Gospel explores the same enigma. If you love your life too much, you will lose it. If you lose it, you will somehow find it. Readiness to die, in the thousand ways that we can die, is essential for moral success. Joshua saw the loss of courage as a total loss of "spirit" (2:11). The prophets had no such loss. They suffered for their vision.

Amos discovered that people "loathe him who speaks the whole truth" (5:10). And this loathing, following the untamed logic of anger, led to murder. Isaiah, according to some traditions, met martyrdom by being sawn in two. When they heard what Jeremiah was saying, the soldiers said: "This man must be put to death" (Jer. 38:4). And they immediately put him into a muddy cistern without water or food. When the prophet Micaiah refused to mouth the royal line, the king responded with: "Lock this fellow up and give him the prison diet of bread and water" (1 Kings 22:27). When Jeroboam brought the prophet's message to King Solomon, the king tried to kill him (1 Kings 11:40). At the inauspicious beginning of Jesus' prophetic mission, the people "leapt up, threw him out of the town, and took him over the edge" (Luke 4:28-30). Eventually this prophet was crucified. John the Baptist was beheaded. And so it continues into modern times, as Martin Luther King Jr. joined the train of prophets and was shot to death while campaigning for the rights of garbage collectors. History is splattered with prophets' blood. We kill the messengers of justice while we enthrone and elect their adversaries.

Courage and the Warmth of Wisdom　　Courage is not just standing firm in the face of danger. Sometimes it is smarter to turn and run. Plato's dialogue on courage, the *Laws,* moves quickly to the point that courage involves more than boldness, that it must be linked to wisdom.[53] Villains and emotionally disturbed people might be dauntless, but their "courage" is not a virtue. Virtues are rooted in moral value. If courage is not wise, it is foolhardy and a vice.

Courage does not relate abstractly to the truth. Like wisdom, courage is always emotionally charged. Both courage and wisdom have an inner core of eagerness. Courage, after all, is an adversative virtue. It addresses threat and resistance. It is unnecessary where all is easy and accessible. If its roots do not reach the passions, it will have no muscle in the face of hardship.

Courage affectively embraces moral truth, and thus it is rooted in the love of persons and their environment. Thomas Aquinas says that courage is the precondition of all morality and virtue.[54] If you do not have it, your commitment to persons and this earth is specious. Courage is love that is ready to risk. Where there is no readiness to risk, there is no love. If we will not risk anything for person- or Earth-related causes, we have subordinated everyone and everything to our own safety. Safety, of course, is a value—but not an absolute value.

If life is full of adversity and challenge, then the inability to risk is the inability to live. Those bent only on survival do not even survive. In saving their lives, they do, in a sense, lose them. All important areas of human endeavor depend on reasonable and sometimes heroic risk-taking. The opposite of courage is pusillanimity, smallness of spirit, languid love. Courage, in contrast, is the full maturation of will. It is the mark of a healthy and creative personality and culture. Most worthwhile goals are arduous and beyond the reach of that moral lassitude that we call cowardice.

In general, western culture does not reward risk-takers and whistle-blowers. Small wonder its thinkers write so little about courage. The modern symbol may well be the toad, from which the blunt word "toady" derives. The toad moves carefully and surely from one safe spot to another, taking no risks. The toad's image will never appear with prophets in creativity's pantheon of daring achievers. Sadly, in many governmental and corporate offices, the toad is king.

6. The Loneliness of Truth-Telling

In a conversation created by Oscar Wilde, two men speak of the lonely dreamer:

> Gilbert: For a dreamer is one who can only find his way by moonlight, and his punishment is that he sees the dawn before the rest of the world.

Ernest: His punishment?
Gilbert: And his reward.[55]

The prophets saw what others dared not see and because they spoke of what they saw, they knew the loneliness of courageous minds. Love of the truth condemns you to stranger status. The world wants to be deceived (*mundus vult decipi*), so those who do not join in the world's dalliance with deception are a threat. If not killed, they are voided. Prophets retreat from collective rationalization into an alternative consciousness. Prophecy always represents an "insurrection of subjugated knowledges."[56]

"I have trodden the winepress alone; no man, no nation was with me," moaned Isaiah (63:3). Jeremiah lamented: "Because I felt thy hand upon me I have sat alone" (Jer. 15:17). His mission seemed a failure: "For twenty-three years . . . I have been . . . taking pains to speak to you, but you have not listened" (25:3). The subjugated knowledge was subjugated for a reason, and no one wanted it resurrected into the currency of conscience. The prophets were on the front lines of "the gigantic struggles between truth and falsehood besetting our bleeding world."[57] Prophecy was, and ever will be, lonely, unpopular work.

7. The Piety Bypass

Martin Buber makes the stunning observation that, according to the prophets, "God does not attach decisive importance to 'religion.'" Other cults "are dependent on a house, an altar, [and] sacrificial worship."[58] Israel was morality-centric rather than religion-centric, in the usual sense of religion. And so its literature contains an amazing array of anticultic texts. Justice took precedence over piety.

This is all the more remarkable since the condemnation of cult was seditious. Cult, or religion, was seen as serving national interest and national security in the world of the prophets. Lambasting it as the prophets did was treason. With this in mind the texts are all the more dramatic.

Isaiah opens his work with bald derision of the worship practices cherished by the pious. Their "countless sacrifices" he declares "useless." Indeed, "the reek of sacrifice is abhorrent" to God. Such ritual is a "burden" to God, something God cannot "tolerate" or "endure." Offer "countless prayers"—it matters not. God "will not listen." Instead God wants the people of Israel to "pursue justice and champion the oppressed; give the orphan his rights, plead the widow's cause" (1:11-17). "For I desire steadfast love and not sacrifice, the knowledge of God, rather than burnt offerings" (Hos. 6:6 RSV). The "knowledge of God" could be realized only by doing *tsedaqah*. Liturgy without *tsedaqah* is not worship.

Amos would have God say: "I hate, I spurn your pilgrim-feasts; I will not delight in your sacred ceremonies. . . . Spare me the sound of your songs; I cannot endure the music of your lutes. Let justice roll on like a river and righteousness like an ever-flowing stream" (5:21-24). Hosea even declares the altars to be a "sin" (8:11). Jeremiah mocked almost all his compatriots who felt the fate of the land depended totally on what went on in the temple. He scorned those who said incantations: "The temple of the Lord, the temple of the Lord, the temple of the Lord. This catchword of yours is a lie; put no trust in it" (7:4-5). This is all the more remarkable since Jeremiah and Ezekiel both came out of a priestly background (Jer. 1:1; Ezek. 1:3). Such blasting texts abound in the prophetic literature of Israel (see Mic. 6:6-8; Jer. 6:20; 7:21-23; Isa. 58:3-12; 61:1-2; Pss. 40:7; 50:12-13; 1 Sam. 15:22). Jesus also attacked the temple, echoing Jeremiah (Matt. 21:12-13), and he too insisted on the precedence of morality over worship (Matt. 5:23-24; 7:21).

Clearly, the prophets sensed that piety and liturgy often take the primary place of justice. They did not object, of course, to the idea of worship, or awe before the mystery they called God. The great Elijah took twelve stones and with them "built an altar in the name of the Lord" and ordered, in the name of God, that liturgies be conducted there (1 Kings 18:32ff.). Jesus was not against prayer—he was against prayer used as a surrogate for the reconciling work of justice (Matt. 5:23-24; 6:5-13). Religion can be the supreme opiate of the people. It can be the epitome of ideology in the Marxist sense and can drape the thickest tissue of lies around unconscionable arrangements in the status quo.

Piety, indeed, would seem to be the first refuge of scoundrels. Some of the worst evils of history have been presented as the will of God. *Deus vult,* "God wills it," was the cry of the Crusaders as they wreaked horrors on the innocent. *Gott mit uns,* "God is with us," was engraved on the buckles of Hitler's troops. Spanish swords slaughtered the Indians of "Latin America" with the sign of the cross on their hilts.

Liturgy can be the grand deceiver, especially since it is a communal event, braced by the force of collective rationalization and group-think. It can suffocate guilt and put in its place a euphoric sense that all is not only well, but blessed by divinity. Group-interest is more impervious to reason than individual self-interest. Liturgies, whether patriotic or religious, dignify the selfish interest of groups with explicit or cryptically religious benedictions. Add to this that it is naturally easier to ritualize noble aspirations than act on them, and you have a dreadful power. The prophets saw this mischief and thrashed it.

8. Tradition and Fidelity

Finally, the prophets of Israel were traditionalists whose power derived in part from their sense of history. There is no story like an old story when it comes to moving people. The prophets were keenly aware of the exciting revolution that brought Israel into being and they tapped these cherished memories, putting words like these into the mouth of God: "I remember the unfailing devotion of your youth, the love of your bridal days, when you followed me in the wilderness, through a land unsown" (Jer. 2:2). They reminded Israel of the time when the yoke of the pharaoh was broken and Israel marched to a historic new freedom. Such images have a universal, classical power. Exodus and resurrection imagery still function today in liberation movements.

American prophets today would appeal to the most generous ideals of our revolutionary beginnings. It is no slight thing to stand at the bar face-to-face with your own professed ideals. We pay repeated homage to "liberty and justice for all." The application of that belief to our poor and to the poor of the third world, whose lot we influence, is prophet's work—until it is adopted by all. We fancy ourselves a generous and goodly people, but our behavior toward the environment and the children of tomorrow is neither generous nor good. Still, even our messianic consciousness, which has had mainly a military expression, might be redeemed. An America leading in causes of ecology and the elimination of world poverty would acquire a new form of international power. Prophets could imagine the United States as admirable for its justice at home and for a foreign policy driven by the goal of eliminating hunger from the planet. Many ideals that blossomed in our founding days would make that dream feel achievable. We are not as selfish in our roots as we have come to be. We once excited the world with our realistically idealistic revolution. We do not now. We are hated and feared in much of the world, as empires always are.

STREAMS OF PROPHECY

Prophecy does not normally appear in any single individual who perfectly embodies all the qualities listed above. It is a complex awakening that appears in streams and interlocks with other movements and triggering forces. Feminism is one modern example of prophecy. Feminism has no single prophet but a rich variety of Miriams, Deborahs, and Huldahs, as well as Jeremiahs and Isaiahs. The movement has historical antecedents in earlier feminist movements and it also draws symbols, often explicitly, from the reservoirs of Judaism and Christianity. It is in debt to the civil rights struggles of people of color, particularly African Americans, and it has shown its own unique genius and developed its own prodigious scholarship.

The eight marks of classical prophecy as outlined above are found in feminism. It (1) seeks justice for the disempowered; (2–4) shocks a nation into healthy guilt by politically and outrageously exposing the outrageousness of prejudice; (5–7) courageously suffers isolation and scorn from the pious protectors of the status quo; and finally, (8) has demonstrated that its roots are deep and representative of the professed foundational ideals of our society. Feminism offers us an alternative consciousness and an exodus experience into a land flowing with mutuality and equality. That is prophecy in its fullness.

Similar prophetic streams are found in international peace and environmental movements. The civil rights movement in the

Chapter Six

IF YOU WANT PEACE, BUILD IT

The ancient world cynically declared what seemed to be the natural law of social evolution: *si vis pacem, para bellum*, if you want peace, prepare for war. In this view, in the tough world we live in, war is the only way to peace. The biblical writers entered a major dissent to this logic. They say: *si vis pacem, para pacem!* If you want peace, you have to prepare it and build it. "Seek peace and pursue it" (Ps. 34:14). You have to plan it and work at it. Peace does not happen because people individually are nice. You can't just pray for it. It is a social, economic, and political arrangement that must be aggressively and ingeniously forged. As the rabbis put it, "All commandments are to be fulfilled when the right opportunity arrives. But not peace! Peace you must seek out and pursue."[1] You will not stumble upon it by luck. Like a city, it will come to be only if it is constructed brick by brick.

This point is one that the human race has generally missed and is still missing. It deserves another look as we emerge from the twentieth century—the bloodiest one yet. The human being, reports Erich Fromm, "is the only mammal who is a largescale killer and sadist."[2] It's unfair to the animals to say that we are acting like them. There is evidence that if we had the same aggressiveness as chimpanzees in their natural habitat, our world would be a kinder place by far.[3]

Our very talent is our undoing—*corruptio optimi pessima*—the corruption of the best is the worst. We are the only animal capable of universal love, the only one that can abstract from differences and appreciate the common essence of all who share this configuration of flesh. And yet only we, by the same genius, can devise myths of enmity that can deny the status of humanhood to nations and classes of people. What is more, and worse, only we can sacralize slaughter. Our unique appreciation of the sacred has been twisted to make a sacrament out of killing. Kill-power is seen in our culture as normal, noble, and blessed. It is our religious duty to "support our troops" while they are killing, not support them by bringing them home to their families. As President John Kennedy once commented, we will not know peace until the conscientious objector has the same status as the warrior. We're not there yet.

War is seen as rational and unavoidable. We have as a species decided that torture is always wrong (though we still commit it). We also accept that rape and slavery are wrong (though both continue to occur). We have not made a similar judgment on war. Police action, which can involve violence, can be defended since it exists in a community context under the restraints of law. The United Nations in its charter envisioned a world where only international police action within the framework of that charter is morally defensible. This was not intended to condemn a defensive response to a direct attack. This was to condemn vigilantism, the unilateral aggressions that mark the history of war. Still, the vigilante syndrome attracts nations. The United States violates that charter regularly and still plays the vigilante, invading whenever it sees fit. The absence of Christian protest is an unholy silence.

Tacitus spoke for much of history when he said that the gods are with the mighty. Royal power, which is always bred of bloodshed, calls its rights "divine." The military option has to our day an almost mystical allure so powerful that it can dissipate self-interest and the instincts of self-preservation. We will empty our pockets buying guns while children starve.

EARLY ISRAEL'S DEMURRAL

Abraham Heschel states this dramatic fact: the Israelites "were the first [people] in history to regard a nation's reliance upon force as evil."[4] Nothing in their setting was conducive to this insight. The sociology of knowledge is hard-pressed to explain how these simple tribes, surrounded by superior and hostile forces, could dream a dream of peace, unmatched to our day—but increasingly seen as indispensable common sense.

The peace protest of Israel, and subsequently of Christianity, illustrates the whole thesis of this book. Ideals don't appear full grown. They are slowly and roughly born. There was no golden age of peace, no smooth, logical progression leading to early Israel's ingenious peace plan. And yet the ideal did get born. A tender shoot broke through the resistant clay and lived, and even cascading armies did not crush it or stifle its promise. It remains relevant. More than ever, given our modern kill-power . . .

The Hebrew Bible does not resort to hints and indirection when it speaks of peace. This epochal breakthrough is blunt and loud. Also, the writers are not speaking about an internal, spiritual peace of soul as subsequent centuries of Jewish and Christians would rather have it. They are neck high in politics and economics and are out to condemn precisely the reliance of nations on weapons. Their position is that trust in weapons for safety will not work and represents a moral failure and a collapse of imagination. They insist that kill-power is not sacred. God is not with the militarily mighty; indeed, God abhors them and will abandon them, not bless them when they seek peace by war.

FROM THE GOD OF BATTLES TO THE GOD OF PEACE

How the peace ideal emerged in scriptures is a study of how ideals get born in this rugged world of ours. The exodus experience shaped Israelite consciousness. As they saw it the tribes were saved not by their own military power—they had none—but by the might of the Lord. This may not seem like progress toward a peace ideal since the Lord is portrayed in the Song of Moses as one tough deity: "The Lord is a warrior . . . majestic in strength" who lets loose "fury" and unleashes the "blast" of divine "anger" (Exod. 15:3-8). Is that the beginnings of a peace ideal? Again, ideals are born precariously, step by step.

Step One: Defrocking Weapons

When the people of Israel were saved, it was not their weapons that saved them, but the power of God. This was the subversive wedge driven into the militarism of the day. Do not trust weapons; trust God. That sounds innocent and pious but it was the first undermining of the weapons-make-us-safe mentality. The prophets thrashed the idolatry of weapons. They scorned the deep human tendency to see weaponry as the ultimate sacrament of safety. "Dismayed are all those whose strength was their God," that is, those who trusted in kill-power (Hab. 1:11). Indeed, violence at times is seen as incompatible with God and the house of God. When David would build a house to shelter the Ark of the Covenant, he was told by God: "You shall not build a house in honor of my name, for you have been a fighting man and you have shed blood" (1 Chron. 28:3).

"Neither by force of arms nor by brute strength" would the people be saved (Zech. 4:6). "Not by might shall a man prevail" (1 Sam. 2:9 RSV). Military power will be discredited. "The nations shall see and be ashamed of all their might" (Mic. 7:16 RSV). "Some boast of chariots and some of horses, but our boast is the name of the Lord." Those who boast of these state-of-the-art weapons "totter and fall, but we rise up" (Ps. 20:6-7). "Their course is evil and their might is not right" (Jer. 23:10 RSV). "The song of the military (ruthless)" will be silenced, and fortified cities will become a ruin (Isa. 25:5, 2).[5] The message is drummed home: violence does not work—it bites back at you.

Reflecting Israel's history, the prime weapons of oppressive royalty—horses and chariots—are despised (see Exod. 14:9, 23; Deut. 20:1; 2 Sam. 15:1; 1 Kings 18:5; 22:4; 2 Kings 3:7; 18:23; 23:11). As Walter Brueggemann puts it: "Horses and chariots are a threat to the social experiment which is Israel. . . . Yahweh is the sworn enemy of such modes of power."[6] God orders Joshua to disarm. "Hamstring their horses and burn their chariots" (Josh. 11:6).[7]

"There is no peace for the wicked" (Isa. 57:21). The inverse of that is that if you do not have peace, it is your fault. You took the wrong approach. "Because you have trusted in your chariots, in the number of your warriors, the tumult of war shall arise against your people and all your fortresses shall be razed" (Hos. 10:13-14). For leaders to ask their people to trust weapons for deliverance is "wickedness" and "treachery" (Hos. 10:13). Weapons beget fear, not peace. You cannot build "Zion in bloodshed" (Mic. 3:10). Therefore, "I will break bow and sword and weapon of war and sweep them off the earth, so that all living creatures may lie down without fear" (Hos. 2:18). Notice that distrusting weapons is seen as a norm for "all living creatures," not just for Israel. War delivers peace to no one. The insight that began to be birthed here—rough and imperfect, but stunning in its implications—was that "just war" is an oxymoron. The so-called just-war theory is only a modification of the primitive theory that war is a normal extension of statecraft—good if certain norms and amenities are observed. The cold presupposition of just-war theory is that the slaughter and mayhem of war, done properly, is rational. Israel pioneered, and early Christianity intensified, the more radical idea that slaughter is never a moral means to decent social goals.[8] There are many modes of power, but in the biblical perspective, violent power is the most delusional and least successful.

Isaiah acknowledged that all of this was "a new thing." Referring to the exodus, he writes with biting irony that "chariot and horse [were drawn] to their destruction, a whole army, men of valor; there they lay, never to rise again; they were crushed, snuffed out like a wick." The way of such warriors is not the "way through the wilderness," that is, you won't get where you want to go by way of war. "Cease to dwell on days gone by and to brood over past history. Here and now I will do a new thing; this moment it will break from the bud. Can you not perceive it?" (Isa. 43:16-20). The beautiful, generative image of the bud suggests the delicate birthing of this new vision.

Insight into the counterproductivity of violence is not limited to Jews and Christians. Three hundred years before Jesus was born, the powerful prince Ashoka dominated much of India by military force. After his last big battle, he walked among the dead in the battlefield where a hundred thousand men had fallen and instead of feeling triumph he felt revulsion. He converted to Buddhism and for the next thirty-seven years he pioneered a new mode of truly compassionate government. He left a legacy of concern for people, animals, and the environment. He planted orchards and shade trees along roads, encouraged the arts, built rest houses for travelers and water sheds for animals, and devoted major resources to the poor, aged, and sick. As Duane Elgin says in his hope-filled book *Promise Ahead: A Vision of Hope and Action for Humanity's Future,* "Ashoka's political administration was marked by the end of war and an emphasis on peace."[9] His governmental officers were trained as peacemakers, "building mutual good will among races, sects, and parties."[10]

The result? His kingdom lasted more than two thousand years until the military empire of Britain invaded India. Britain's empire, which was based on superpower thinking, did not last, nor did that of Alexander the Great, Caesar, Genghis Khan, Napoleon, or Hitler. Historian H. G. Wells said that among all the monarchs of history, the star of Ashoka shines almost alone.

It need not shine alone. The formula is simple. Violence begets violence. Again Isaiah pleads: "Can you not perceive it?" (43:20).

Step Two: The Justice Link

Although the God in Israel's literary history was often portrayed as warrior, once the Israelites had become suspicious of military might, their rethinking of power took a quantum leap.

The God of Israel was not automatically pro-Israel—not, as other national and tribal gods, automatically a patriot. When Israel sinned by showing "no pity, no mercy or compassion," God said: "I myself will fight against you. . . . I will turn back upon you and your own weapons" (Jer. 21:7, 5, 4). When Israel did wrong, "then was he changed into their enemy" (Isa. 63:10). The god of Babylon was not the true God, even though he had been victorious. God was with the just, not the mighty. Justice, not weaponry, was the sacrament of God's favor. History was thereby challenged as never before. The pedestals of the national gods were shaken. If peace is truly our ultimate goal and we Christians take our biblical tradition of justice seriously, then justice is the ultimate power. But if, in the United States, we do conduct unjust wars and say that we are killing for peace, we should fear the wrath of God more than any terrorist when we sing "God Bless America." Weapons will not redeem Zion. *Tsedaqah* will.

Gradually it became clear that God's weapon of choice was justice. "Justice will redeem Zion" (Isa. 1:27). Justice "shall yield peace" (Isa. 32:17). Redemption—for which peace is another name—would not be a divine trick. It comes about when we abandon the ways of war and follow the path of *tsedaqah*. Because justice shall redeem Zion, says Isaiah, "all nations shall come streaming to it" to learn this approach to peace. "They shall beat their swords into mattocks and their spears into pruning knives; nation shall not lift sword against nation nor ever again be trained for war" (Isa. 22:4; Mic. 4:24). Hostility is not intrinsic to the species. The day can come when "they shall not hurt or destroy in all my holy mountain" (Isa. 11:9). That is, the whole earth must be taught to abandon this madness before it self-destructs.

As this theology develops, Yahweh undergoes a personality change. Yahweh becomes "the Lord of peace" (Judg. 6:24). The covenant becomes "a covenant of peace" (Isa. 54:10). Note the process: Yahweh in the myth of exodus assumes the military function. But justice is God's cause and Yahweh will war against the Israelites if they are not just. Justice then begins to assume ascendancy over Yahweh's battling prowess, and scorn for all the instruments of warring grows. Then, climactically, there is the vision of swords beaten into plowshares and all the nations of the world reject slaughter as a moral option.

All of these changes are not just moral, they're practical. How can the evolution of the species go forward if the nuclear swords are not melted down? Modern kill-power has made qualitative leaps and can lay no rational claim to use, and yet we sacrifice everything to continue increasing it. The old reasons for war are obsolete—opening sea lanes, crossing borders, rights of passage. National economies and global product manufacturing are thawing national borders. Economics is leading politics as it internationalizes. War is becoming increasingly unfeasible. Superpowers who try to impose themselves on others by sending their armies overseas find themselves in quagmires. Isaiah and Micah are suddenly people of the hour . . . not dreamy idealists but pragmatists who saw that justice, not military power, brings peace.[11] Ashoka and Isaiah, not Caesar, had it right.

PEACE IN THE JESUS MOVEMENT

Christian scholars have often neglected the peace message of the Hebrew Scriptures. In effect, to aggrandize Jesus, they distorted his religion. The Christian Scriptures take it up, but the peace message is undeniably in the very Scriptures Jesus used. As Elisabeth Schüssler Fiorenza says: "The earliest Christian theology is sophialogy."[12] Jesus was seen as the messenger or child of Sophia, Wisdom. The message of gentle *sophia* is the message of *tsedaqah* and the reign of God. In this sense, a difficult text finds its meaning: "The reign of God suffers violence from the days of John the Baptist until now and is hindered by men of violence."[13]

The God of the Christians is, once again, a "God of peace" (Heb. 13:20). The Sermon on the Mount, especially the insistence on loving enemies, radically subverts the military instinct. The call to nonviolence in these writings, as one study concludes, is "overwhelming."[14] The Christian Scriptures do not, any more than the Hebrew Scriptures, give a coherent philosophy of peace. They, too, have contradictions and texts that can please both warmakers and peacemakers. But Jesus, unlike the violent Zealots of his time, did not require violence for the commencement of the reign of God. The reign was already dawning without the Zealots' military preamble (Matt. 12:28).[15] But men of violence impede it.

The message is clear: "If you go on fighting one another, tooth and nail, all you can expect is mutual destruction" (Gal. 5:14). As Jesus said, right before his death, "Put up your sword. All who take the sword die by the sword" (Matt. 26:52). If a military solution were in order, his Father would send "more than twelve legions of angels" (v. 53). But that is not the way of God. The reign that Jesus represented was not of this world, this *kosmos*, this order, this system. If it were, said Jesus, "my followers would be fighting to save me" (John 18:36). Fighting and the reign are incongruous. Jesus' authority was, he said, "from elsewhere." And in that elsewhere, the rule is "how blest are the peacemakers; God shall call them his children" (Matt. 5:9). If you follow the traditional rules of conflict, "all you can expect is mutual destruction." (Gal. 5:14)

THE REALISTIC VISIONARIES

The position of the Israelite and Christian prophets is sound. If we are afraid to walk any distance from our homes at night, if the world is immersed in wars and rumors of wars, if our budgets are bled by the endless mustering of horses and chariots, if a quarter of the world's children are hungry, the prophets would only say: "You trusted your horses and chariots and you shall be destroyed. You squandered your trust and money on gods of metal, on military towers of Babel, and created despair. And from despair come desperadoes. Beat those swords into farming tools and turn the earth green with hope and not red with the horror of shed blood."

Jesus and the prophets of Israel were realists. Their insight into the weakness of the sword is born out every day. Mohandas Gandhi, Martin Luther King Jr., and Nelson Mandela are famous for showing the power of nonviolent resistance. Almost bloodlessly dictators, such as Ferdinand Marcos and at least seven Latin American despots have been driven out. As Walter Wink writes: "In 1989–90 alone fourteen nations underwent nonviolent revolutions."[16] Gene Sharp lists 198 different types of nonviolent actions that are on the historical record, but neglected by historians and journalists who prefer to report on the flash of war.[17] "Britain's Indian colony of three hundred million people was liberated nonviolently at a cost of about eight thousand lives. . . . France's Algerian colony of about ten million was liberated by violence, but it cost almost one million lives."[18]

Compare these successful cases of nonviolent resistance with the American quagmires in Vietnam, Afghanistan, and Iraq and ask:

who are the realists—the prophets of Israel, Jesus, and Gandhi, or the Pentagon warriors?

THE SUPERPOWER FICTION

For those whose God is found in the barrel of a gun, talk of peacemaking seems pathetically naïve. Let's see who is naïve. By all accounts, the United States is a superpower unmatched in all of history. Isaiah and the prophets would ask: "Does that make you secure?" Let facts give the answer:

September 11, 2001, proved that a handful of people with nothing more than box cutters and penknives as weapons could destroy the Twin Towers of the World Trade Center and severely damage the Pentagon, symbols of American economic and military strength. This signaled the end of nation-versus-nation warfare as in World War II. As Karen Armstrong says, "It was an attack against the United States, but it was a warning to all of us in the First World." It made us aware of "a new nakedness and a raw [and new] vulnerability."[19] If our policies inspire hatred around the world, and they do—see *Why Do People Hate America?* by Ziauddin Sardar and Merryl Wyn Davies—the angry of the world have the means to get at us.[20] The National Security Strategy of the United States in 2002 admitted that America is now threatened less by conquering states than by failing ones, "less by fleets and armies than by catastrophic technologies in the hands of the embittered few." A recent estimate by information warfare specialists at the Pentagon reveals how vulnerable developed nations are. The study estimated that a well-prepared attack by fewer than thirty computer whizzes with a budget of less than ten million dollars "could bring the United States to its knees, shutting down everything from electric power grids to air traffic control centers."[21]

The meaning of "protected borders" has changed, which changes everything regarding "security." Nothing is fully protectable by borders: our 1,000 harbor channels; our 3,700 passenger and cargo terminals; the 7,000,000 cargo containers moving in and out of all parts of our ports; our factories and refineries; our fish

farms and megafarms; our chemical plants and nuclear energy fa-
cilities. To penetrate any of this is to penetrate us and they are all
penetrable. Ponder the vulnerability of the eight million daily rid-
ers on New York's subways: are we ready to subject all of them to
the scrutiny now given in airports? Even airport security is full of
leaks. The idea of protected borders has become obsolete. A single
rifle in the hands of two men could change life for twenty-two days
in the nation's capital and in Virginia. Mere hundreds of trained and
motivated persons could paralyze our nation with catastrophic effect on all commerce.

Recall too that the nuclear genie is out of the bottle and for
sale on the international market, with nations like Pakistan called by
some "the K Mart of nuclear weapons." The nuclear club is burgeon-
ing, with interest being shown in Saudi Arabia, Iran, Japan, Argentina,
Brazil, Australia, and South Korea. In the United States, with its huge
caches of nuclear and other weapons, to preach disarmament is like
the village drunk urging sobriety. We have made nuclear weapons the
coin of the realm. Countries that have them, like Pakistan and North
Korea, we do not attack. Countries that do not, like Iraq, we invade.
We bless Israel's weapons of mass destruction and invade Arab states
on the mere suspicion they might want them.

Atomic devices that fit in a suitcase or can be easily hidden
in huge cargo containers are now technically feasible. Angering
nations by our aggressive policies motivates those with access to
use them *and we should anticipate their use in the United States if present trends continue.* President Bush, in his 2001 State of the Union
address, said that our safety is due to "the might of the military." On
the contrary! Our military, with its weapons of mass destruction,
is now the model for any nation that wants to be taken seriously.
Israel understood that, and Arab states, among others, of course
want to follow suit.

We are in this mess because of our naïve faith that more weapons and bigger military budgets bring security and because of our
arrogant belief that we have no need to find out why people hate
us enough to die hurting us. The biblical prophets would scorn us:
"You have trusted your horses and chariots and failed in justice,
compassion, and wisdom. You shall be destroyed."

PACIFISM VERSUS PASSIVE-ISM

As we have seen, the process of translation is by nature traitorous. The ancients put it this way: *translator traditor*, the translator is a traitor. Some have done a lot to betray Jesus, especially in this text from Matthew 5:38–42: "You have learned that they were told, 'Eye for eye, tooth for tooth.' But what I tell you is this: Do not set yourself against the man who wrongs you." [Nrsv: "Do not resist an evildoer."] If someone slaps you on the right cheek, turn and offer him your left. If a man wants to sue you for your shirt, let him have your coat as well. If a man in authority makes you go one mile, go with him two" (neb). This text has been interpreted so badly that it became "the basis for systematic training in cowardice, as Christians are taught to acquiesce to evil."[22] It has been used to urge cooperation with dictators, submission to wife battering, and helpless passivity in the face of evil. Associating Jesus with such pusillanimity is an outrage.

Walter Wink puts the meaning back into these texts. "Turn the other cheek" was not in reference to a fist fight. The reference is to a backhanded slap of a subordinate where the intention was "not to injure but to humiliate." The striker desires abject submission. Turning the other cheek was the opposite of abject submission. Rather it said: "Try again. . . . I deny you the power to humiliate me." The striker is a failure, his goal not achieved. His "inferior" is not cowering but is trivializing the insult.[23] Gandhi understood, saying that "the first principle of nonviolent action is that of non-cooperation in everything humiliating."[24] This is courageous resistance, not passivity.

Similarly, the person being sued for his clothing is an example of a frequent horror in Jesus' day. The poor were strapped with debts and through debt would lose their land, their homes, and even their clothing. As Wink explains, if a man is being sued for his outer garment, he should yield it and then strip himself naked and say, here take my inner garment, too. "Why then does Jesus counsel them to give over their undergarments as well? This would mean stripping off all their clothing and marching out of court stark naked! Imagine the guffaws this saying must have evoked. There stands the creditor, covered with shame, the poor debtor's outer garment in the one hand, his undergarment in the other."[25] Nakedness was taboo in that society and the shame fell less on the naked party than on the person viewing or causing the nakedness (Gen. 9:20-27). This again was not submission, but deft lampooning. It was nonviolent resistance.

As for going the second mile, by law, the Roman occupiers could force a person to carry a soldier's heavy pack, but only for a mile. The mile limitation was a prudent ruling to minimize rebellion, and it provided two advantages for the Roman soldier. He could hand over his 85- to 100-pound pack and gear and also reduce the occupied person to the status of a pack animal. But when they reach the mile marker—and the soldier could be punished for forcing more than a mile—the victim says, "Oh, no, I want to carry this for another mile!" "Imagine the situation of a Roman infantryman pleading with a Jew to give back his pack! The humor of this scene may have escaped us, but it could scarcely have been lost on Jesus' hearers, who must have been regaled at the prospect of thus discomfiting their oppressors."[26]

Again, this is not submission but an assertion of human dignity by the apparently powerless. Jesus knew that violent resistance to the Roman empire was fruitless and recent history in his own region showed that. A more recent example might be the people of Denmark during World War II who did not try to fight the German army, but allowed it in. Every day their king would lead a quiet walk through the city of Copenhagen with the citizens in good order behind him. It was peaceful, but it said to the occupiers, "You do not own us and you have not captured our spirits." This had to affect even the minds of the occupiers, as nonviolent resistance always seeks to do. The same spirit showed through when the Danes got word from a friendly German officer that the Nazis were coming for their Jews. Using everything that could float, the Danes transported their Jewish compatriots over the sea to neutral Sweden, saving most of them.

What Jesus was saying was, "Don't retaliate against violence with violence because it will get you nowhere, but you must oppose evil in any way you can." Even Gandhi said that if there were only two choices in the face of evil, cowardice or violence, he would prefer violence, but there is the third option of ingenious, persistent, creative nonviolent resistance, and this, in biblical terms, is "the way of the Lord."

Chapter Seven

PEACE: HOW IDEALS DIE ...
AND CAN BE REBORN

Early Christians grabbed the revolutionary biblical peace concept and ran with it. The chorus of early writers is almost unani-
mously antiwar. The words of Jesus to Peter in the garden of Gethse-
mane, "all who take the sword die by the sword" (Matt. 26:52), were
much quoted and treated as a literal ruling. Origen, commenting
on this text at the end of the second century, says that the rule for
Christians was to beware lest "for warfare, or for the vindication of
our rights or for any occasion, we should take out the sword, for
no such occasion is allowed by this evangelical teaching."[1] Tertullian
was equally unambiguous:"Christ in disarming Peter disarmed every
soldier."[2] Lactantius, writing as late as 304 CE, said that "participation in warfare therefore will not be legitimate for a just man."[3] Early
Christian regulations reflect this same attitude. The Canons of St.
Hippolytus treat the question of military service. One canon said that
a catechumen who showed military ambitions was to be rejected,
because "[this] is far from the Lord."[4] (Soldiering also presented the
danger of enforced idolatry.) Arnobius naïvely thought that the calm
of the *Pax Romana* should be credited to Christ's teaching: "The
ungrateful world owes to Christ this blessing that savage ferocity has
been softened and hostile hands have refrained from the blood of a

kindred creature."[5] Roland Bainton observes that "the outstanding writers of the East and the West repudiated participation in warfare for Christians."[6] Practice, of course, did not always follow theory and accommodations were made, especially as order broke down eventually at the edges of the empire.

Starting around the year 170 CE Christians began to appear in the army. However, it was in 312, with the victory of Constantine at the Milvian Bridge—under the alleged auspices of Jesus—that Christians began their epochal turn to a new morality of war and peace. As their social status changed swiftly from persecuted to preferred, a new world order came into view. Peaceful idealism was a heady wine and the ideal of peace teetered and began to collapse under the comforts of imperial favor. The befriending sword was not about to be beaten into a plowshare. In an error replicated throughout history and even in our modern times, a political leader or faction who provides material comforts is taken to be the vanguard of the reign of God. Eusebius was beside himself with joy at the idea of a "Christian" emperor. "The God of all, the supreme governor of the whole universe by his own will appointed Constantine."[7] Lactantius, forgetting what he had recently said about Christian commitment to nonviolence, rejoiced that divine power could have appointed so superior a person "as its agent and minister."[8] Music to Constantine's ears! This militant emperor promised to do battle against Jesus' enemies and he was as good as his word. Eusebius tells us jubilantly that Constantine chastens the "adversaries of the truth" with the usages of war.

So Jesus had come full circle, married to the empire that killed him—the Prince of Peace become the Lord of War, with a Roman emperor killing in his name.

"Jesus" was immediately active in his new career as war lord. A fourth-century bishop of Nisibis reports that in response to prayer, the Lord routed the Persians by sending a cloud of mosquitoes and gnats to tickle the trunks of the enemy's elephants and the nostrils of his horses.[9] Clearly the new Jesus was not just tough, but versatile. Christian abhorrence and avoidance of military service faded so far that by 416 you had to be a Christian to serve in the Roman army according to the Theodosian Code![10]

Writers such as Augustine and Ambrose masked the new realities by baptizing the just-war concepts of Plato and Cicero. While admiring those who died as martyrs rather than fight, Augustine still yielded and allowed that wars could be fought, though insisting that this should be done in a mournful mood. His lethal conclusion, however, revealed an attitude more redolent of the library than of the battlefield: "Love does not exclude wars of mercy waged by the good."[11] That, of course, is the illusion of all warriors. That is why just-war theory does not have rules for the other side against whom "the good" are doing righteous battle. The other side is presumed wrong and bad and there are no rules for being wrong and bad.

ONWARD, CHRISTIAN SOLDIERS

A little more of the history of the collapsed peace ideal is instructive. With the "just-war theory" nicely in place the *Pax Romana* broke down as the so-called barbarians arrived. These robust people admired the empire that they overran and found the Christian faith of that empire attractive. They converted in droves but the waters of baptism did not wash away their zest for battle. The mythical St. Michael, with his sword, replaced Wotan, their former god of war, as the patron of battle. In their liturgies they praised Peter, who used his sword to strike at the offending Roman, apparently not bothering to record Jesus' immediate rebuke.

Just-war theory soon became an irrelevant abstraction. Battles were fought on any pretext and "Christendom" became a cauldron of violence. In a well-meaning but ineffectual effort to stem the violence the Truce of God was instituted in the tenth century. The terms of the Truce are starkly revealing. It banned all killing for several months around the feast of Easter, for the four weeks before Christmas, and on all Fridays, Sundays, and holy days, of which there were many. Church properties and the clergy were always to be exempt from violence (the clergy, of course, were making the rules!) as were peasants, pilgrims, agricultural animals, and olive trees. From age twelve on, everyone was bound to take an oath to obey the Truce and, with bizarre irony, to take up arms against those who would not conform.[12]

One of these oaths comes down to us from Robert the Pious, a designation that implies he was a cut above the rest. Its cagey wording tells much of the state of things. "I will not burn houses or destroy them, unless there is a knight inside. I will not root up vines. I will not attack noble ladies nor their maids nor widows or nuns, unless it is their fault. From the beginning of Lent to the end of Easter I will not attack an unarmed Knight."[13] So much for the "pious" Robert. As Stanley Windass comments on the Truce of God: "The disease was too radical to respond to such first aid."[14]

The next and fatal step was the consecration of violence in the Crusades. In effect, the violence that could not be contained was diverted. At the end of the eleventh century the Crusades received formal blessing at the Council of Clermont. The slaughterous fury of these wars is reflected in the dictum of John Calvin: "No heed is to be paid to humanity when the honor of God is at stake."[15] Today, much of the Crusading spirit is found in the Christian Right. Theirs is the big-bang theory of the return of Jesus, giving apocalyptic war a sacral role in the redemption scenario. It is the most frightening part of their religious faith.

It is not just the Christian Right that can be indicted, of course. President Eisenhower called the Second World War a "crusade" and George W. Bush used the term to describe his unconstitutional assault on Iraq. If, as Teilhard de Chardin said, nothing is intelligible outside of its history, the stunning lack of Christian resistance to warring presidents and leaders—indeed the enthusiasm of many self-proclaimed Christians for military slaughter—reflects a Christian history drenched in blood leaving us all too inured and receptive to violent solutions.

The main work of religious education, theology, and preaching should be to recover the lost energy of abandoned ideals.[16]

COMMON SENSE
AND RECOVERING IDEALS

Paul the apostle almost rivals the Chicago School of Economics in cynicism about human motivation when he tells the Philippians that "people always pursue their own interests" (Phil 2:21, my translation). It is not too cynical to say that appeals to self-interest have tremendous clout. The Gospels are certainly right in saying that our treasuries show where our hearts truly are (Matt. 6:21). How we spend our money is a vivid clue to our values. Let's see how the United States, a nation avowedly committed to moral, family, and Christian values, spends its dollars. What an example it gives of the gap between self-perceived piety and incompatible action.

The United States, avowedly and unavowedly, is committed to enhancing its own power. If we can show that our spending choices to enhance our power are actually enfeebling and endangering us, then the wisdom of Jesus and the other prophets might seem freshly relevant. Common sense might come to the rescue of Gospel values.

First, let's visit the U.S.S. Kitty Hawk, the nuclear-powered aircraft carrier. It is impressive: almost three football fields long and towering as high as a twenty-story building. On board it has six thousand crew and seventy state-of-the-art aircraft. And it is never lonely. As a "carrier battle group" it is accompanied by an Aegis cruiser outfitted to knock down incoming missiles, several frigates and destroyers, and one or more submarines and supply vessels. "The United States has thirteen of these carrier battle groups. No other country has even one."[17] That should be embarrassing. It is like having the greatest football team in the world and no opponents. It is, of course, the product of the *more-arms-equals-more-secure* illusion that undergirds American faith and foreign policy. Let's probe that illusion with an exercise of creative imagination, our supreme moral talent.

The U.S. economy has come to spend more than $31 million per hour—over ten thousand dollars per second—on its military. Even the collapse of Soviet Communism, the designated enemy, did not stay this wasteful profusion. An undefined "terrorism" has taken its place as the *bete du jour*. We must prophetically be prepared to ask: how could all that profligate and misguided economic power be redirected into plowshares?

Putting aside my own view that 10 percent of the United States military budget would be adequate for all our reasonable purposes, I submit more conservative figures. Long before the collapse of Communism in the Soviet Union and Eastern Europe the Center for Defense Information estimated that one-third of our expenditures served no military purpose. Some even estimated that one-half of the budget would provide for all imaginable military needs. Since the collapse of Communism others have joined in even lower estimates. Thus, it is conservative to say that at least $10 million per hour (of the more than $30 million per hour now spent) could be diverted to nonmilitary purposes. Starting with the first $1 million, here are some possibilities to stoke our moral-political imagination and allow us to follow more faithfully the wisdom of *tsedaqah*.

The First Million

With the first $1 million per hour, coming to $24 million a day, we transform American education. Through history we have honored the teachers of our children, and, relatively speaking, starved them. We could end that shame by immediately doubling the salaries of K–12 teachers. By removing this money from military misuse we can remove school aid from inequitable and inconsistent property tax schemes. We institute fully paid sabbaticals for K–12 teachers to let them keep up with the latest developments in their field, thus allowing, in some cases, for major retooling.

We put some of our idle explosives to good use by combining them and many bulldozers to raze every inferior school structure in the nation—putting in their place buildings full of light, beauty, practicality, and hope. (We could allow the girl who writes the best essay to push down the dynamite trigger plunger that razes the old school!) We cut the teacher-student ratio and lower it further for students with special language or other needs. Some of our liberated monies will flow to the universities since our need for teachers will at least double. The genius now present in our overworked teachers will be allowed to explode as they themselves decide how to improve teaching. Prematurely retired people who have forgotten that financial security without fulfillment can lead to death by boredom could be lured back into part-time teaching.

Increasingly the lower economic classes are being priced out of college education. Why not heed Adolph Reed's suggestion of "a GI bill for everybody"?[18] Under the GI Bill, Second World War veterans usually received full tuition support and generous stipends (up to $12,000 in 1994 dollars). A 1988 report by a congressional subcommittee on education and health estimated that 40 percent of those who attended college would not otherwise have done so. The report also found that each dollar spent educating that 40 percent produced a $6.90 return due to increased national output and increased federal tax revenues resulting from the more educated citizenry. For less than $50 billion a year (the cost of six months of fighting the second Gulf War) all public college and university tuition would be free for all qualified students.

The economic and security gains from all of this? A highly skilled workforce. There would be alternatives to despair in the ghettoes and barrios. Lower unemployment would follow as buildings are constructed and equipped, and new teachers get hired. We could anticipate technological advances from better-educated researchers. When it comes to creativity, "fortune favors the prepared mind." More taxpayers, less despair, less crime, more genius empowered for our enrichment—in a word, more security! That's just one option. It awaits us, or do we prefer to stay with current policy . . . more and more bombs?

The Second Million

With the next $1 million per hour, we could seed the private sector to find new energy sources, creating more jobs at the same time. The first goal of this industry would be to put solar paneling on every suitable roof in this country in X number of years. The supply of oil is finite and therefore environmentally benign substitutes are necessary. Generous grants, free training programs, and low-interest loans could be made available to aspiring entrepreneurs. Scholarships for technical schools and funds for research universities would be made available. We could begin to catch up in the search for new forms of energy. In April 1988 a Soviet passenger plane, the TU 155 (comparable in size to the Boeing 727), took off from Moscow airport on a test flight powered by hydrogen rather than petroleum-based fuel. We did not respond to this event as we did to Sputnik because we believed that, unlike Sputnik, the TU 155 had little military importance. We are more responsive to fear than to hope—current budgets show that. With 71 percent of our federal research monies allotted to military purposes, there has been little left for anything more beneficent.

The Third Million

The next $1 million per hour could be directed toward redirecting the work of the many good people who make a living on military contracts. Our purpose is not to put them and the military contractors out of business. The gracious and feasible goal of Torah is: "There shall be *no* poor among you!" (Deut. 15:4). We direct these people to transportation, first turning bomber-makers into train-makers. American trains are among the least developed in the world. Press reports advise us that they are frequently off the tracks, and when on the tracks they go nowhere very quickly. Meanwhile, trains in Japan, Germany, and France move at speeds of 180 miles per hour. Japanese scientists have tested the magnetic levitation train at 319 miles per hour. Although the idea for this train was born in the United States it was shunted aside in favor of weapons research. (Actually I think that 319 miles an hour is too fast. You could not even see the cows! "Was that a cow?" "No, I think it was Chicago.") We have spent 170 times as much on space travel in recent years as on terrestrial transit. The results are painfully visible in cluttered airports and abandoned rail tracks, and on the 40 percent of our bridges and 60 percent of our roads in serious disrepair since the beginning of the 1990s.[19]

The Next Few Million

Other problems of health and well-being could be met by redirecting several other military millions. We could eliminate the category of the "uninsured patient" from our health care lexicon. The government should become the insurer of last resort, as works well in the other industrial nations of the West. We could consider making all medical schools tuition-free, with admission based on talent and commitment alone. In return, new doctors would be required to serve for two or three years in medically deprived areas—something that would give them clinical experience they would not get elsewhere. We could supply the number of drug treatment centers that are actually needed—while not forgetting that the best drug treatment is a job-filled economy.

Scientists redirected from war to peace could help plan for future major earthquakes in California and elsewhere. Poisoned lakes and groundwaters could be redeemed, topsoil restored, fish sources replenished, and forests saved. The technology is already available to turn deserts into gardens, as illustrated by projects in Israel and elsewhere. The deserts can rejoice, as the biblical poets imagined.

We could address the pressing population crises. Projections show the world's population growing to as many as 8, or even 11, billion people by 2050, almost all of them in poor nations.[20] Hope is the best contraceptive. Education, health care, and access to food are the ingredients of hope, and without it people will not plan reasonable birthrates. If decency does not move us regarding the calamities afflicting people who live in the third world, fear should. For the first time in history the poor can hurt us because poverty is now as global as finance. While the rich are rapid ecology-wreckers, the poor do it slowly as they denude their land out of desperation and the results come home to us in the air, the water, the beef, and the strawberries.

Solving all this is not beyond our fiscal reach, though it seems to be beyond our moral grasp. Let's not forget the possible solutions already on the table, like economist James Tobin's Nobel Prize–winning suggestion of a 0.5 percent tax on all transactions in foreign exchange. The Tobin tax on foreign exchange transactions would help dampen speculative international financial movements but would be too small to deter commodity trade or serious international investments. The money could be used to retire the unwieldy debts of poor countries and it could finance the efforts of the United Nations and other agencies and non-governmental organizations to bring education, soil conservation, water-purification, microloans for cottage industries, family planning, fighting of AIDS, and improved communications throughout the world. If the United States took the lead in all of this, it would have nothing to fear from terrorism. As historian Howard

Zinn often reminds us, generous and modest nations have nothing to fear from terrorists.

This list gives only a few of the benefits that come when the human spirit is freed of the military stranglehold. The result is peace, in the sense of the Hebrew *shalom,* which means more than just the absence of war. It implies fullness of life and a triumph of human intelligence in a community where needs are met and joy is possible. Peace is the only rational goal of economics or politics. The ultimate purpose of these disciplines is that life might survive and thrive. There is really no economics of war—that would be necro-economics. Likewise, war is not an extension of politics, but its collapse. Deuteronomy's prescription is so obvious and so tragically avoidable. We can choose life or death, and we are urged to choose life for the sake of our children. "Choose life and then you and your descendants will live" (Deut. 30:19).[21]

Again, Howard Zinn: "Should we not begin to consider all children everywhere as our own? In that case, war, which in our time is always an assault on children, would be unacceptable as a solution to the problems of the world. Human ingenuity would have to search for other ways."[22] Such a simple idea, and it would transform the world. Again we hear from afar the plaintive cry of Jesus and the prophets: "Have you eyes and cannot see; have you ears and cannot hear?"

HOW TO APPEAL TO CONSERVATIVES

The ingenious Constitution of the United States decided that the president has no power to declare war or to use the military on his own authority. Article 1, Section 8, of the Constitution gives Congress and only Congress the right "to declare War." As for presidents assuming this power, Justice William O. Douglas said, "There is not a word in the Constitution that grants that power to him. It runs only to Congress."[23] The "Commander-in Chief" does not have the power to move the country from peace to war unless the Congress so moves. But Congress has abdicated its war-making powers with trust-the-president resolutions like the Tonkin Bay Resolution and the vote to let the Presidents Bush make their wars on their own.

Congress has limply allowed "all presidents since Harry S. Truman to use military power on their own authority."[24] We have not had a constitutionally declared war, with the appropriate debate it requires, since World War II. The quagmires of Korea, Vietnam, Laos, Cambodia, Iraq, and Afghanistan show the wisdom of the Founding Fathers. James Madison wrote: "In no part of the Constitution is more wisdom to be found than in the clause which confides the question of war and peace to the legislature, and not to the executive department."[25]

It seems a very conservative thing to defend the Constitution, and according to that Constitution we are not at "war on terrorism." We are not "at war" since war has not been declared in accord with the Constitution, and "terrorism" cannot be defined, although it often refers to those in occupied countries like Iraq, the Palestinian territories, and Chechnya who are fighting the occupation. Those who die in these undeclared American non-wars are victims of impeachable presidential misconduct.

Senator Sam J. Ervin, an expert on the Constitution, wrote: "The only security America has against anarchy on the one hand and tyranny on the other is to be found in reverential obedience to the Constitution by those entrusted with governmental power."[26] What a refreshing thought for conservatives and liberals alike.

Chapter Eight

TRUTH AND THE TINCTURE OF THE WILL

My brother Joe was a chaplain with the Marines during the Vietnam War. When he went there he took with him the long-established rationale for why America goes to war and why we were in this one: we were over there to do good and we wouldn't be back until it was over over there. As a Catholic priest in the military he had been shaped by two authoritarian systems: pre–Vatican II Catholicism and military culture. Thus the controlling myth.

Suddenly he was set free and truth arrived unannounced. He was waiting to cross a road on which American trucks and military vehicles were lumbering noisily past. He looked to his right and saw that he had been joined by a little Vietnamese girl. He looked down at her and then started at what he saw on her leg: a festering growth the size of half an orange. The dust from the passing trucks was caking on it. "Bubonic plague," someone explained to him later. And then the light of truth clicked on with the illuminating power of lightning, and he thought, "Millions of dollars of American military equipment are roaring past. What are they up to that is more important than this little girl's diseased leg and body for which they are doing nothing!" He could never view the war the same way again. A military chaplain moved from hawk to dove. The bruised human preciousness beside him was a solvent for the falsity of long-tenured myths.

There are many routes to the truth. Until heart and head are married, we miss most important truths. Such is the mystery of human knowing, and the biblical authors plunged into it with gusto and more than a little success.

The passion for truth drives every pen. Truth-hunger is the engine that powers thought. The social standing of truth would thus seem to be beyond challenge. Who could bear to be called or thought of as a liar or a fraud? But, wait! The moral traditions of Judaism and Christianity entered a gentle and insightful demurral. They were convinced that our love of the truth was not marital in kind, but flirtatious at best. Given the chance, we betray the truth. We make bargains with it, and truth loses. The biblical writers even stand close to Tertullian, who said that "the truth appears to be instinctively hated."[1]

"There is no truth . . . in the land," says Hosea (4:1).[2] "Go up and down the streets of Jerusalem and see for yourselves; search her wide squares: can you find any man who . . . seeks the truth?" (Jer. 5:1). False "prophets prophesy lies and priests go hand in hand with them, and my people love to have it so" (Jer. 5:31). The people order visionaries to "have no true visions." Instead, they say, "give us smooth words and seductive visions. Turn aside, leave the straight path" (Isa. 30:10). All this is acted out: "Truth stumbles in the market-place and honesty is kept out of court, so truth is lost to sight" (Isa. 59:14). The Bible agrees with the ancient saying: *mundus vult decipi*, people want to be deceived. Biblical cynicism would also stand with Søren Kierkegaard, who said, "It is far from being the case that [people] in general regard relationship with the truth as the highest good, and it is far from being the case that they, Socratically, regard being under a delusion as the greatest misfortune."[3] Scripture has a complicated answer to Pilate's question: "What is the truth?" (John 18:38).

The beginning of all wisdom is in knowing how we know. There is a strong tendency in the western world to think of truth in merely abstract terms, as the accurate refraction of reality in the mind. Clearly that is part of it, but there is so much more. We process everything that we receive, so nothing is pure upon delivery to the mind. Our interests process incoming data.

Beyond that, reality is bigger than our minds so we know only in part. The mind is not a camera that takes snap shots, with no affective or mythic filters intervening. There is no disinterested knowing. Vision, like evolution, is selective. Truth is more of a challenge than simple rationalists can believe.

HARD TRUTH

The biblical classics cannot be accused of rationalism. They saw truth as an intricate challenge and an awesome but precarious good. They start by paying truth their supreme compliment, saying it was one of the marks of God. God is a "God of truth" (Deut. 32:4; 2 Chron. 15:3; Ps. 31:5; Jer. 10:10). Truth is the mark of the presence of God: "I will dwell in Jerusalem. Jerusalem shall be called the City of Truth" (Zech. 8:3). Truth, however, is not seen as a hallmark of our history or our personalities. The Bible works from the assumption that we are compulsive architects of falsehood. We manufacture false gods, false prophets, and even false truth, which we prefer to real truth, or what the biblical authors called "God's truth."[4] God's truth has to be on the job all the time to oppose the web of lies in which we have chosen to wallow. "God must be true though every man living were a liar" (Rom. 3:4). The real drama of cognition occurs as real truth tries to cut into our self-serving versions of it.

To "walk in the truth" might seem natural, but it is not. First of all, the truth is hard to find: "Thou hast hidden the truth in darkness" (Ps. 51:6). Truth is not easy prey: certainty is not easily captured. It is often hidden in the tangle of ambiguity and paradox.

On top of that, the biblical writers assumed the unpopularity of truth. We have to be commanded to speak it (Ps. 15:2), seek it (Jer. 5:1), and walk in it (2 Kings 20:3). Our inveterate avoidance of the "path of truth," the way of God, is the heart of the human tragedy as this literature sees it (Ps. 119:30). Jeremiah tried to serve the truth and learned the penalty: "I have been made a laughing-stock all the day long, everyone mocks me" (Jer. 20:8). Fabricated truth has more fans.

HEART TRUTH

Another biblical point is that truth is not purely cognitive in a detached, intellectual way. The attunement to reality, and that is what knowledge is, is also an affective, volitional enterprise, and this thickens the plot considerably. The truth is not just something to be known or contemplated. Volition is involved in getting to the truth. For moral truth, doing and knowing are conjoined. Truth has to be done and even obeyed (John 3:21; Gal. 5:7; 1 Pet. 1:22). Truth is paralleled with justice (Jer. 5:1) and coupled with love (2 John 3). Non-commitment to the truth is a moral disaster and so sinners are "strangers to the truth" (1 John 1:8). Truth does not just inform; it transforms us into people "of the truth" (John 18:37; 1 John 3:12). "The truth becomes our very nature."[5]

The truth also has its own power and attractiveness. Ezekiel pictured himself as being fed the truth by God, who had written it on a scroll. "Open your mouth and eat what I give you. . . . Swallow this scroll. . . . So I ate it, and it tasted as sweet as honey" (Ezek. 2:8; 3:3). Truth refreshes our being when we finally let it seep in. And when it does, the urgency to communicate it can be irresistible. Jeremiah said his sense of the truth became "like a fire blazing in my heart, and I was weary with holding it under, and could endure no more" (20:9). Truth, when found, is like "the true bread from heaven" that has an aura of being imperishable. It is the bread that "brings life to the world," and it has in it the scent of "forever" (John 6:32-33, 51).

Israel was confident of the charismatic power of truth. It saw itself as the world's teacher who will teach the truth of justice. Speaking of God's servant Israel, Isaiah says with confidence: "He will plant justice on earth while coasts and islands wait for his teaching" (Isa. 42:3-4). Israel's grasp of God's truth will become "a light to the nations, . . . salvation to earth's farthest bounds" (Isa. 49:6). The power of truth, in spite of human obduracy, is almost irrepressible.

ELEMENTS OF A PHILOSOPHY OF TRUTH

The biblical traditions saw truth as far more a limpid mental mirroring. Indeed, our mirrors are sullied and bent. Truth is also a sol-

vent that dissipates the protective social and personal lies that en-
case our meaner purposes and drape our exploitative—or at least
insensitive—arrangements with respectability. As such, truth is an
unpopular threat and a complicated one. Remarkably, the biblical
authors got to some of its most striking and enigmatic characteris-
tics, especially (1) the imperfection of our grasp of it, (2) the affective, active, and social nature of experiencing it, and (3) its hopeful
power.

Dim-wittedness

Reinhold Niebuhr pinpointed a human imperfection when he
said that we can neither know the truth fully nor avoid pretending
that we know it.[6] Miguel de Unamuno has an even lower estimate
of our power to comprehend. He says that whatever is living is
thereby "absolutely unstable" and therefore "strictly unintelligible":
"The mind seeks what is dead, for what is living escapes it: it seeks
to congeal the flowing stream in blocks of ice; it seeks to arrest it.
. . . Science is a cemetery of dead ideas, even though life may issue
from them. . . . My own thoughts, tumultuous and agitated in the
innermost recesses of my soul, once they are torn from their roots
in the heart, poured out into this paper and there fixed in unalter-
able shape, are already only the corpses of thoughts."[7]

Our ideas of the truth are like nature scenes painted by children. They suggest more than they portray. The children, however
gifted, can no more do justice to nature than our ideas can do justice to reality. The written gospel always betrays the gospeler—who
already had only part of the truth. We do not grasp truth; at best,
we are grasped by only a bit of it. Our minds are not an infallible
measure of the real.

Modesty, therefore, is the badge of wisdom. A skilled, experienced physician is often more modest than the newly minted
doctor who does not yet know the frequency of surprise or the
narrowness of science. Political theorists and economists deal in
yet a more recalcitrant subject matter: human behavior and its
possibilities. Every religion in history has merited Unamuno's
complaint. The "flowing stream" of the original charisma gets
frozen into "blocks of ice," and the religionists end up with a dog-

matic cemetery of dead ideas. Those whose thought is important enough to spawn a system will be betrayed by their followers— Marx by Marxists, Freud by Freudians, Isaiah by Jews, and Jesus by Christians.

The cause of this common failure is thinking that truth can be reified, packaged, boxed, and handed on in manageable, even infallible, nuggets. In fact, imperfect as our minds are, our contact with reality involves a tortuous process of attunement. If we take the truth as finished, it dies in our hands. If we take it as an active process into which we are grafted, it may live and grow in us. As John Milton wrote in his *Areopagitica:* "A man may be a heretick in the truth; if he beeleve things only because his Pastor sayes so, or the Assembly so determines, without knowing other reason, though his belief be true, yet the very truth he holds becomes his heresie."[8] He accepts packaged truth claims, but he does not join the search; he does not enter into the process of attunement to this emerging corner of reality. He mistakes part of the successful quest for the quarry. The river moves on, and he has in his hands the congealed remnants of an earlier flow of insight. Many brilliant scientists, philosophers, and theologians are "hereticks," as the very truths they immobily hold become their "heresie."

Truth received begins—it does not end—a journey. In the pursuit of truth, fortune favors the restless and humble mind. The confident "heretick" underestimates the size and the elusiveness of the truth.

THE TINCTURE OF THE WILL

Francis Bacon, in his *Novum Organum,* wrote: "The human understanding resembles not a dry light, but admits a tincture of the will and passions, which generate their own system accordingly, for [people] always believe more readily that which [they] prefer."[9] Something demanding like *tsedaqah*, something that challenges our egoism, will be almost instinctively resisted. Reality is refracted through a filter of interests—personal, social, and class, among others. Ideas are not purebred; there are no "ideal observers" in matters human and moral. As Juan Luis Segundo says, "Anything and everything involving ideas . . . is intimately bound up with the existing social situation in at least an unconscious way."[10] Nothing escapes the tincture of the will. Suspicion, therefore, is mandatory equipment in the quest for truth. Everything from religious doctrines to national constitutions must be viewed with alert suspicion. Special interests roam ubiquitously, and, like metastasizing cancer, they destroy good flesh.

George Orwell's novel *1984* imagined a Ministry of Truth whose job was to repaint reality, past and present. This literary image is really an extrapolation from human experience generally. We construct our reality imaginatively, rather than seeing it as it is. Disciplines such as social psychology and the sociology of knowledge study this conditioning process of human social awareness. In other words, we decide as a group what will pass as truth, and we excommunicate those who would dare say that our emperors aren't wearing any clothes. There is a politics of truth in which bargains are struck, with truth as the loser.[11]

We can, of course, hide from truth individually through private rationalization. Collective rationalization, however, is more binding and more impervious to correction. We humans have a well-demonstrated clubbing instinct whereby we bond together in falsity. Such social conspiracies are common and powerful. Class consciousness is the clearest example of that. Advertisers say that if they know your zip code, they can tell what you eat, buy, and almost what you think. In terms of morality, they could say, show us your zip code and we will tell you what your social conscience is and how much of it is a mental concoction to protect your privileges. Others in your privilege group share the concoction and so it seems even more like the truth.

FEAR OF FLYING

Once we have fabricated a tidy little view of reality we don't want it disturbed. New ideas are aliens to be shunned because, at the very least, they threaten our ease. If an idea appears that would shake up our comfort zone, let it be anathema! When Charles Darwin's major paper on the theory of evolution was first read to his peers in the Linnean Society they yawned and missed the point. The "club" was not open to the novelty, to the creative moment. At the end of that year, the president of the society wrote in his annual report that "the year which has passed . . . has not, indeed, been marked by any of the striking discoveries which at once revolutionize, so to speak, the department of science on which they bear."[12]

During the eighteenth century, the French Academy of Science stubbornly denied all the evidence for the fall of meteorites, which seemed massively obvious to many other scientists. Many museums in Europe threw away what precious fragments they had of these meteorites, given the prestige of the French Academy. In a similar way, medical scientists refused to accept the evidence of hypnosis and denounced F. A. Mesmer as an imposter, insisting that all reports of his work be stricken from the minutes of the meetings of the Royal Medical and Chirurgical Society. Dr. Esdaile, in the nineteenth century, performed over three hundred major operations using mesmeric trance and could not get the results published in any medical journal in India or England.[13] What passed for the truth was preferred to the truth. It usually is.

Premodern psychology and philosophy pictured the mind as a passive recipient of information. Psychologist Rollo May refers to the work of Immanuel Kant as the "second Copernican revolution": "Kant held that the mind is not simply passive clay on which sensations write, or something which merely absorbs and classifies facts. . . . Kant's revolution lay in making the human mind an active, forming participant in what it knows. Understanding, itself, is then constitutive of its world."[14] The problem is that the mind as an "active forming participant" may fabricate fantasies. We get together and impose a meaning that often is not there, and then we conspiratorially insist on our version of reality.[15]

For example, it passes for truth among many white people that African Americans are "shiftless" and lazy, do not want to work, and would rather get handouts by way of welfare. The Brookings Institution noted that this has hardly been challenged by social scientists. In a careful study its researchers found that there were "no differences between poor and non-poor when it comes to life goals and wanting to work."[16] Asked whether they would prefer to receive money for working or as welfare while unemployed, from 72 to 80 percent of respondents said they would prefer to get the money by working.[17] I have found it difficult to convince students of this, since this study contradicts the popular and self-serving version of the truth. We fall madly in love with our lies.[18]

J. Glenn Gray wrote of an experience he had during the Second World War. He was with the American army fighting in Italy. One day on a mountain ridge, he met an old hermit. They exchanged greetings while in the distant background the sound of shelling could be heard. After a discreet interlude, the hermit asked him what the shelling was all about. Gray realized he was face-to-face with a man who had not heard about the Second World War. He explained that the Germans, English, and Americans were fighting, with some Italians fighting on both sides. The old man's perplexity grew, and with it Gray's inability to explain it even to himself. "For a few minutes," he later wrote, "I could observe this spectacle through the puzzled eyes of the old hermit, long enough to realize that I understood it as little as he."[19] Gray was disarmed by meeting someone who had not married the dominant lies of the day and his ideological casement was torn irreparably. He could not view the war in the same way again. The incident is a parable for the human plight.

THE VITAL PROMISE

Good writers know that they must pierce "the tissue of lies" (Marx's term) that society wraps around our minds. Jean Sulivan, the French novelist, sees this as the writer's calling. He writes, he says, so that he might lie less. In his stunning novel *Eternity, My Beloved* he says that the healthfully angry, not the blandly enslaved, will find their way to truth: "The anger born out of the heart of life is often the only way to break open the path of truth."[20] Eibhear Walshe sees the literary artist as having the "eye which can still find, underneath all the falsehoods, the vital promise."[21] The hope of our erratic species lies in the possibility that truth, the real truth, has an allure and a charisma that draws us, that we cannot, after all, give ourselves totally to that which is false. Falsehood, however convenient, jars the polygraph. We pay a price for our lies.

"The truth will set you free" (John 8:32). That thought contains a promise and a threat. Just as we fear real freedom, we fear real truth, and yet we want it still. With superabundant cynicism, the biblical authors thrashed our love of the lie, and yet their final word was resurrection. There is some indestructible good at the center of human life, and these writers stretched for it with heroic reach. They judged us as suicidal and at ease with enslavement, and yet they concluded: "You will indeed be free!" (John 8:36). The contagion of that hope is our best prospect.

Openness to truth is the heart of honesty and humility. It allows us to face our weakness and meanness and opens us to the call of the reign of God. A final word from the novelist Jean Sulivan:

> If streetwalkers precede us into the Kingdom, it's not because the Son of man is giving them a reward; he is simply verifying a fact. The prostitute is more truthful, more authentic, than most of us because of the knowledge and consciousness she has of her wretched situation; because she's more capable of humility. On the other hand, there is no end to the prostitution of the highly placed; they go on pretending, issuing statements, organizing justice, charity, morality, even the love of God, for their own profit. It's all done so skillfully that it takes a miracle, the greatest of all miracles, for a self-righteous person to awaken to a realization of his wrongdoing and iniquity.[22]

Chapter Nine

WHEN FREEDOM IS A VIRTUE

How much better it would have been if the United States greeted immigrants in New York harbor with a Statue of Justice, rather than a Statue of Liberty. Much American iniquity is done in the name of freedom. "Freedom" is often a tool of propaganda, used by the American empire to justify its military ventures. It is best to remember that freedom is not intrinsically a virtue. After all, even criminals want it. The Bible speaks wisely to freedom, but it is not the freedom that scoundrels and weak consciences lust after. The philosopher Georg Wilhelm Friedrich Hegel actually concluded that freedom was the dowry of biblical religion to modern civilization.[1] However, only when freedom is married to justice can we make an honest virtue out of it.

In the ancient view of kingship, only the supreme potentate was the "image of God." Israel's democratizing declaration that God created us, each and every one of us, "in his own image" (Gen. 1:27) was a foundation-shaking, liberation revolution that has left history rocking in its wake ever since. As Hegel saw it, the belief that the least of us is born in the image of God was a seed planted in Israelite antiquity, a seed able to come to bloom only in the modern era.

Freedom is strong drink, and few are they who have the stomach for it. Despite all the hackneyed praise of it, real freedom is scary; most people prefer their chains whether they acknowledge them or not. Even in the freedom revolutions of Israel and Christianity, the call to freedom was dulled by time and timidity. After pioneering political and religious freedom in a unique and revolutionary way, Israel eventually succumbed to the lure of royalty, and the revolution dimmed in spite of prophetic protest. Christianity, in its first three centuries, saw *freedom* and *gospel* as synonyms. This ended, largely under the eventual magisterial tutelage of Augustine, and humanity was seen not as royal or full of potential but as corrupt and terminally in need of authoritarian control.[2] That the ideal perished is sadly normal. That it ever existed is a blessing to be revisited.

THE DIMENSIONS OF FREEDOM

The value of freedom need not be preached to moderns. Though our homage to it is flawed, it remains the sacred beacon of modern times. The modern era might be said to have begun when Copernicus and Galileo dashed our geocentric hubris and "condemned" us to freedom. We were no longer the central darlings of the universe. It was a terrible abandonment. The old and placid order was gone, with its myths and principles. As Walter Kasper writes: "Since there was now no pre-established order, humans had to create their own." Humankind became "the point of departure and the norm." Modern notions of freedom thus arrived in the form of autonomy, with freedom seen "from now on [as] something unconditioned and ultimate, the calculus by which all else was to be measured."[3]

This epoch-making cult of freedom was not sterile. It spawned reverence for human and civil rights, and stimulated the expansion of art, science, and communication. But freedom also came to be seen as mastery (i.e., we were now free to master others) and the fruits of this corruption were bitter. The "empire syndrome" was born. "In the West," as Douglas Meeks writes, "this has been manifested in terms of the male's mastery over nature, over his own body, and over women and the white male's master over people of color."[4] The danger with freedom is that it is a formalistic notion susceptible to any content. Indeed, freedom is a natural charlatan, and thieves as well as saints aspire to it. Bourgeois ideas of freedom are often only masks for egoism. Exploitation often parades as free—*free* trade, *free* market, *free* love. Freedom without morality is toxic. In the absence of morality, freedom remains merely privative, a matter of being absolutely unregulated. Massive systems of law exist precisely because of the practical need to give freedom some moral content and direction. Freedom and just rules are not antithetical since justice relates to freedom like the potter to the clay.[5] Justice is the shape that humane freedom takes.

Freedom does bespeak a privation, but a happy privation. We do not speak of being free from food or free from respect. The word *freedom* cheerfully implies the negation of a hostile limit. There, however, is the ethical rub. We are capable of perceiving morality itself as hostile to our purposes and of seeking to escape its limits. Heaven and Earth might well beware the soldiers of this kind of freedom.

Fortunately for us, modern freedom is not a newborn. Neither is it an orphan. The freedom movements of early Israel and early Christianity have been stocked in the active memory of western culture and have often been explicitly invoked in modern freedom movements. Contemporary notions of freedom, washed anew in these ancient springs, can prosper and deepen. The ancient seers looked and saw deeply into the variegated nature of domination.

BIBLICAL FREEDOM

The biblical writers hyperbolically burst the tired barriers of the mind when they sang their song of freedom. They saw domination as pandemic and struck at all its forms. Liberation, not creation, was God's identifying act: "I am the Lord, your God, who brought you out of Egypt, out of the land of slavery" (Exod. 20:1). "They shall know that I am the Lord when I break the bars of their yokes and rescue them from those who have enslaved them" (Ezek. 34:27). The early Israelites were fed up with the oppressive strictures of the Egyptian empire and the Canaanite city-states. As Norman Gottwald says, they "were not willing to pay taxes, to be conscripted into the city-state armies, or to be debt-obligated. They asserted the full and free use of their own labor products, and they did so within the context of a society and culture where coopera- tion took precedence over competition."[6] As they saw it, liberation is God-work. It is freedom that will reign in the reign of this God, freedom from every undue limit.

These movements spoke of freedom in a spirit of "staggering amazement."[7] They sensed the possibility of a newness that sur- passed all previous understandings (Phil. 4:7). Any serious historical revolution of consciousness breaks through the strictures of menial expectation and glimpses the possibility of "a new heaven and a new earth" (Rev. 21:1). These movements did just that, going into rhapsodies on freedom and offering a broad framework for apply- ing it to every phase of human life. The Bible offers a "fundamen- tal and normative framework for our thinking about the mystery of human possessing," but it does not offer a systematic theory of property.[8] It takes a similar approach to freedom. It offers a new and profound framework for our thinking about freedom.

This literature introduces mind-blowing symbols and category- dissolving insinuations and ideas that have the power to relativize the oppressive meanness that reigns in place of God. "You were called to freedom" (Rom. 5:13 RSV). "Refuse to be tied to the yoke of slavery again" (Gal. 5:1). "Do not become slaves of other humans" (1 Cor. 7:23).[9] The biblical story began with our per- sonhood being found by imaging God (Gen. 1:26). Certainly that means freedom "from the present evil age" (Gal. 1:3 RSV) with its constraints and strangling limits. It also means freedom from a love- inhibiting understanding of law (Rom. 7:8; Gal. 5:13-15), from the demonic grip of money (Matt. 6:24), from guilt (Rom. 6:12-23), from sexual relationships if we so wish (1 Cor. 7), from arbitrary diminishments of status (Gal. 3:28), and even, in a way, from death (Rom. 5:21; 6:21-23). Paul, the wildest poet of freedom, goes so far as to say that "the whole created universe groans" to be liberated from its current restraints as an aborning child seeks to be freed from the womb (Rom. 8:22).[10]

With all this ebullience, the biblical writers knew that freedom without a qualifier is not a virtue. Freedom is a transitive noun. Talk of freedom that does not specify *from what* and *for what* is morally ungrammatical. Exodus moved from something to something else. In the spirit of the energetic imagery of the reign of God, the prime rubric of biblical morality, biblical freedom is freedom *from* everything that restrains the flourishing of human life on this "very good" Earth. In different language, it is freedom *from* "sin"—from everything that hobbles the human spirit and wounds the Earth. On the positive side, freedom is freedom *for* joy, which is the natural destiny of the kind of beings we are and of the kind of earth that bore us. As the paean of liberty unfolds, freedom takes on flesh, intelligibility, and, as we shall see, an identifiable agenda.

TEMPERING POWER

Not surprisingly since Israel was born in the melee of politics, early Israel's liberationists stormed the ancient forms of political authority. The old modes of royalty fell before the blast as Israel stunned the tired old world with its kingless revolution. God alone was king; all other claimants to authority were subordinates, pale adumbrations of the invisible, benevolent Ruler. All authority was derivative and subservient to the God whose passion was *tsedaqah*. All power was under the judgment of the Holy One who was a lover of compassion, justice, and peace. Power that did not reflect these qualities was spurious and ungodly. The words of Israel attacking royalty were, as Martin Buber says, "unparalleled in the literature of the ancient Orient for their liberty of spirit."[11]

Elaine Pagels says: "The Hebrew creation account of Genesis 1, unlike its Babylonian counterpart, claims that God gave the power of earthly rule to *adam*," to humankind, and not to pharaohs and kings.[12] Small wonder that early Christian Scriptures include a king searching "for the child [Jesus] to do away with him" (Matt. 2:13). Jesus was party to a historic Israelite subversion calculated to undo the despotic power of kings. Gregory of Nyssa was only following an old rabbinic tradition when he wrote that God had created the world "as a royal dwelling place for the future king," and that humanity was created "as a being fit to exercise that royal rule" precisely because human beings were made in the image of the Creator. Gregory's language is exorbitantly independent: "The soul shows its royal and exalted character . . . because it acknowledges no master, and is self-governed, ruled autocratically by its own will." It is against our nature, Gregory declared sweepingly, to be "in bondage to any power."[13] Early Israel had only scorn for what would be called "the divine right of kings."

In the political spectrum Israel was at the opposite end of those who preach or assume absolute obedience to political authority. Utterly un-Israelite was the Mesopotamian who wrote: "The command of the palace, like the command of Anu, cannot be changed. The king's word is right; his utterance, like that of a god, cannot be changed."[14] Humans—even supposedly very secular and sophisticated modern humans—have a dreadful tendency to sacralize their political leaders. Even the obnoxious and truculent Henry VIII was pictured as divine. One devotee of his royalty said that people "dare not cast [their eyes] but sidewise upon the flaming beams of [the king's] bright sun, which [we] in no wise can steadfastly behold."[15] Another enthusiast compared the despot to the "Son of Man."[16] "Nonsense," Israel would reply, insisting that royalty, for all its pretensions and finery, has its historic roots in slaughter. Royals kill their way to power. Modern theories of "executive privilege" and "national security" and "fighting terrorism" still house presumptions of divine right and devoted citizens will still rush to their death when the leader beckons. Light and heavy brigades still run to ruin on the most fatuous of orders.

Israel looked at kings and saw not the face of God but a bull full of "pride, . . . arrogance and vainglory." In Isaiah's ironic terms, an honest king would have to say: "By my own might I have acted and in my own wisdom I have laid my schemes; I have removed the frontiers of nations and plundered their treasures, like a bull I have trampled on their inhabitants. My hand has found its way to the wealth of nations, and, as a man takes the eggs from a deserted nest, so have I taken every land" (10:13-14).

Israel insisted that there is a kind of "yielding to men" that is "as evil as idolatry" (1 Sam. 15:23). When the people wanted Gideon to be king he spoke the faith of Israel: "I will not rule over you, nor shall my son; the Lord will rule over you" (Judg. 8:23). There was no cult of obedience here. The divine role was not to shore up political authority, but to break those forms of political power that are oppressive or unresponsive to the needs of the poor. God was by definition a liberator: freeing was the divine passion. "They shall know that I am the Lord when I break the bars of their yokes and rescue them from those who have enslaved them" (Ezek. 34:27). This was seditious talk. Small wonder Israel was so threatening to the surrounding kingdoms that attacked it—with all the viciousness of a President Reagan going after little Nicaragua and its modest social experiment or the paranoid American response to tiny Cuba that dared to try living a different way. Royalty, even in modern dress, has a horror of innovation, especially innovation that might challenge the perquisites of current power arrangements.

The Hebrew idea of freedom reignited in Christianity. All terms of authority were to be questioned. Its theological principle was the same as Israel's: God is the one authority—all other claimants are fraudulent. "You must not be called 'rabbi'; for you have one Rabbi, and you are all brothers. Do not call any man on earth 'father': for you have one Father, and he is in heaven. Nor must you be called 'teacher'; you have one Teacher, the Messiah. The greatest among you must be your servant" (Matt. 23:8-12). "You were bought at a price; do not become slaves of men" (1 Cor. 7:23). "You see, then, my brothers, we are no slave-woman's children; our mother is the free woman. Christ set us free, to be free people. Stand firm, then, and refuse to be tied to the yoke of slavery again" (Gal. 4:31—5:1). "Where the Spirit of the Lord is, there is liberty" (2 Cor. 3:17). Some early Christians saw baptism as a kind of *apolutrosis*, a term referring to the judicial process of releasing a slave.[17] These texts stalk that love of slavery that seems to be a temptation endemic to the human spirit. The forms of slavery vary with the economics and politics of the age, but in every age we proffer obeisance too readily to convention and fad and to the currently reigning status quo. It is almost as though we have been made to be empire's listless pawns.

Especially in an age when the praise of freedom is a required civic ritual, we are slow to admit that it is frightening. But the early Christians, like the early Israelites and the prophets, daringly applied this freedom-talk especially to its most dangerous target, politics.

Human dignity is insulted by political despotism in any form. As Minucius Felix put it:"How beautiful is the spectacle to God when a Christian . . . raises up his liberty against kings and princes, and yields to God alone . . . when triumphant and victorious, he tramples upon the very man who has passed sentence upon him!"[18]

FREEDOM FROM RELIGIOUS POWER

This liberationist advance was directed also to the abuse of religious power. With remarkable precocity Tertullian pioneered the concept of religious liberty:"It should be considered absurd for one person to compel another to honor the gods, when he should voluntarily, and in the awareness of his own need, seek their favor *in the liberty which is his right.*"[19]

In the fourth century the radical Christian bishop John Chrysostom had a message for the grand inquisitors who inhabit every age, reducing religion to authoritarian control:"We do not have authority over your faith, beloved, nor do we command these things as your lords and masters. We are appointed for the teaching of the word, not for power, nor for absolute authority. We hold the place of counselors to advise you. The counselor speaks his own opinions, not forcing his listener, but leaving him full master of his own choice in what is said. He is blameworthy only in this respect, if he fails to say the things that present themselves."[20] What healthy lessons are in these words for popes, Ayatollahs, and other ministerial demagogues. This form of freedom dissolves absolute power claims. As for *freedom from* and *freedom for,* this was a freedom *from* all tyrannies, religious and political, and freedom *for* joyful self-realization in a community unbound by unnatural or artificial constraints.

This biblical love of freedom displays a stubborn optimism about human nature, an optimism that relates closely to hope, joy, and justice. Such commitment to freedom presumes that hope is valid and that joy is normal. This freedom is not anomic, since the guiding principle of this entire moral vision is justice, with its many distinctive Hebraic nuances. What is rejected is any authoritarian shortcut to human good. A case may be made for restrictions of freedom—and both Judaism and Christianity acknowledged the need for order, law, and direction in society—according to justice. The difference is one of accent and burden of proof, and that difference is massive and revolutionary. Judaism and Christianity placed the burden of proof on those who would limit freedom.[21]

This assignment of the burden of proof crashes against the servile assumptions that grip most people and most societies most of the time. Political and religious leaders seem endemically tempted to substitute control for leadership. Tyranny (which is the abuse of power) is the seemingly permanent and in-sinewed bane of civil and religious authority. Israel and Christianity assaulted this mulish malignancy head-on, and in so doing they shook the symbol-base and presuppositions of despotic and distrustful power.[22]

FREEDOM FROM CLASS

The word *class* is common. We all know its prefixes: upper-, middle-, and so on. What we usually don't know is how controlling it is of most people's lives and how "un-free" they and we are as a result. As Professor Mary Hobgood says, class is "the way that groups consolidate social, political, and economic power." It's the way deals and arrangements have been set up so that some get and others don't. "People largely get their poverty or their wealth depending on their location in the class system."[23] Your location in the class system also strongly influences whether you will serve in the army, do menial jobs, attend good or poor schools, live close to or far from toxic waste dumps, get good or poor medical attention, have access to legal aid, and even the ability to "keep hope alive." Class creates the slave base that services the empire and its elite.

Class, the modern form of slavery, has many tiers. The polysaturated elites at the top of the imperial pyramid depend on the compliant, underpaid middle class and the middle class depends on the sweat-shop class below. Again Mary Hobgood: "The blood, sweat, tears, and suffering [of the lower classes] . . . are carefully hidden from us" as we consume and bow our heads for grace.[24] Our freedoms are bought by their unfreedoms. Pious people giving thanks to God for their "blessings" must check to see if those blessings are stained with the blood, sweat, or tears of the poor. Biblical liberty—like everything in the biblical moral creed—brings us back to Deuteronomy: "There shall be no poor among you" (15:4). If there are, our privileges are likely cut from their flesh and neither they nor we are free.

FREEDOM FOR AND FROM WORK

Sculptors were not supreme in Israel. The preferred symbols were not spatial and crafted of matter. Rather, the stuff from which Israel's artists created was history and time. Judaism, says Abraham Heschel, "is a religion of time."[25] The main themes of this faith are temporal. The new moon, the festivals, the jubilee year, the remembered times of exodus, the giving of the law at Sinai, the messianic hope for future fulfillment, and, of course, the sabbath were the cathedrals of ancient Israel. The sabbath tradition was the masterpiece. It is, perhaps, the supreme temporal monument built by these religious poets. Like any monument worthy of the designation, it must be articulate, and it was—volubly so.

The sabbath was a breakthrough of moral intelligence to which modern western civilization stands in debt, not only for its "weekends" but for its overall appreciation of leisure.[26] Historically Jews have been criticized for their solemn insistence on sabbatical rest. Juvenal, Seneca, and others saw in it an unworthy indolence.[27] Aristotle spoke for the dominant view of work and rest: "We need relaxation because we cannot work continuously. Relaxation, then, is not an end; for it is taken for the sake of activity."[28] To the dissenting Jewish tradition, Aristotle was a heretic. We do not rest and celebrate in order to work better. It is labor that is the means to an end. Joyous celebration is our holiest destiny. Labor that does not recognize itself as a means is drudgery and even idolatry.

Clearly, the biblical tradition is not opposed to work. We were given the Earth "to till it and care for it" (Gen. 2:15). That is work, and it was thoroughly compatible with the paradise of Eden. Indeed, a long work week was still the norm: "You have six days to labor and do all your work" (Exod. 20:9). Work was part of the covenant and it was seen as a positive good: "Love work!"[29] The depth of the sabbath insight is lost if we define it in terms of *not* working. We have an unfortunate practice of describing good in negative terms: *peace* as the absence of conflict, *freedom* as the absence of restraint, and the *sabbath* as the absence of labor. Such privative definitions are impoverishing.

The sabbath was a rich symbol of biblical freedom. It served to recapitulate the very meaning of freedom in this tradition. It liberated us from our idol gods. But we often demonize and absolutize relative goods—work, money, technology—and they remain good until they are endowed with an ultimacy that puts means in the shrine reserved for ends. Then the means that should serve our freedom become a slaver. The worker becomes a workaholic.

There are at least three liberating aspects to the institution of the sabbath: (1) smashing idols as the path to joy, (2) peace, and (3) harmony with others and with nature. Each frees us from demons that are ever on the ready. Each makes the sabbath, as Jews call it yet, a "day of freedom." The ideas of this day, however, are not limited to the weekly celebrations of some religions, but are the ingredients of a rich humanism of universal appeal.

1. Joy

The sabbath was conceived as a "day of joy." Joy was the reason for suspending the usual asperities of survival. Leave time for joy "by not plying your trade, not seeking your own interest or attending to your own affairs" (Isa. 58:13). All those things were important, and had better go on most of the other six days, but they are not supreme in value. The needed tool is easily bent into a manacle. The very necessity of work lends it the potential to dominate and define us. Our work can wizen life and bring us to a premature death without our having pressed the grape of joy to the palate of our lives.

The sabbath is an idol-smashing day, when priorities are re-ordered and the joy of life is given its due. With the tone thus set, even work will be different and, if it is joyful, more efficient. Even productivity is subject to the natural law that joy, not misery, is life's destiny and meaning and we are not productive without it. There is a message for all modern managers in this.

Even passing money was seen as a desecration of the sabbath. The Silas Marner syndrome is as contagious as the common cold. The purpose of money is lost in its accumulation, as hoarding in all its modern and ancient forms replaces both the moral and the economic purposes of money. The result is bondage, not freedom. The money owns us.

2. Peace

Strife too is contagious. It can reproduce itself with a chain effect. The sabbath was to break that chain and give peace a fresh chance. The ancient rabbis pondered a seeming inconsistency in the scriptural accounts of creation. Exodus says that the Lord "rested on the seventh day" (20:11). Yet Genesis states that on the seventh day, before resting, "God finished his work" (2:2). The conclusion was that the sabbath was something quite positive and the making of it was the work of the seventh day. What was created on that day was *menuba,* meaning tranquility, serenity, peace, and harmony.[30] *Menuba* is a state without discord, fighting, fear, or distrust. It is the essence of the good life. The sabbath should exemplify it and short-circuit countervailing hostilities in the society. Disharmony can be interrupted before it destroys us. Again, peace does not just happen. The sabbath reminds us that God had to make peace and so must we. And peace does not happen if our brothers and sisters are in need. Peace requires sharing and *tsedaqah. We cannot call it peace when wealth and hunger co-exist.*

3. Harmony

The sabbath was the original Earth Day. The harmony it sought was not limited to humans. Earth people cannot be at peace if they are only at peace with one another and not at peace with the Earth. Aside from the weekly sabbath, every seventh year was sabbatical, a sabbath for the land: "The land shall keep a sabbath of sacred rest, a sabbath to the Lord. . . . For six years you may sow your fields and for six years prune your vineyards and gather the harvest, but . . . the seventh year . . . shall be a year of sacred rest for the land" (Lev. 25:3-5). The community of the sabbath extended also to animals.

The oxen, the asses, and the cattle were all to share in the rest and harmony of sabbath (Deut. 5:13).

So the sabbath was more than respite from work. It was a reminder that the harmonies of the Garden of Eden were not part of a historical past, but were rather a symbol of what could yet be. We could live at one with one another and with the earth. We are meant to thrive, not just to survive—to dance as well as to toil. We are not slaves to other persons, to patterns of enmity, or even to the laborious necessities.

The sabbath is a humanistic poem of hope written on the scroll of time. Or, to change the image, like the steeples of a cathedral—it points us toward the more that we constantly bury in less. Sabbath joy puts work days in perspective, reminding us that celebration, not labor, is our truest genius. *Homo gaudens* ("the joyful human being") has precedence over *homo laborans* ("the working human being"). Time points toward sabbath, toward our being free for joy.[31]

Chapter Ten

HOPE VERSUS THE CRINGE

When my son Tom was almost three, lightning struck a huge tree near our home and split it in two, leaving half of it lying in the street. I picked Tom up and carried him on my arm over to the spot a block away, convinced he would find it of interest. He was chatting all the way over, as was his wont (we called him "the speaker of the house"). When we reached the scene, Tom stiffened in my arms and went silent. He didn't say a word the whole way home. I offered no comment, knowing that inside that little head, theology was going on. When we got home, I sat beside him in silence, not imposing any interpretation on him, convinced as I was that theology begins at birth. Finally he broke the silence, to voice his theology of hope. "Daddy, when God came up out of the ground [where Tom had located divine power], he wanted to send the lightning down to play with the tree." I asked Tom: "So, what happened?" With great sadness in his little voice Tom replied: "Sometimes God can't get his lightning straight." Tom already knew that when God made his brother Danny, who was terminally ill with Hunter's Syndrome, that God had already shown that he could not always get his lightning straight.

So there was Tom's theology. It was determinedly hopeful. Ultimate power, ultimate reality could not be malignant. Inept, yes, but well-meaning, intent on play, not misery. The fallen tree had challenged Tom's essential hope in *the reliability of reality. He replied with the best of his imagination, which is all that any of us can do to keep hope alive.*

Hope, I believe, is all too rare. Unlike smile-button optimism, it is not easy. Optimism turns away from trouble; hope wrestles with it. Hope stands tall. It is the antidote to the cringe, the posture of most people most of the time and many people all of the time. Cringing people not only don't try to change things, they avoid information that might stir them to action, and they don't even vote. They don't see citizenship as a vocation to care for the common good. It is instead a burden to be sloughed off. Their attitude is that of slaves bent to the ground by forces they dare not challenge. They are literally desperadoes. They are the delight of empire-builders and whatever else they are, they are unbiblical.

Any literature that imagines seas parting to give slaves an avenue to freedom; that armies will crumble before the power of justice; that deserts can bloom with verdure; that resurrection, not death, is the end of life; and that the power that guides the stars loves us with an everlasting love—such a literature is unabashedly hopeful. But such a literature might also be mad. Hope is the primal energy of life, but it lives on the brink of simpleminded optimism. Hope, if it is to serve in a world where tragedy abounds, must always stand judgment before the bar of cynicism.

Still, hope remains the energy of the living. It's the motor center of the *elan vital* and the activator of human will. Its opposite is paralysis and catatonia. Even at the level of living cells we can see a power analogous to hope, a protoplasmic force reaching "hopefully" for success within the narrow framework of mysteriously ingrained goals. Cells relate conspiratorially to other cells, and organisms cooperate with stunning success. Robin Morgan, in her poem "Peony," writes of the flower that begins life encased in a thick, stubborn rind. The peony has no resources to escape the grip of the rind and bloom into loveliness. Tiny herbivorous ants come to the rescue, eating that rind, working relentlessly, getting washed away by the well-meaning gardener and then returning, and not even living to see the final explosion of beauty that they released. The poet sees an analogy to us in those insect-liberators as we nibble, hopefully, with intermittent success, at "this green stubborn bud some call a world."[1] Hope in some form spans the universe of the living.

Biblical literature specialized in hope. It is a theme that runs with myriad variations through these classics. No classical envisioning of life could fail to deal with the phenomenon of hope. Pinchas Lapide says that hope is "the most Jewish of all emotions—the irrepressible urge to make yesterday's dream tomorrow's reality."[2] Ancient Israel's theory of hope was wrapped in its God-talk. There, God and hope "are almost identified," as John Macquarrie says.[3] Hope was another of those moral terms Israelites used to express ultimate and basic reality. God is the "hope of Israel" (Jer. 14:8). "Thou art my hope, O Lord, my trust, O Lord, since boyhood" (Ps. 71:5). This tradition would have no part with the pessimism chanted by the chorus in Sophocles' *Antigone:* "Pray not at all since there is no release for mortals from predestined calamity."[4] For the Israelites, hope, not calamity, is the name of God, and therefore in this symbolism, hope is the hallmark of our reality.

The Christian Scriptures echoed this, also naming God a "God of hope" in whose presence we should "overflow with hope" (Rom. 15:13). The mood of the early Jesus movement reflected the hopes of early Israel. Some think Jesus was convinced he was living "at the turn of the ages,"[5] when a shocking new system would supersede the fading old one.

Underlying the theistic language used in this literature is the morally crucial conviction that reality is ultimately reliable, that the possibilities of good outweigh the possibilities of evil, however formidable the latter may be. The Israelites were not naïve about evil, but hope remained one of their dominant moral motifs. The moral significance of that orientation for politics, economics, and definitions of power is dramatic. Hope is the womb of creativity and the power-center of every successful ideology—and every flourishing personality.

The Hebrews were in a good position to hope for new things. Abraham left his "own country," his "kinsmen," and his "father's house" to set out in search of a new mode of existence (Gen. 12:1). Israel was born not in the cities, mired in the constructions of its past, but in the wilderness where the rules had not yet been written and where new thoughts required no passports.[6] Israel began as a journey of hope. Its hope was not unfocused or abstract. What the Israelites wanted was very concrete and down-to-earth: "a time of justice, good government, freedom from oppression, a time of plenty, good crops, harmony and peace."[7] They wanted a new politics and a new economics in which poverty and oppression and the tyranny of empire would be eliminated, and they were willing to break all the old rules to find an alternative future with a new mode of social organization.

They specifically and precociously hoped for a world without war. "They shall beat their swords into mattocks and their spears into pruning-knives; nation shall not lift sword against nation nor ever again be trained for war" (Mic. 4:3). They hope for an end to deprivation. The political and judicial systems that would function with genuine justice (Isa. 1:26; 28:6; 32:1). All of these things would be "good news to the poor," bring "release for prisoners," and allow "broken victims" to go free (Luke 4:18-19). The Israelites were not overwhelmed by the unlikelihood of this. It might be like turning a field of dry bones into a living throng, but it can be done. The power to do it is available to us (Ezekiel 37). (This image of the dry bones coming to life was not some spacey spiritual imagery but was applied by Ezekiel to the politics of the day.) If Israel had an ideology, its name was hope.

In one sense, for both Judaism and Christianity, the past was definitely prologue. The mythic marvels of the past set the hope-tone for the present and the future. The exodus was not a one-shot miracle, but a living theme to be celebrated yearly at Passover by "you and your children for all time" (Exod. 12:24). Similarly, the resurrection of Jesus was not a past-tense wonder, but was to be liturgically relived in some new way, never to be forgotten. Both of these "events" are rich myths, presented in a literary genre that was not strapped to historical facts. Biblical writing was not reportage; it was an explosion of human imagination. Ideas and ideals were being born here that would be like "living water" issuing "from Jerusalem, half flowing to the eastern sea and half to the western" and benefitting "all the earth" (Zech. 14:8). Once again that stunning sense of destiny that charged the batteries of the biblical writers.

MORAL FUTURISM

"The dominant reality is necessarily in prose."[8] Those who benefit from the status quo want the future to mirror the present. It is not in their interest to imagine a new future that is radically discontinuous with present luxury, however inequitably based. The poetic imagination that could envision a "new heaven and a new earth" (Rev. 21:1) is a drastic threat to those made royal by today's arrangements. Biblical literature is a poetic burst of hope that would dare to believe that "every ravine" could be "filled in," "every mountain and hill" could be "leveled," "the corners" could "be straightened, and the rugged ways made smooth" (Luke 3:5). (When military research budgets dwarf research monies for environmentally benign fuels, our prime political need is hope, hope that this and other mountains can be "leveled" and that such "rugged" and noxious nonsense can "be straightened" and "made smooth.")

Scriptural hope offers what Erich Fromm calls "alternativism."[9] The resurrection hope of Christians and the messianic hope of Jews, says Fromm, have many possible symbolic meanings but one of the most important is the need for constant resurrection in human life and the tireless discovery of alternatives. "Every moment existence confronts us with the alternatives of resurrection or death; every moment we give an answer."[10] The exodus and the resurrection were not "big bangs" in the past meant to stir us to ineffectual wonder. The Bible is totally misunderstood if it is reduced to a history of past stunts. Rather, these "events" were symbols illustrating the promise of history itself. They uncovered the inherent potential of life, "the plan of the mystery hidden for ages" (Eph. 3:9). The biblical imagination did not act outside the limits of human reality, nor did it indulge in dreams of magical cures. It simply expressed "the implicit promise already present in the human vocation to personhood and community."[11] As one of the most hopeful lines in the Bible puts it: "What we shall be has not yet been disclosed" (1 John 3:2). Paltry expectations are repugnant to these traditions. As Gregory of Nyssa said, there is "no limit to progress in perfecting."[12] The heroic biblical moral tradition condemns us for the paucity and parvity of our pallid hopes.[13]

Persons fully alive to their potential would not destroy one another and the Earth, nor would they settle so passively for current morally undeveloped social conditions. They would hear the compelling wisdom of Deuteronomy that holds the keystone of all morality: "I offer you the choice of life or death, blessing or curse. Choose life and then you and your descendants will live" (Deut. 30:19). The writer almost becomes sarcastic in making the point that should be obvious: this moral rule "is not too difficult for you, it is not too remote. It is not in heaven, that you should say, 'Who will go up to heaven for us to fetch it and tell it to us, so that we can keep it?' Nor is it beyond the sea, that you should say, 'Who will cross the sea for us to fetch it and tell it to us, so that we can keep it?' Is it a thing very near to you" (Deut. 30:11-14). The wisdom of this advice would seem, indeed, to be indisputable. Life is preferable to death. Yet our perversely pessimistic species seems bent on killing itself and the Earth that is our maternal womb.

In matters moral the obvious is most often ignored. Life is better than death, yet we spend our money and genius on death rather than life. Those who critique this are dismissed as fuzzy-minded dreamers, lacking in realism. The common wisdom in most cultures embodies a shallow and shortsighted ideology of hopelessness. To such an ideology, the biblical writers enter a thunderous dissent and unfurl the possibility of progress.

THE NATURE OF HOPE

Hope is ignition. There is "a tacit hopefulness" in all human activity.[14] Even Sisyphus had to be hoping for something or he would have left the stone where he found it. And hope, like all things basic, is mysterious. When fleshed out, it is a cosmology, an epistemology, as well as an ideology, if the reader will indulge the cumbersome terms.

Hope as Cosmology

Hope is an affirmative response to the universe into which we have been cast. It takes a stance on three cosmological challenges that everyone must wrestle with: (1) fate, (2) tragedy, and (3) suicidal temptation.

Fate The fatalist is conservative. *Quod est, est, que sera sera*—what is, is, and what will be, will be. Hope rides on the conviction that what is, is becoming, and that we, within limits, can shape the future. Being is an open-ended process. It bears the mark of plasticity, not inevitability. Early Christians were reflecting their inherited Israelitic hope when they clashed against the Platonic theory of cycles. Origen scorned the notion that things will just repeat without sense or hope, that "in another Athens another Socrates will be born who will marry another Zanthippe and will be accused by another Anytus and another Meletus."[15] In contrast, the biblical view of history is linear. Though the lines are not straight, there is the possibility to transcend the past and to become what we had only begun to be.

Humanity, and therefore history, is not a fixed and given essence, or a pre-plotted set of patterns. Rather, in the words of A. E. Taylor, humanity "is something that has to be won."[16] He quotes Friedrich Nietzsche's injunction *werde was du bist*, "become what you are," and calls this "the supreme 'categorical imperative'" of life. Nietzsche's view, which fits snugly with that of the biblical, is that humanity is "something that must be surpassed."[17] The biblical view is: "What we shall be has not yet been disclosed" (1 John 3:2). The better is implicit in the good. Being is permanently pregnant. Those who marry a fatalist cosmology deny this and part company with the biblical searchers who find more *yes* than *no* in life. In so doing, the biblical authors open the door to freedom and creativity.

The biblical belief is that we are made in the image of God. In biblical language, we are stewards (or administrators) who make managerial decisions, not slaves ruled by inexorable decree (see 1 Cor. 4:1).[18] We are not pawns of fate being moved about hopelessly in a game of chance. In Thomas Aquinas's hope-filled phrase, we are "participants in divine providence," not its passive witnesses.[19] Subsequent theology would call us co-creators and co-redeemers, all to the same effect. It is no accident that the technological imperative—for good and for ill—has been most pronounced in biblically influenced lands. All these symbols are counter-fatalistic and conducive to a take-charge mentality. As co-creators, if the heart fails, we create another. If the liver lags, replace it. We are "stewards"; we are in charge. Of course, in the biblical perspective, stewardship is to be exercised in a way that cherishes and nourishes the Earth and its interrelated inhabitants.[20] The creative impulse, like all good things, can go mad.

Pharaoh's rule is that "what is, must be," and it operates in every sphere of life—politics, economics, the professions, and academic disciplines, and so on. Power is always prone to myopia. It rewards preservative immobility. The seas will not part, slaves of old ways and old ideas cannot escape, and the plagues of unsettling perceptions must not trouble us. Tradition, necrotically conceived, rules. Such fatalism is rampant, but we have the antidote: hope.

Tragedy Tragedy is so real that it easily makes hope seem unsustainable. Thousands of children are born each day brain-damaged and broken. Hurricanes, tsunamis, and tornadoes strike with cruel indiscrimination. By no means is all evil the fault of humans. As one Anglican priest put it, "God has a lot to answer for." There is a well-known story about a group of Jews who conducted a trial of God at Auschwitz, found God guilty, and then, with Jewish paradox, repaired to worship their guilty God. After earthquakes, the camera shows us orphaned and bleeding children looking out from the rubble that was their home. Their stunned faces and broken hearts are the face of tragedy. Tragedy is the crushing of hope and they exemplify it. In the sight of tragedy what value is there in traditions that babble on about their "God of hope"?

Horrid tragedies leave no theodicy, no theory of evil, in peace. We imagine that if we were powerful gods we would do better—at least we would spare the children. But reality as we see it is at times unyieldingly cruel. No theology should pretend to understand it, nor should it retreat to the obnoxious insipidities of calling the tragedy a "blessing in disguise."

Some years ago in Milwaukee, I met a man who had just heard me speaking of my twenty-two-month old son who had just been diagnosed with a terminal illness. The man, sobbing, told me of his son of the same age who, some months before, was in Chicago with his mother. They were standing on a March day beside a building waiting for a bus. The child kept moving out from the mother, and she would protectively draw him back. During one of these gentle forays, a fifty-pound chunk of ice detached from the top of the building and crushed the child to death. The man wept, and I wept with him, and he asked me where comfort lay in the face of this. "Do not tell me," he pleaded, "that this was a blessing in disguise." "The only blessing," he continued, "would be for it not to have happened." Bitter experience had taught this man and me that the cosmos into which we are born bears the cruel and bitter mark of the tragic.

Biblical hope is not romantic. It rails against God and reality whenever it is appropriate. Elie Wiesel showed this when he said of his time at Auschwitz: "Why should I bless His name? The Eternal, Lord of the Universe, the All-Powerful and Terrible, was silent. What had I to thank Him for?"[21]

Biblical morality responds to tragedy by first rushing to the aid of its victims. This is the heart of *tsedaqah*. It knows that hope in this kind of world is precarious. Yet we struggle, with bloodied grip, "never to be dislodged from the hope" we have achieved (Col. 1:23). Rather, the goal is to fix our pained vision on the preciousness that coexists with tragedy and seems ultimately more real. This kind of hope does not descend to bland optimism, and it is compatible with streams of despair. This sturdy hope lives amid chaos and bears the wounds that are the insignia of that chaos. Ultimately, it is impressed with good more than with evil, with what can be more than with what is not. It is convinced that whatever chaos is, it is not the name of God. Tragedy is not the ultimate reality.

To return to my autobiographical note, I boldly urged the grieving man in Milwaukee to go home and have another baby, to reinvest in the mystery. His loss was beyond remedy, but the miracle could be re-created. This pain-filled reality of ours is ambiguous to the core, but hope sees its enduring promise and stays stubbornly faithful to its possibilities. Bloodied by life, it reinvests in life. Such is the way of hope.

Suicidal Temptation   Hope has an activist, interventionist quality in the biblical ethos. It rises as the vigorous alternative to the suicidal temptation. As existentialist philosopher Gabriel Marcel says, genuine hope "underpins action or it runs before it." It is the most active people "who carry hope to its highest degree." Thinking of hope as an inactive, expectant state of the personality comes "from a stoical representation of the will as a stiffening of the soul, whereas it is on the contrary relaxation and creation."[22] Such a hope does not stand on the sidelines, pining for the best. In this sense hope is the antithesis of the suicidal temptation. I do not refer here to the physical termination of life, but to the gradual, psychological withdrawal from life by persons or whole cultures that are more impressed by life's negativities than by its possibilities.[23] The marks of this temptation are the marks of death: detachment, coldness, insensitivity, inability to listen, to respond, or to create. Overwhelmed by the anomalies, the suicidal temptation says "No." Hope, the struggler, says "Yes." Hope is the rejuvenator, the badge of youth, and in some people its youthful expansive joy can survive even into old age.[24]

The Epistemology of Hope

Awash as it is in hopeful symbols, the Bible is keenly attentive to the possibility of false hope. It asks the fair question of the hopeful: "What ground have you for this confidence of yours?" (Isa. 36:4–5). It chides the Israelites for putting false hope in certain political alliances or military schemes (Isa. 31:1-3; 36:4-9; Hos. 10:13). This shows an awareness of a cognitive factor in hope. Real hope is not dumb. Genuine hope is linked to the truth as a lens that enhances vision—it helps us know. False hope is a bad connection to the truth because it springs from falsehood and causes more of the same.

Small wonder that Aquinas says that drunks and young people are filled with hope.[25] In hope, the truth connection can be broken. Hope is a joyful and pleasant good and we can try to buy it "on the cheap." Inexperience, superficiality, and stimulants can give us a hopeful high. Some good can come of such hope since all hope is a reaching and even misguided reaching can know success. *Ex falso sequitur quidlibet,* from falsehood, anything might follow. But false hope is an unreliable friend. Hope grounded in truth opens the eyes. It reaches for a good that is "arduous but possible of attainment."[26] Hence all hope is suspended between fear of the difficulty and elation at the possibility we sense. If we succumb to the fear, we shrink. The cringing mind does not see far. "The fearing mood clings to the familiar," says John Macquarrie.[27] The lack of hope is crippling. Psychologist William Lynch says hopelessness is "perhaps the most characteristic mark of mental illness."[28]

Militarism is the most common symptom of a culture that tips from hope toward fear, the prime emotion of militarism. Fear is antisocial, withdrawn, and hostile. It is bent not on the transformation but on the destruction of adversity and adversaries. It calls for preemptive strikes, not intelligent mediation of differences. Fear animates what has come to be called "the conservative mind." Fear of other nations, of the other gender, of other races, classes, or ethnic groups, or of other sexual orientations. The conservative mind is shackled with fears and hence is open to tyranny if that tyranny offers protection.

If, however, the love of the possible overcomes fear, hope is joined by another virtue beloved of the ancients but largely ignored by moderns—magnanimity. Aristotle and Aquinas both called magnanimity "the jewel of all the virtues," an expansion of spirit that makes all our powers greater.[29] Magnanimity is the aspiration and enlargement of the spirit to great things . . . *extensio animi ad magna*.[30] The ancients saw it as a part of courage, and linked both to hope.[31] Hopeful minds are not trapped in the familiar but raise their view to the horizons, *ad magna*. Hopeful intelligence is filled with what Josef Pieper calls "courageous unrest" because it has caught the scent of greatness missed by the timid.[32]

Because it is truth-linked, then, hope is not a blind impulse of the will. The truth connection saves hope from simpleminded optimism, arrogance, and illusion. It also commits hope to planning. As theologian Jürgen Moltmann says: "Without planning there can be no realistic hope."[33] Hope without homework is sterile. Hope draws us to a possible but arduous future *ad astra per aspera*, "through the rough ways to the stars." No one reaches the stars without tedious work and calculation. If hope would enter the gritty realm of politics it must join with working intelligence or fizzle. Utopian schemes without planning die. They may linger as a symbol and an inspiration for other hopes, but fulfilled hope is always in debt to rationality. Hope without plans is an idle dreamer.

Hope as Ideology

An ideology is a collection of myths, emotions, and thought patterns through which we somewhat systematically organize our interpreting and thinking.[34] It is something we construct to make sense of things. Ideologies are, as Andre Dumas says quite simply, "methods of thought."[35] There can be no end to ideology—we are ideologues by nature. Hope, with cognitive, emotive, and mythic components, has all the stuff of ideology.[36] Hope can also become ingrained as a habit, a frame of mind that conditions all evaluation and interpretation.

H. Richard Niebuhr portrays Jesus as a hopeful, counterfatalistic ideologue:

> [Jesus] sees as others do that the sun shines on criminals, delinquents, hypocrites, honest men, good Samaritans, and VIP's without discrimination, that rains come down in equal proportions on the fields of the diligent and of the lazy. These phenomena have been for unbelief, from the beginning of time, signs of the operation of a universal order that is without justice, unconcerned with right and wrong conduct among [people]. But Jesus interprets the common phenomena in another way; here are the signs of cosmic generosity. The response to the weather so interpreted leads then also to a response to criminals and outcasts, who have not been cast out by the infinite Lord.[37]

Note the ethical product of this hopeful ideology. Unconcern is not the heart of reality. Rather, "deep down things" there is love, supreme artistry, and gracious creativity. This good news calls for replication in human behavior. Reality is promising, not ultimately a menace. Enhancing the good, not resigning to evil, makes the most sense. Cynicism has its place, but not on the throne of a personality or a culture. When the human race has made progress it is because hopeful ideologies and myths won out.

The elixir of hope can congeal and cease to energize the arteries of the will. The symbols of hope can dry up. Theologian Rosemary Radford Ruether observes that Christianity and Marxism are two examples of this. Both were revolutions of hope. "As in Christian history, Marxism begins with the announcement of the apocalyptic day of wrath and the speedy advent of the kingdom of God, but ends in the indefinite prolonging of the era of the Church, which can justify all persecution and suppression of liberty in the name of that final liberation which never comes but to which it is the exclusive gateway."[38] The enlivening hope of early Israel can succumb to a tribalistic, isolated *concept* of Israel that could then, like historical Christianity, contradict its own native hopes for humankind. A modern Israeli state that feels it must occupy other people's land to be safe, that it must have one of the world's most powerful armies including nuclear weaponry, has lost the hope that gave it spiritual birth. And with all its weaponry and the support of the world's only military superpower it knows no peace, nor will it until it returns to Isaiah's insight: only justice brings security (Isa. 32:17). Occupying people is not a form of justice; it is, rather, a crime. The United States, while pretending to be a Christian nation with Bibles in its hotel drawers, has, like the State of Israel, surrendered hope and adopted fear as national policy. Despite possessing more kill-power than any empire in history it is increasingly insecure, in a constant state of alert, demonstrating again that fear is not the underwriter of peace. Most of the world sees the United States as an empire and empires inspire no love. It makes enemies and, once again, those enemies have tactical advantages over the superpower: invisibility, versatility, and patience. When Osama bin Laden declared war on the United States, critic Thomas Friedman noted what a stunning new world this is: "The United States [under President Clinton] fired 75 cruise missiles, at one million dollars apiece, at a person! That was superpower against a Super-empowered angry man."[39] We missed our target but when he replied, he did not miss. Clearly, this is a seismic shift in the meaning and nature of power.

SURPRISES FEED HOPE

Hope dies if it forgets success stories and happy surprises. Conservative, squinting, cringing eyes are cynical and cynicism is self-fulfilling. Good surprises are antidotal to cynicism. As the hopeful David Korten writes:

> Consider the ridicule that would have been heaped on the visionary prophet who dared even in 1988 to predict that by 1991 the Soviet Union would peacefully dissolve itself, Germany would be reunited, the Berlin Wall would be gone, and the leadership of the former 'evil empire' would be inviting the United States to help dismantle its nuclear arsenal . . . [or] that in 1994 Nelson Mandela would be elected the president of South Africa in an open multiracial election. Perhaps even more remarkable than the fact that these events occurred at all is the fact that we already take most of them for granted, quickly forgetting what extraordinary events they were and how rapidly impossible dreams are becoming accomplished fact.[40]

In another grand surprise, women have arrived with unprecedented power. In 1997, a woman named Jody Williams, armed with nothing more than e-mail, won the Nobel Prize for peace because of her efforts to push the international ban on land mines by uniting 1,000 different human rights and arms control groups on six continents. The women of Kenya's Greenbelt movement have set up 1,500 grassroots nurseries and planted over 10 million trees. Japanese women operate a 200,000-household Seikatsu Club Consumers' Cooperative that works with suppliers to ensure that they are gentle to their workers and to nature.

In large numbers women have entered the most democratic movement on the planet, the non-governmental organizations (NGOs) that have, among other things, revolutionized the United Nations. "By the time of the 1994 International Conference on Population and Development in Cairo, the women's movement demonstrated that it was the first among the citizen movements to truly master the UN meeting process."[41] Dissenting governments and the Vatican were put in the position of quibbling about the nuances of certain phrases because the women had set the agenda.

THEISM AS MEDIUM OR MESSAGE

Is the hope of early Israel and early Christianity translatable for modern theists and non-theists alike? Clearly, in this literature God was the grounds for hope. Still, this vision is adoptable, even by modern non-theists, for two reasons: First, the hope of Israel was never just perceived as a God-show. It was based on a covenant. Human participation was essential. Without appropriate human behavioral changes, there would be disaster. The prophets left no doubt about that. In spite of some flourishes of apocalyptic literary imagination, this literature was not based on salvation by miracle. The miracle was us, made in the image and likeness of God—humans were seen as divine in their potential. That is the biblical anthropology. A non-theist could appropriate the spirit and direction of that vision. The fact that such a hope "has appeared in this universe of ours is itself a ground for *hoping that hope is at home in the universe.*"[42]

Second, religious language, reaching as it does for the ineffable, is always poetic at its core. "Logically prior to every particular religious assertion is an original confidence in the meaning and worth of life. . . . The primary use or function of [the word] 'God' is to refer to the objective ground in reality itself of our ineradicable confidence in the final worth of our existence."[43] God-talk is always an interpretation of reality at its depths. It is a task that theists and non-theists share; it's just that they explain it differently. Biologist Edward O. Wilson does not think of God as a being but as a product of human creative imagination. That imagination itself gives him hope. He ends his book *The Future of Life* by asserting that the Earth-wrecking problems he has outlined "can be solved. Adequate resources exist. . . . A civilization able to envision God and to embark on the colonization of space will surely find the way to save the integrity of this planet and the magnificent life it harbors."[44]

The theistic hope of the Bible is not beyond anyone's poetic grasp. Theists and non-theists together can know that beyond all the horrors of our world are the first smiles of infants, the undefeatable growth of greenery from volcanic ash, the ingenuity of evolution, the historic realization of many bold dreams, the beauty of minds and sunsets and human love. The *yes* is mightier than the *no*. Hope is at home in our universe.

Chapter Eleven

EXPLORING LOVE

Late in his life Jean-Paul Sartre met some former students in a park in Paris. They had their three-month-old baby with them. Sartre took the baby in his arms and wrote later that he realized, with a kind of mystical poignancy, that if you took all of his life's work (which was considerable since he was the best known philosopher of the twentieth century) and balanced it against the smiling preciousness he held in his arms, his achievements would seem almost weightless by comparison. The word sacred *attempts to describe such moments.*

"Why is this flesh so precious?" I would ask myself as I cradled my ten-year-old son Danny in my arms. His dwarfed body was wasted and limp and he was near death, but I handled him with all the reverence with which I used to handle the sacraments when I was a priest. Some of our value experiences are literally ineffable; we can't explain them. Such experience is mystical, the word that the medievals reserved for our deepest and purest experiences of what we call "love." "Sacred" is the highest encomium in the human lexicon, the superlative of precious. It is where love dips into mystery. The artisans who gave us the Bible did not leave this peak expression of the human spirit unexplored.

The anthology of writings called "the Bible" has been compared to the cathedral of Chartres, France. Variant and often discordant artists from different moments each produce a masterpiece that—with the blessed fortuity that characterizes all great art—coalesces with other masterpieces into a wholesome and rich unity. The comparison holds fast for the biblical treatment of that spiritual energy we limply call "love." Like the Chartres cathedral, the biblical portrayal of love is marked by creative boldness, surprising use of materials, and hundreds of nooks and crannies that could be easily missed, even by professional tour guides.

The biblical authors stretched their minds on the subject of love. As Friedrich Nietzsche said, there is a kind of "consecration of passion [that] has perhaps never yet been represented more beautifully . . . than by certain Jews of the Old Testament: to these even the Greeks could have gone to school."[1] In fact, the whole thrust of Israelite religion is toward the recovery of the broken human capacity to love. Its treatment of justice, of the reign of God, of prophecy, and of hope can be understood only within the felt need of this movement to "revive the heart" (Isa. 57:15). These writers were convinced that the world will perish unless there is "a new heart and a new spirit" (Ezek. 18:31). This insight is not dated. What makes the Bible's treatment of love all the more striking is the antiquity of the literature. When we reflect, for example, that the prophet Amos preceded Socrates by three centuries and Aristotle by four and that the roots of some biblical writing are centuries earlier, the product is all the more fascinating.

To put the sense of this ancient literature in modern terms, we can begin by acknowledging that our capacity to acquire information and technical skills is not now in question. But that kind of knowledge will not save us. It can only leave us repeating with Robert Oppenheimer, during the first atomic bomb test, the words of the Bhagavad Gita: "I am become Death, the shatterer of worlds." Knowledge without caring is deadly; brilliance without love shatters. As Abraham Heschel insists: "In the Bible, callousness is the root of sin."[2] The human capacity to be uncaring and unfeeling about the values of personal and terrestrial life is the constant and central target of the whole moral revolution called Israel.[3] In an overpopulating world people worry about our going beyond "the carrying capacity" of this finite planet. The biblical artists worried about *the caring capacity* of the human caretakers of the planet.

RESCUING LOVE

It is tragic that the word *love* is such a smothered cliché in our parlance. It is a word, however, that must be rescued from mushy banality because the root insight of Israel was certainly valid; if politics, economics, ethics, and religions are not grounded in the caring affection called love, they "become Death, the shatterer of worlds." It is in the heart that wisdom has its roots, and survival its possibility. The hope for "a new heart" is the only hope we have.

So it is not easy to write of love, even with this vibrant literature at hand. The chill human perversity that allows the ravaging of our children, waters, lands, and air seems indomitable. Robert Heilbroner's pessimism seems to reek of realism: "The outlook for [humankind], I believe is painful, difficult, perhaps desperate, and the hope that can be held out for [our] future prospect seems to be very slim indeed."[4] Even the language of "civic virtue" is distasteful to our times. The capacity to know *and feel* the preciousness of all human flesh and of all the miracle of life of which humanity is but a part is arrested at tribal, egoistic, and species-ist level. We wreak abuse on the earth when only cherishing and enhancement would do justice to the miracle. Even the robust theism of centuries past, with a provident and potentially punishing God on duty full-time, did not civilize the human animal. What chance is there now, in a secular age, with God increasingly sequestered into metaphor, to rally the love potential of egoistic humans? Even the language of civic virtue is out of fashion now.[5] In modern secularity, efficiency is god, but efficiency focuses on means, and there is no value-consensus to give the means direction. Means without ends are blind. Still, the challenge will not go away. We either tap and enhance the love potential of this species or we will all perish.

HOPE FOR LOVE?

The First Epistle of John may have been right in saying that "there is no room for fear in love" (1 John 4:18), but fear can nonetheless elicit love for something about to be lost—proximity to apocalypse stirs us to moral attention. The new fragility of our setting is spawning glimmerings of ecological and political sensibility. We are double-basting the planet with carbon in a way that could trigger an irreversible decline of earth life. Physics professor Marty Hoffert does not discount the possibility of terminal ecological disaster. He says that "somebody will visit in a few hundred million years and find there were some intelligent beings who lived here for a while, but they could not handle the transition from being hunter-gatherers to high technology."[6] After many ignored warnings, the feeling that we must love the earth or lose it is at last denting our obtuseness. There is hope in that.

Further, we have to believe with Martin Buber that we are capable of giving ourselves totally to good but not totally to evil. We have to credit the insight of Dag Hammarskjøld that there is a center of indestructible good in everyone, a center that can resonate with the truth and feel its exhilaration. Truth has its own embattled charism. If its appeal could not reach our affect we would never have made the moral gains that mark our history. We have heard and been warmed by "pioneers in morality," figures like the Buddha, Lao-tzu, Confucius, Isaiah, Jesus, Muhammad, Marx, Gandhi, and Martin Luther King Jr. To some slight but crucial degree we recognized that for such geniuses life holds "unsuspected tones of feeling like those of some new symphony, and they draw us after them into this music that we may express it in action."[7]

Each of the figures just mentioned was, we can assume, intelligent. But that was not the quality that made their music. It was the development of their love capacities that gave them powers of discernment, and so they opened doors that merely brilliant minds never knew existed. The biblical symphonies of love should be listened to again for they are classical imaginings of a possible future. Its authors were geniuses of affective discernment, "geniuses of the will" in Bergson's choice phrasing. Such geniuses are fascinating and shocking, and they have the power to "draw us after them."

CENTERING IN ON LOVE

According to the biblical literature *being moral* is *loving well.* As Paul says of morality, "The whole law is summed up in love" (Rom. 13:10). It is on love that "everything in the Law and the prophets hangs" (Matt. 22:40). All virtues, including justice, are blooms from the plant of love. People are good or bad depending on the quality of their love. Since God-talk always shows what people think is really real, it is no surprise that Christianity, a love-centered religion, would conclude that "God is love" (1 John 4:16). And such a judgment, in this eminently practical religion, has a moral bite. God is the model for love (Matt. 5:48). So how does God love? God cares for "widows and orphans and loves the alien who lives among you, giving him food and clothing. You too must love the alien" (Deut. 10:18-19). "Your heavenly Father's goodness knows no bounds," and so "there must be no limit to your goodness" (Matt. 5:48). Not even enemies or aliens are excluded.[8] That is the divine model and human mandate. "Love thus means recognition of the common humanity of all persons" and, we must add, the recognition of humanity's humble place in the unfolding of this universe.[9] As for other humans, you must love your neighbor as yourself (Lev. 19:18). The Bible *neighbor* is to be understood not tribally, but universalistically and with particular reference to those in need. This incipient, wild idea was at the heart of the moral revolution of early Israel.

Love is multidimensional in the Bible. Among other things, it is (1) universalist, (2) individualized, (3) action-oriented, (4) mystical, and (5) creative.

CHALLENGING NARCISSUS

Biblical love is a mutation. It represents a break with the forces of natural selection. Early in their history humans made their way by huddling together within families and clans. In a hostile world nothing else seemed sensible. Kinship marked the safe confines of love. The Bible parted company with this tested wisdom. It called for a break from family and clan by mandating love of enemies. As biblical scholar Gerd Theissen says: "The tendency of biblical religion to go against selection can hardly be expressed more sharply than this."[10]

It seems natural to love the near and dear and to place all others somewhere on a spectrum ranging from indifference to hostility. The Bible pioneers the view that this is humanly abnormal. The family and the clan can be merely narcissistic extensions of individual egoism. The biblical assault on this narrowness was radical. It traces back to the refined monotheism of the prophets who stripped Yahweh of family ties. Originally, Yahweh, like all the gods, had a wife at his side. She was called Asherah (2 Kings 23:7) or the queen of heaven (Jer. 44:25). The prophets broke up this family, producing a nonfamilial God. When the female element returns, it is as Sophia, or Wisdom, "not as an independent person alongside God, but as an expression of another dimension of the one God."[11]

God is always the ultimate model or symbol of reality. Theissen is correct, therefore, when he argues that "the step towards belief in the one God without a family, without wife and children, without kith and kin, is an important step beyond the [usual] bond between human beings and their social environment."[12] The family model is no longer ultimate or divine. Familial and tribal gods were divisive. The decision not to make a familial image of God, says Theissen, "is a constant reminder that human beings are called to free themselves from the way in which they are stamped by the family."[13] Other stories highlight the fragility of the clan structure. Cain kills Abel, Abraham is seen as ready to kill his son, Jacob deceives his brother Esau, and the brothers of Joseph hand him over to the Egyptians. Clearly this is not a literature romancing the family or the clan.

This antifamilial spirit advances in the Jesus movement, and it does so in stunning terms of love and hate: "If anyone comes to me and does not hate his father and mother, wife and children, brothers and sisters, . . . he cannot be a disciple of mine" (Luke 14:26). Because of allegiance to Jesus, parents and children will be turned against one another and siblings will be divided (see Mark

13:12-13). Families will be broken up because of commitment to the reign of God (Matt. 10:35; Luke 12:49-53). Those who leave their families and lands will receive "a hundred times as much" (Mark 10:30). In a text appearing in all three synoptic Gospels Jesus dramatically rejects his mother and his brothers and sisters in favor of the voluntary community united with him in the work of the reign of God. Rather than acknowledge his biological mother and siblings he points to his colleagues in the reign and says: "Here are my mother and my brothers. Whoever does the will of God is my brother, my sister, my mother" (Mark 3:35). Jesus was a product of the Hebrew Bible he used. Strangers are your brothers and sisters because you have a common parent, and you shall love them as you love yourself (Lev. 25:35-37; 19:34).

The theological grounding for this antifamilial—or, better, preter-familial—outlook is clear. "Do not call any man on earth 'father'; for you have one Father, and he is in heaven" (Matt. 23:9). Just as the ancient Israelites relativized royal power by saying there was only one real king, Yahweh, and just as they relativized private property by claiming universal ownership by Yahweh, the family too is put in its place. Family and clan are seen as tendentially egoistic groupings that can seal us off from other humans who share the wonder of our being. Family and clan can also feel protected from concern for the needs of others.

The parable of the Good Samaritan defined moral humanity in terms of responsiveness to strangers in need. "Go and do as he did" (Luke 10:37). Familial, clannish, and nationalistic pockets of self-interest will not bring peace. Because of this conviction, as Elaine Pagels says, "first-century Christians saw themselves participating at the birth of a revolutionary movement that they expected would culminate in the total social transformation that Jesus promised."[14] "The whole frame of this world is passing away" (1 Cor. 7:31). Love is the solvent of all hostile barriers. "There must be love, to bind all together and complete the whole" (Col. 3:14). Only when the "whole body" of humanity, "with all its joints and ligaments," is "knit together" can it grow "according to God's design" (Col. 2:19).

HOSPITALITY

Biblical love is an insurrection against the usual definitions of status. The roles of enemy, foreigner, and all separated "others" are recast. Hostile divisions between "Greek and Jew, circumcised and uncircumcised, barbarian, Scythian, slave and free" are subverted (Col. 3:11).

Hospitality is a central theme of biblical morality but it is not presented as the mark of one who has a flair for domestic entertaining. It is redefined in a way that makes it a symbol of a new kind of human solidarity. In Judaism, Abraham became the symbol of hospitality because of his lavish entertainment of the three guests in his tent by the oaks of Mamre (Gen. 18:1-15). Though the visitors were unknown to Abraham, the patriarch literally commandeered them into a visit. "Do not pass by my humble self without a visit" (18:3). It was indeed in the context of hospitality that the promise to Abraham was made, a promise that he and "all nations on earth" will be blessed (18:18). Job and Lot were also marked out as heroes for their unstinting hospitality (Gen. 19:9; Judg. 19:22; Job 31:31-32). There is no little symbolic import in the fact that the whole hope of Judaism is set in a context of munificence to strangers. At its birth, Israel was not xenophobic.

The Hebrew people were told not to forget that their ancestors were nomads whose lives were lived as guests or hosts.[15] As always, God-language sets the moral tone. God is the epitome of hospitality. "The land is mine," God said, and the Israelites were Yahweh's invited guests (Lev. 25:23). "I am thy guest as all my fathers were," the psalmist acknowledged (39:12). The consummation of the history of the world is symbolized as an opulent meal to which "all the peoples" and "all the nations" will be invited (Isa. 25:6-8). All nations, races, and ethnic groupings will break bread together and enjoy "well matured wines strained clear" and "richest fare" (25:6). Job and Lot were also marked out as heroes for their unstinting hospitality (Gen. 19:9; Judg. 19:22; Job 31: 31-32). The universal symbolism of this was shocking in a tribal and divided world. But there it was, this status revolt, at the very center of this bold religion.

This pivotal emphasis on hospitality carried over into early Christianity. Jesus appears to have found festive hospitality very compatible with the reign of God. Recall that Jesus, unlike his mentor, John the Baptist, was not known for fasting (Luke 7:31-34). Indeed, he was accused of excess. His parties were lively, and Jesus was called a drunk and a glutton (Luke 7:34). Also, the guest list at his social gatherings was an affront to the status norms of his society. "This fellow entertains sinners and eats with them" (Luke 15:2).[16] Jesus' advice: "When you are having a party for lunch or supper," do not leave out the untouchables, "the poor, the crippled, the lame, and the blind" (Luke 14:12-13). "Tax gatherers and sinners," beggars and tramps, they should all be there (Luke 7:34; 19:1-10). Notice that the focus is not just on the appropriate joy of the reign of God but also on the dissolution of status and exclusionary claims. Baptism, in fact, was a status-dissolver. Natural family relationships were superseded by a sibling relationship with all.

Such a notion of love marks the end of unity through enmity. When Herod and Pilate got a common enemy, "that same day [they] became friends" (Luke 23:12). A lot of bonding is built on shared hatred and fear. But such social unity is a house built on sand (Matt. 7:26). Hence the revolutionary call that climaxed in Matthew's Gospel: "Love your enemies!" (5:44). This was the sharpest break with those processes of natural selection that had guided the species from its inception. "Unite against the enemy" was a maxim that served us well up to a point. The biblical trailblazers saw that that point had been reached and that now the dissolution of enmity, not the destruction of enemies, was the only feasible route to peace. The state of excessive modern militaries only makes this insight more obviously true. Destruction of the other and impunity for self are no longer compatible goals. The military is no longer the department of realistic defense.

And so this "unnatural" reorientation toward enemies is dunned in the biblical pages: "Love your enemies and pray for your persecutors; only so can you be children of your heavenly Father, who makes his sun rise on good and bad alike, and sends the rain on the honest and the dishonest" (Matt. 5:43-45; Rom. 12:9-21). "Do not repay wrong with wrong, or abuse with abuse; on the contrary, retaliate with blessing" (1 Pet. 3:9).[17] However radical, such ideas of the Jesus movement were thoroughly traditional in ancient Israel. It is an anti-Jewish prevarication to say that the maxims of the Sermon on the Mount were uttered in contradiction to the religion of Israel. They were a flower from the Jewish stem. A volume of parallels to the Sermon on the Mount can be found in the Talmud and other Jewish sources: "I presented my back to the smiters, and my cheeks to those who pulled out my beard" (Isa. 50:6). The very law of Moses had the same message: "When you come upon your enemy's ox or ass straying, you shall take it back to him. When you see the ass of someone who hates you lying helpless under its load, however unwilling you may be to help it, you must give him a hand with it" (Exod. 23:4–5; Deut. 22:1–3). "If your enemy is hungry, give him bread to eat; if he is thirsty, give him water to drink" (Prov. 25:21).

The message of Leviticus 19 is clear: the Israelites had been in Egypt and people hated them and did not heed the value of their humanity. From that Egyptian experience, Israel was to learn the lesson of love and discern the shared wonder of humanity in stranger and enemy alike and thus become a model for all nations. But, as Pinchas Lapide says, there are "Egypts" everywhere.[18] African Americans exist in a white American "Egypt" and homosexuals, women, and others exist in their own Egypts. Love is the power of exodus from these lethal segregations.

The value of this moral mutation was appreciated not only in Judaism and Christianity. Epictetus says that the good Cynic is to love as his brother anyone who strikes him.[19] The author of Second Isaiah and his Greek contemporary Xenophon of Colophon came to the socially unifying idea of monotheism at the same time. Indeed, according to biblical scholar Norbert Lohfink, "monotheism only arrived in Israel when it was also announcing itself everywhere else. This fruit was also growing on the tree at that time in Persia and in Greece."[20] There is no need to say that when a breakthrough of moral consciousness occurs, it occurs only in one place. Ripeness is rarely localized. But, clearly, the rethinking of enmity and the diagnosis of separatism reached high levels of development in early Israel and in the Jesus movement. Early Israel felt itself called to be "a witness to all races" and an "instructor of people," including "nations you do not know and nations that do not know you" (Isa. 55:4–5).

The basic idea in this is that *solidarity* is a requisite if this species is to evolve in peace—solidarity with other humans, especially victims and outcasts, and solidarity with the Earth. This moral insight screams its contemporaneity and urgency. A narcissistic humanity will be short lived—it will not match the dinosaurs in longevity.

NARCISSUS MATURES

Aristotle could say with ease at the beginning of his *Politics* that "the state is by nature clearly prior to the family and to the individual, since the whole is of necessity prior to the part."[21] It was common wisdom that the titanic state was more divine than the individual. Rome was more sacred than the Roman. Before and after the Athenian there was Athens. The individual citizen was like a wave. It rose, crested impressively perhaps, but then it sank without leaving a trace. The ocean remained. In times when death seemed ever crouched under the lintel and ready to strike, the precarious value of individual human life was easily subsumed into the more stable collectivity. Hannah Arendt credits the Jewish and Christian emphasis on the sacredness of life with subverting this perception. She particularly credits the Christian belief in immortality with changing the political sphere of symbols. "The Christian 'glad tidings' of the immortality of individual human life had reversed the ancient relationship between [human beings] and the world and promoted the most mortal thing, human life, to the position of immortality, which up to then the cosmos had held."[22] The wave in this new imagery would live at least as long as the ocean. It could make its claims now before the behemoth of the state with something like equal stature. The ancient rabbis did not shrink from saying that "whoever destroys a single soul should be considered the same as one who has destroyed a whole world. And whoever saves one single soul is to be considered the same as one who has saved a whole world."[23] Politically speaking, the individual never had it so good.

A destabilizing fault had thus materialized in these traditions beneath the pretensions of statist absolutism. Modern bills of rights defending individuals are in debt to this critical shift. Narcissus, obsessed though he was, did have a point. The self and other selves have an irreducible value that may not be simply cancelled out when measured against the state. The common good and the private good have a tensive relationship in which one does not dissipate the other. Absolutized statism (in left- or right-wing forms) is as wrong as absolutized individualism.

The biblical insistence that all individuals must be loved is not just a lyrical personalism. It does indeed insist on the preciousness of individual personhood. You shall love the other as you love yourself (Lev. 19:18). Each self is infinitely valuable: "Are not sparrows five for twopence? And yet not one of them is overlooked by God. More than that, even the hairs of your head have all been counted. Have no fear; you are worth more than any number of sparrows" (Luke 12:6-7). As Martin Buber says, a human being "is *Thou* and fills the heavens."[24] But this rhapsodic exaltation of the person is set in a broad attack on all personal and collective egoism. You have to lose your personal life to find it (Matt. 10:39). Affectively, you have to leave your homeland like Abraham, and your family like Jesus, to find your soul.[25] This condemnation of narrow definitions of self-interest is intrinsic to the biblical definition of love.

The individual is valued not as an *ens a se*, a being unto itself, but as a correlative to others. Personal reality is social, not atomistic. Again, Buber: "I become through my relation to the *Thou*: as I become *I*, I say *Thou*. All real living is meeting."[26] Egoism is the negative gravity of the soul. It puts us on a death trajectory by denying the essential correlative affirmation of others. An egoist is not fully person-ed, but remains at a lower level of evolution. Richard Dawkins, author of *The Selfish Gene*, says nature and culture present a conflict between genes and memes (ideas). The genes are selfish replicators by nature; the memes give birth to morality and distinctively human consciousness. "We alone on earth can rebel against the tyranny of the selfish replicators."[27] We alone can cross over the threshold into morality. We alone are capable of ethical altruism. The hive, the pride, and the pack are clannishly selfish and would not survive if they morally transcended this selfishness. For us, the opposite is true. If we do not transcend our selfish groupings, if the memes do not defeat the genes, we will not survive. This is what underlies the Bible's philosophical offensive against egoism. You have to lose your life to find it. If you settle for ethnic, religious, national, or familial groupings, you will die.[28] "By gaining his life, a man will lose it; by losing his life, . . . he will gain it" (Matt. 10:39).

The tribe-busting universalism that appeared in early Israel so presciently—and with the literary force to make it stick—was an evolutionary event. Self-love untamed by Other-love is lethal. It is a lesson in economics and politics as well as in ethics. Selfish, elitist groupings, neglectful of or hostile to others, are by nature positioned for short-term gain and eventual disaster. *Person* is a political term and the *polis* to which it has intrinsic reference is humankind. *Person* is also an ecological term because it is irrational egoism to ignore the sustaining Other that is our parent, Earth.

Biblical personalism, which heralds the sublime value of every person, never loses its social sense. The individual is unique, precious, and may not be trampled by *raisons d'etat*. The king (or government) must be endowed with *tsedaqah,* sensitivity to every individual, especially the weakest (Ps. 72:1). Such is the value of every human being, a value "that fills the heavens." But sociality is the setting of individuality. By relationships are we individuals made, and by relationships will we be saved. The biblical writers insist, with their hard-nosed practicality, that if we miss this message we will perish. They are not expressing pious wishes, but a profound sense of reality. The alternative is apocalypse.[29]

LOVE AS ACTION

In the main biblical perspective love and justice are not opposites, but coordinates, manifestations of the same affect. Translating *tsedaqah* as "justice" is something of a betrayal because *tsedaqah and its synonyms* are suffused with merciful love in a way that our word "justice" does not connote. It is not a case of iron-fisted justice versus the soft arms of love. The various words for *justice* and *love* in both the Hebrew and Greek scriptures are linguistically interlocking. But both *justice* and *love,* in any language, are alternatives to egoism. Both look to the private and public good, both respond to need. So, just as one could not mistake justice for mere warm feelings, so in this literature, love is never without issue. It is a *doing* virtue.

The Bible, of course, does not portray love as a steely, grim resolve to go about staunchly doing good. It is marked by "delight" and "filled with tenderness" and yearning (Jer. 31:30). It is brimming with ardor, "burning and tender," and with "zeal" and "valor" in the cause of the beloved (Isa. 63:15). Love is enduring: "I have loved you with an everlasting love" (Jer. 31:3 RSV). The "bonds of love" bring union, "harnessing" the beloved "in leading-strings." Love finds you tenderly holding the loved one in your arms and lifting her or him to your cheek as one would a child (Hos. 11:3-4). Recalling that God is the moral exemplar in the Bible, it is significant that all of the above poetry is given to describe how God loves. Human love, then, when fully alive, would have all those ardent qualities as well. But it would also be hardworking.

Love is an energy that must be incarnated in action. Love and the moral commandments are linked right at Sinai in a *love-and-do* fashion: "Love me and keep my commandments" (Exod. 20:6). There is no piety bypass through lofty but sterile "good intentions." Loving the God who is called *Tsedaqah* means immersion in the works of justice. How do you love and serve God "with all your heart and soul"? "This you will do by keeping the commandments . . . which I give you this day for your good" (Deut. 10:13). (Notice again the practicality. Keeping the commandments is "for your good." It works. It produces peace, *shalom.* Nothing else will.) The anticultic texts in the Bible were directed against reducing love to feelings or ritual, however pious: in the Bible "love is to be expressed in ethical terms."[30] That makes love taxing, since biblical ethics means such things as loving enemies and giving preference to the forsaken and the hapless. A detached piety would obviously be easier.

In the Christian Scriptures the preferred term for "love" is *agape,* a word rarely found in prebiblical Greek. Other words were available, such as *philia* and *eros,* words that had the philological advantage of connoting greater warmth and intensity. What *agape* had, however, was the associated meaning of *"showing* love by action."[31] Again, with Jesus, that very traditional rabbi, active love has a priority over worship. You contact God by loving people. *Morality, not liturgy, is the sacrament of encounter with God.*[32] If you are at the altar but not at peace with your brother, "go and make your peace with your brother, and only then come back and offer your gift" (Matt. 5:24). Again, liturgy without lived love is not worship. Lived love is the only holiness. "God is love; he who dwells in love is dwelling in God, and God in him" (1 John 4:17). There can be no vertical love between us and God. We can only get to God horizontally through love of people. "If a man says, 'I love God,' while hating his brother, he is a liar" (1 John 4:20).

FROM LOVE TO MURDER

The biblical philosophy of love as necessarily active has other practical implications. This tough viewpoint concludes that a line can be drawn from inactive love through hate all the way to murder. The person who "does not love" is described as "one who hates his brother," and everyone "who hates his brother is a murderer" (1 John 3:15). In this argument you are either among the *tsaddikim,* the "doers of justice-love" or among the *resa'im,* the "merciless ones."[33] A benign "fare thee well" to the poor is not benign; it is complicity in murder. Omission is almost the prime sin in the Bible.[34] If you do not actively love, you are "in the realm of death" (1 John 3:14). The classical sinners, or unjust persons, in Matthew's judgment scene and in Luke's parable of the Good Samaritan were "decent" people whose love did not respond actively to need (Matt. 25:31-46; Luke 10:29-37).

People have a strict right in justice to be enabled to fulfill their essential needs.[35] Essential needs are those that must be fulfilled in order for respect and hope, the indispensable requisites of human life, to endure. The opposite of respect is insult; the opposite of hope is paralysis. We require large doses of respect and hope to be normal. That is why they are essential needs. We have many frivolous needs that can be denied without moral tragedy, but if our essential needs are unmet, and we lack the power to meet them, it is because others have not responded to the question: "Where is your brother?" (Gen. 9:4). The blood from your brother's unmet needs "is crying out to me from the ground" (Gen. 9:10). If you do not hear this cry, you are "in the realm of death" (1 John 3:14). If we ignore the unmet essential needs of the powerless poor we are treating their humanity as insignificant. Our inaction is hate-full. Action is the only test of sentiment. By "their fruits" are true lovers known. Those who merely cry "'Lord, Lord' will [not] enter the kingdom of Heaven, but only those who do the will of my heavenly Father" (Matt. 7:21).

The non-doers face the strongest curse found in the Christian Scriptures: "I never knew you; out of my sight, you and your wicked ways!" (Matt. 7:20-23). The contrary blessing is given in Jeremiah's signal text to those who "dispensed justice to the lowly and poor; did not this show [they] knew me?" (22:16). This thoroughly biblical insight was better received by some Marxists than by people of the book. The Marxist Koschelava scorns "the hypocritical sighs for the unenviable lot of [humankind]." Such sentiments, Marx says, can only be saved by "the heroic and selfless struggle for the genuine equality of [all people.]"[36] The Bible agrees.

THE JUSTICE LINK

Justice is part of love's link to action. Justice and love do not relate as opposites or alternates. They are not even a progression, as though we start with justice and grow to love. Rather, as José Miranda says, "love is not love without a passion for justice."[37] Aristotle missed something that the Bible did not: "Friends have no need of justice," he said.[38] But they do. The biblical writers have the better part of wisdom in not sharply dividing love and justice. Justice ensures the mutuality of love. Justice saves love from condescension. "The supreme delicacy of charity is to recognize the right of the person being given to."[39] The alternative is paternalism or maternalism. If love's gifts are from on high, from an unshared *noblesse,* the recipient is demeaned.

The justice link also saves love from optionality. If you respond in love to my need you are not simply doing me a favor out of the sheer surfeit of your nobility. You owe me the help that I need. Our shared humanity and shared planetary destiny make active love a minimal mark of humanhood. Responding to the cry of the needy privileges us. It signals that we have crossed the threshold of moral being. We have been morally birthed. "The other's call or appeal" is "the privileged instance which opens up the original meaning of morality itself."[40] Prior to such response we are premoral beasts.

THE ART OF FORGIVENESS

Hannah Arendt gave Jesus too much credit when she wrote: "The discoverer of the role of forgiveness in the realm of human affairs was Jesus of Nazareth."[41] The value of this supreme manifestation of human spirituality was appreciated before Jesus. She is more correct when she says that many of the insights of movements such as the Jesus movement are ignored "because of their allegedly exclusively religious nature."[42] That has been the argument of this entire book. Forgiveness is a creative and curative force permitting human interaction. Insight on it from any source should be welcome.

Long before Jesus the Book of Genesis ended its pages with an epic of forgiveness. Common sense would have allowed Joseph to seek vengeance against the brothers who betrayed him viciously. Instead, he redirected events by forgiving the malfeasants. Joseph states: "Do not be afraid. I will provide for you and your dependants." And "thus he comforted them and set their minds at rest" (50:15-21). When he forgave, "Joseph wept. His brothers also wept" (Gen. 50:17-18). Everything changed. As Arendt put it, the freedom that forgiveness affords is "the freedom from vengeance which encloses both doer and sufferer in the relentless automatism of the action process, which by itself need never come to an end."[43] (The tensions in Ireland and the Middle East will never be eased without forgiveness by all parties. The forgiveness process led by Archbishop Tutu and others in South Africa showed that, since history cannot be rewritten, forgiveness is the only route to a peaceful future.) Forgiving the debts of impoverished nations is not a high-minded gesture. It is the only practical way to a future of well-being on a small planet. The God who was the summation of all moral norms for Judaism set the pattern of morality: "I will forgive their wrongdoing and remember their sin no more" (Jer. 31:34). To accept such a God as your model commits you to forgiveness as an essential of life.

Jesus strengthened this tradition: "Forgive your brother from your hearts" (Matt. 18:35). He even said that God's ability to forgive, which was a cornerstone of his own Jewish theology, was conditioned by our readiness to forgive others (Matt. 6:12-15). God cannot forgive an unforgiving people! Jesus also ties forgiveness specifically to love: "Where little has been forgiven, little love is shown" (Luke 7:47). Paul's classic song of love highlights the view that love is "not quick to take offense" and that it "keeps no score of wrongs" (1 Corinthians 13). Valuing people—which is love—requires that stroke of social amelioration called "forgiveness." The unforgiving heart has not yet begun to love.

Forgiving the debts of impoverished nations is not a high-minded gesture. It is the only practical way to a future of well-being on a small planet.

SURPRISES

That the gravitational pull of egoism is ever defeated is astonishing. That it is at times totally routed in heroic self-sacrifice is almost beyond philosophical explanation. We cannot completely explain the behavior of the young German soldier in Holland who was ordered onto an execution squad to shoot innocent hostages but stepped out of rank and refused his assigned duty. He was accused of treason and immediately executed with the hostages by his erstwhile comrades.[44] He may never have heard Socrates say that it is better to suffer injustice than to perpetrate it, or Immanuel Levinas say that morality begins when a person is more concerned about not committing murder than about avoiding death.[45] He had probably not been instructed by Albert Camus that "it is better to suffer certain injustices than to commit them even to win wars."[46] Yet the young soldier embodied all those insights and lived them to their heroic, mortal conclusion. The story of this event spread through the war zone. It was like a blazing, hope-filled star in the darkness of a terrible night.

Were that young soldier our son or brother we would say that the beauty of his death explained the depths of our grief. His dying showed the beauty of his person. We see his death as not only moral but as supremely noble. We build monuments to people like that. And yet, here is a case where morality seems totally unpractical. His death was not "cost effective." His action led to more murder and more injustice, not less. And yet his action was described as "inspiriting" by the author who reported it, and we share readily in that reaction half a century later.[47] "There is no greater love than this, that a man should lay down his life for his friends" (John 15:13).

Is there not a certain admirable madness in the "logic" of love? In love we affirm the unconditional significance of empirically conditioned persons. We even fly to words related to divinity, infinity, and worship to try to do justice to our phenomenology of preciousness. Persons are worth so much that expressing their value brings us to the edges of language where even symbols and metaphors flag as they try to body forth our experience. Ultimately we have to conclude with Vladimir Solovyev that "we can assert unconditional significance only by faith, which is the assurance of things hoped for, the conviction of things not seen."[48] Love is grounded in a belief in "things not seen." We are plunged into mystery by the experience of a love that we cannot explain. Theologian Gregory Baum touches the essential nerve when he asks "why the men and women who struggle for justice should take upon themselves so many hardships, even though they expect their movement to be successful only at a future time when they will be gone."[49]

Not everyone, of course, has appreciated or risen to such love. Aristotle felt that status differences precluded friendship, which, by definition, is a process of enduring love.[50] Baum says that Marx had little regard for the hopeless vagrants sleeping under the bridges of Paris. They were not functional in his view of the working economy. But, as Baum observes, such coldness would be fatal today for the masses of people in third-world countries who "are precisely the marginal, the dispossessed, . . . excluded from participation in the process of production."[51] How can we love them as we love ourselves? How can we say of them, "this is my body; this is my blood"? And at this point, practicality and enlightened self-interest return. If we do not so love them, we will not know peace. They will not forever go off quietly into the bush to die. Wars of redistribution are the main threat of this century. Love, hard-working love, is thus the most practical of emotions.

Practical arguments, however, do not dissolve the mystery. The question remains as we look at our panhuman siblings: Why is this flesh so precious? Theists have long explained it in terms of God. They are precious because they are made in the image of God. But does that explain it, or merely push the mystery back a notch? Why is God so precious and why does the lovability of God refract onto the dispossessed? Does this explanation not fly to ultimate causes, bypassing all proximate causation? And certainly at the level of persuasion, this explanation did not impress atheist Michael Harrington but, even with terminal cancer, he worked to his final days for the poor, and for justice and peace.

Does immortality explain it? Can we love persons unconditionally because they will live forever? Possibly. Is it true we suffer and maybe even die for persons but do not commend the supreme sacrifice for petunias or poodles however highly we regard them. But immortality is only a hypothesis, and many who love heroically do not subscribe to it. Also, in what sense does immortality make us worth more? Would the petunia be worth dying for if we knew it had an afterlife? The scent of a reductionist rationalism rises with the immortality explanation of the supreme sacrifice.

The answer to this mystery of love remains beyond our explanatory reach. The experience cannot be unfolded into tidy conceptual categories. All that we are is not within our ken. Our intelligence is small and surrounded by *terra incognita*. Our affective powers stretch from the superficial to the mysteriously profound. If someone confides to you that he likes Chiclets you might appreciate the confidence but you will not feel that you are the recipient of big affective news. If, however, he tells you that he longs and works for the dismantling of the white male monopolies or for the ending of world hunger, you will sense that you have been invited into the deepest sanctuaries of his heart. The medievals referred to affection at this level as *mystical*. The word comes from the same

Greek root, which means "to lie hidden," as *mystery*. The mystical levels are the deepest levels of the soul. The love that produces self-sacrifice and altruistic generosity is mystically deep. We can never fully find its enigmatic roots. We must, with Solovyev, speak of "faith" to explain it.[52]

Michael Harrington struggled with his own moral self-portrait. He said that his was a "religious nature without religion." Though not crediting any supernatural explanations, he called himself "a pious man of deep faith."[53] When Jean-Paul Sartre realized that all of his works could hardly be measured against the smile of a baby, he was not telling us that he liked Chiclets. He was not discussing the economic value of the baby's biochemical components. He experienced the baby's personal worth and, in Buber's phrase, "it filled the heavens." His experience deserves a special word and again that word is *mystical*. It reached into the unplumbable depths of human prizing, appreciating, loving. Such penetrating loving is the foundation of our morality and the hope for our survival. Mysticism is not a rare or freakish psychic event. It is the seed of humanhood and the source of moral consciousness. Affections that do not reach mystical levels are fluff.

LOVE AND GROWTH

Psychology assures us that love is the good news that must greet us at birth. If it does, we grow; if it does not, we wither. Even nutriments without love will not nourish us. The baby who is not hugged will not thrive. The uterus is the womb in which the human body develops but love is the womb in which personhood is formed. Where that love is lacking we will have neither the ability to love others nor the ability to love ourselves. We will not be fully personed. Biology adds to this the observation that sex-love and the multiplication of species have an inverse relationship. In the lower species, multiplication is profuse, but sex-love and bonding do not seem to exist. As we move to the human end of the biological spectrum multiplication diminishes or even disappears, but sex-love and bonding increase in intensity and constancy, suggesting a different and crucial relational role for love.[54]

The biblical authors needed no lectures on this. We can love because we have been loved. "We love because he loved us first" (1 John 4:19) is the core of biblical psychology. Israel attributed its special greatness to its being loved: "The Lord cared for you and chose you," therefore, you are "special" (Deut. 7:6-7). Love gives increase: "He will love you, bless you, and cause you to increase" (Deut. 7:13). And the way of divine love is the model of human love in the Bible. Love gives increase. There is no other route to maturity.

Erich Fromm interprets the myth of Jonah quite plausibly as a message on the creative power of love. Jonah does not love the people of Nineveh so he runs away rather than helps them at first. As Fromm says, he is "a man with a strong sense of order and law, but without love."[55] As he attempts to escape he finds himself imprisoned in the belly of a whale. After God saves him he goes and helps the people of Nineveh and they thrive, but Jonah is not content. He sits angrily, sweltering in the sun. To help him God causes a "climbing gourd" to give him shade and some contentment. But a worm eats the gourd and Jonah returns to his angry lamentations. Then God delivers the message of the tale. Jonah had more sympathy for the gourd that he did not even have to tend and help to grow than for the people of Nineveh. But God's sympathy was with "the great city of Nineveh, with its hundred and twenty thousand who cannot tell their right hand from their left, and cattle without number" (Jon. 4:6-11).

Fromm uses this story to illustrate his own principle regarding the nature of love: "Love is the active concern for the life and the growth of that which we love."[56] In other words, love is not something we fall into, but something dynamic and creative. God's reply to Jonah says in allegory "that the essence of love is to labor for something and to make something grow."[57] Even Jonah's reluctant love had turned the people away from their "habitual violence" and "wicked ways" (3:8). They grew like the gourd grew when loved by God.

The Bible also recognizes that love transforms the lover. You become what you love. "Ephraim became as loathsome as the thing he loved" (Hos. 9:10). So love is good for you or bad for you depending on its object. Love begets love, as Goethe said. Love bounces back; *redamatio* is Aquinas's word for it.[58] This may seem ironic, that the most generous of our endowments has a reward for the self. The Bible, however, saw nothing at all wrong about self-love. Indeed, it is the paradigm for Other-love. You love your neighbor *as you love yourself* (Lev. 19:18). Thus, egoism can be resisted *for selfish reasons.* It is not good even for you. Its marks are constriction and frost. According to Aquinas, one of the effects of love is, *liquefactio,* "melting." Love is a unifying force, a fusion of vitalities. But solids cannot be blended together so love promotes union through the melting of barriers. It does so without squelching individuality. True love accentuates our differences as it bonds us into a fruitful union and is a boon to both lover and beloved.[59]

WHEN LOVE GOES PUBLIC . . .

Respect is the first step to love. At the political, international level love appears as respect, the soul of diplomacy. We can't tell diplomats and international actors to love one another, but the incipient love of respect is not just possible but essential. Talk of love in international relations would certainly sound fatuous in a cynical world. Talk of respect does not. If persons shy from saying they "love" nature, they surely at least can respect it and in so doing the pathway to full loving is opened. Respect for the rest of nature is the beginning of ecological sanity and well within everyone's reach.

There are many modes of love. The music of love pervades all human relationships, only changing in its linguistic melodies. Small wonder the biblical writers made it the summation of all morality and the heart and center of their moral creed.

Chapter Twelve

SONG OF JOY

Among the lessons I learned from my son Danny was one on the natural-ness and normalcy of joy. I used to ride every day past the lovely lagoon of Lake Michigan on my way to Marquette University. My mind was taken up with ponderous thoughts, to be sure, but I wasn't looking. One day I took Danny down to see the ducks at that lagoon. He stepped out of the car, looked with wonder at the beautiful mallards and water birds of every kind, and he grabbed my leg and shouted with booming delight: "Daddy, Look! Look!"

I see Danny's exclamation as his valedictory address to the world, the plea he left to us who are more retarded than he. We don't look and so we rejoice too little. We don't look at this generous Earth that has been provided for us, an Earth that we are progressively wrecking. We don't look at the hungry of the world and those bereft of joy. Our joy is shallow if we can ignore them. "Let us share our joy" (Phil. 2:18). The Gospel writers join Danny's brief: "Look at the birds of the air. . . . Consider how the lilies grow in the fields" (Matt. 6:26, 28).

Blasé is perhaps the most evil of words. The person who is that way is like a broken violin. There will be no more music. Let's be honest. Pleasure and fun have gotten a bum rap in much of Christian history. That history did not always match the wisdom of our Jewish parents.

Sometimes a worldview shines through a single sentence. It happens in this famous Jewish saying: "We will have to give account on the judgment day of every good thing which we refused to enjoy when we might have done so."[1] Given the ascetical gloom to which religions easily succumb, it might be hard to believe that a mandate to have fun could claim religious roots at all. Yet no theory of life can be profound if it cannot decide on the place of joy. Sorrow and joy are competing gravitational pulls. The question confronting any philosophy of morals is: Where does the accent fall? If joy is *normatively* normal, if it is what *ought* to be, then its absence calls for action. If misery is normality, then pain in the world deserves at best a sympathetic shrug.

Joy, which can easily be downgraded to a superficial effervescence, is actually the consummation of morality. The position you take on the normativeness of joy—that is, joy is what ought to be—sets the course for your politics, economics, and religion. If joy is meant for everyone, if ecstasy is our destiny, if both buds and babies are born to blossom and bloom, then, while sorrow has often to be endured, joy must be championed. If joy is what ought to be, then it enters the precincts of social conscience—with prophecy, justice, and hope in its close-knit entourage. Healthy joy cannot be full while sisters and brothers are in misery. Joy in a surrounding context of misery is insulted and undone. Inevitably, every worldview and every person must opt, implicitly or explicitly, for the normativeness of either joy or misery, and the results are massive. The Bible is clear: "The harvest of the Spirit is love, joy, peace . . ." (Gal. 5:22).

Erich Fromm notes that in the principal humanistic religions, "the prevailing mood is that of joy, while the prevailing mood in authoritarian religion is that of sorrow and guilt."[2] Among the "humanistic religions" he includes Buddhism; Taoism; the teachings of Isaiah, Jesus, Socrates, and Spinoza; and certain streams of historical Judaism and Christianity. These religions, he observes, all push for the development of our power to love others and ourselves and all encourage "solidarity [with] all living beings."[3]

Their aim is empowerment and growth, not obedience and control. Obviously, deviant forms of these religions indulged heftily in obedience and control. Fromm, however, discerned something of a more hopeful spirit centered in these explosions of human consciousness.

A MINORITY REPORT

An accent on joy is not in the majority report submitted by humankind. For most people pessimism and gloom seem more normal and truly reflective of reality. A melancholy fatalism reigns even where it is not thematically professed. The presumed normalcy of misery is the badspel (or antigospel) of any culture in which childlike hope is atrophied and the sense of Earth's possibilities is numbed. Seeing joy as the goal of being is a minority report filed instinctively by little children and thematically by humanistic religions and by the great philosophers and artists.

The minority report on joy as normative, that is, joy as what ought to be, is thoroughly biblical and well planted in the best parts of both the Jewish and the Christian traditions. Misery and sorrow in the biblical view are not the product of some inexorable karma or of an all-powerful, unfeeling fate. They are rather the objects of prophetic assault. Only with this in mind could we make sense of Rudolph Schnackenburg's comment about the prophet Jesus, a comment that would otherwise seem superficially lyrical: "What Jesus in fact wanted was not to revive penitential practices wherever he went, but to spread joy."[4] In this light, Abraham Heschel's words also take on full meaning. In Judaism, he says, joy is "the very heart of religious living, the essence of faith, greater than all the other religious virtues." "Merriment," he insists, "originates in holiness. The fire of evil can better be fought with flames of ecstasy than through fasting and mortification."[5] This note is regularly struck in both the Hebrew and Christian Scriptures.

First a look at the hopeful persistence of the theme of joy in the biblical pages. Then, because joy without reason would be weird, it will be worth seeing where the Bible found grounds for joy in a world where "the peak of beauty is the beginning of decay" and where both cold- and hot-blooded violence seem more familiar than celebration.[6]

BIBLICAL DELIGHT

Joy is a natural part of a biblically based moral creed. As the Bible sees it joy is the first fruit of the creative Spirit of God (Gal. 5:22) and the whole purpose of creation itself: "Rejoice and be filled with delight, you boundless realms which I create; for I create Jerusalem to be a delight and her people a joy" (Isa. 65:17-18). Rejoicing is mandated in the law of Moses: "You shall rejoice before the Lord your God with your sons and daughters" (Deut. 12:12). The reign of God, the prime metaphor for the plan of God for reality, is linked to joy. The appropriate response to it is "sheer joy" (Matt. 13:44). God's reign is like a "wedding supper," the happiest of Israelitic events: in Paul's vision, in fact, the minister is one who contributes to the joy of the community (2 Cor. 5:18).[7] God's reign is like a "wedding supper," the happiest of Israelite events: "Happy are those who are invited. . . . Exult and shout for joy" (Rev. 19:6-9).

Even those who followed the old custom of fasting in response to the reign should do so without looking unhappy: "When you fast, do not look gloomy. . . . Anoint your head and wash your face, so that men may not see that you are fasting" (Matt. 6:16-18). Suffer we will, but that gives no grounds for gloom. Indeed, suffering should be accepted with "gladness and exultation" (Matt. 5:12).[8] As Abraham Heschel reports, good people, "even when they are bedridden, manage to sing."[9] He drew this from Psalm 149: "Let them sing for joy upon their couches" (v. 5). If we delight in the right things, we can "be always joyful" (1 Thess. 5:16), whereas the "glee" of the mean-spirited is "short-lived" and "lasts but a moment" (Job 20:5). Now, obviously, this irrefutable joy must be grounded, or it would be but manic madness.

The Bible's joy is based on enthusiastic response to the miracle of life on Earth and fed especially by the beginnings of that life in childhood. Biblical joy is not a gossamer strain of otherworldly spirituality; biblical spirituality is of the Earth and earthy. The Earth, upon its completion, was seen to be "very good" (Gen. 1:31), and upon completing it, God took a day off to rest and enjoy it (Gen. 2:2). As we saw in chapter nine the idea of joy has remained prominent in subsequent Jewish sabbath celebration. The Earth is so full of fruit and promise that it, with all its animals and plants, should also celebrate: "Let the heavens rejoice and the earth exult, let the sea roar and all the creatures in it, let the fields exult and all that is in them; then let all the trees of the forest shout for joy" (Ps. 96:11). There is hope even for the unflourishing parts of the Earth: "Let the wilderness and the thirsty land be glad, let the desert rejoice and burst into flower" (Isa. 35:1-2). In this ecological vision, there is hope even for the wastelands. Water will "spring up in the wilderness, and torrents flow in dry land. The mirage becomes a pool, the thirsty land bubbling springs" (Isa. 35:6-7).

Children, too, are a major source of joy, "a gift from the Lord" and "a reward." Happy the one who has a "quiver full of them" (Ps. 127:3-5). The Bible is not abstemious in its praise of the things that bring happiness to our embodied selves. Sexual joy was well appreciated. The liturgies of sexual passion were so explicitly praised in parts of the Bible that many Catholic and other religious orders in the past were forbidden even to read those sections. The Song of Songs, of course, is an anthology of erotic poems that picture sexual passion in luxuriant bloom without bothering with details such as whether the lovers were married. Skittishly blushing commentators rushed to cover its obvious import with allegorical interpretations but their chastity was more impressive than their exegesis. These texts were not so interpreted in their early history and the fact that these blazing poems were attributed to the wisest king of Israel shows the respect in which they were held.[10] Proverbs gives advice that moderns would shy from using in a wedding toast: "Have pleasure with the wife of your youth. . . . May her breasts always intoxicate you! May you ever find rapture in loving her!" (Prov. 5:18-19; Anchor Bible). The classical prophets of Israel used marital imagery to describe the reality of God. Sexual joy is at home in the biblical vision.

The Bible also did not engage in the prohibition of drink. It praised God for making grass for the cattle, trees for the birds, high hills for the goats, and "wine to gladden [people's] hearts" (Ps. 104:13-18). Jesus, of course, was criticized for feasting and partying while John the Baptist had fasted (Mark 2:18-19). "'Table-fellowship' has loomed large in recent discussion of Jesus."[11] The fact that people reclined at the table during these meals showed that they were feasts or dinner parties.[12] "These dinner parties were such a common feature of Jesus' life that he could be accused of being a drunkard and a glutton."[13] "Unlike the Baptist, Jesus drank wine and alcohol at the homes and 'taverns' of the day."[14] It is remarkable that the synoptic Gospels all agree that Jesus, right before his death, looked forward to having a drink in the kingdom of God (Matt. 26:29; Mark 14:25; Luke 22:18)![15] "I tell you this: never again shall I drink from the fruit of the vine until that day when I drink it new in the kingdom of God." Jesus attached great importance to festive gatherings. Indeed, he wanted to be remembered in exactly that kind of a context. Those who survived him were to do this sort of thing in memory of him (1 Cor. 11:24-25).

The Bible was clearly not epicurean, but it certainly appreciates earthiness and a sense of human embodiment although many theologians over the centuries have tried to spiritualize and desexualize its joy. Neither God nor morality was a killjoy in these traditions. Biblical morality is geared toward happiness. Morality is not a crushing imposition on our nature. Rather it is to us what water, sun, and air are to plants. Happy is the person, says the psalmist, who delights in the law. She is "like a tree planted beside a watercourse, which yields its fruit in season and its leaf never withers" (1:1-3). True morality is "sweeter than syrup or honey from the comb" (Ps. 19:10). Morality, understood at its depths, is music. Morality's beckoning can be sung: "Thy statutes are the theme of my songs" (Ps. 119:54). The life-affirming hopefulness of these traditions was grounds for joy, as Paul reminded his readers: "Let hope keep you joyful" (Rom. 12:12). The consummation of morality was *shalom,* which, for the Hebrews, was the fulfillment of our capacity for rejoicing.

Even God, in the Israelite conception, is an object of joy. Liturgy was to be lively, if not outright fun. "Let Israel rejoice in his maker and the sons of Zion exult in their king. Let him praise his name in the dance. . . . Let them shout for joy as they kneel before him" (Ps. 149:2-3, 5). There will be joy in the "house of prayer" (Isa. 56:7). King David had set the tone for this by dancing "without restraint, . . . leaping and capering" before the Ark of the Covenant. He was even rebuked by his wife Michal for carrying on wildly "like any emptyheaded fool." David was unrepentant and promised more of the same (2 Sam. 6:14-23). In the opening of Luke's Gospel this dancing moment is invoked when Mary visits Elizabeth, but here it is the fetus in the womb that does the dancing (Luke 1:39-45).[16] In the second-century document *Acts of John* the story of the last supper was revised so that Jesus invites his dinner companions to sing and dance with him.[17] Such is the stress on joy that in the *Apocalypse of Peter,* Peter has an unlikely vision of Jesus "glad and laughing on the cross."[18]

THE JOY OF LAUGHTER

Whatever pompous sophisticates may say, no great literature is devoid of laughter. Laughter is in the Bible, playing a key role in some of the major stories. The announced arrival of Isaac, the mythical child of promise, is framed in laughter: "God has given me good reason to laugh, and everybody who hears will laugh with me" (Gen. 21:6). Those are the words of Sarah, the expectant mother who found it ridiculous to be pregnant at her advanced age. She even called the baby "Laughter," which is the meaning of "Isaac."

A key moment in Jesus' mission is also marked with comedy. His ludicrous entrance into Jerusalem—riding an unsaddled colt with his little band of followers throwing their garments on the path before him—was laughable. "If there were any semblance of a powerful entry into Jerusalem, the Roman legions quartered in Jerusalem during the fast would have rushed out to immediately crush them."[19] Jesus was acting here in the bizarre tradition of the prophets.[20] Matthew and John, in fact, relate the incident to the prophecy of Zechariah. That text, like Jesus' mock triumphant march, was a spoof on power, including military power. The words of Zechariah are pointed: "Rejoice, rejoice, daughter of Zion. Shout aloud, daughter of Jerusalem; for see, your king is coming to you, his cause won, his victory gained, humble and mounted on an ass, on a foal, the young of a she-ass. He shall banish chariots from Ephraim and war-horses from Jerusalem; the warrior's bow shall be banished. He shall speak peaceably to every nation and his rule shall extend from sea to sea" (9:9–10). Riding on the young of a she-ass, this "king" will destroy the most advanced weapons of the day. The joke was on power as defined by paltry, cowering minds. Mocking military pomp, Luke has the disciples singing hymns of "peace" and "glory." It is all quite unexpected, cosmic, and unruly, this unseemly band mocking the stunning parades of power that marked the reign of the Caesars and singing a new song of joyful peace.

Verses later, illustrating the natural relationship between joy and sorrow, Jesus weeps because the city he approached so ludicrously did not know "the way that leads to peace" (Luke 19:38). The same message is made, once in joy and clowning, and once in sorrow.[21]

In the Psalms even God is presented as laughing at the powerful, strutting nations of the world. "Why are the nations in turmoil? Why do the peoples hatch their futile plots? . . . The Lord who sits enthroned in heaven laughs them to scorn" (2:1, 4). Other parts of the Bible are seen as comic literature, including the books of Ruth, Jonah, and Ecclesiastes.[22] Ruth and Jonah poke fun at the stupidity of narrow nationalism and ethnic pride. Ecclesiastes should jolt all intellectuals, including theologians, as it mocks the pseudowisdom of the learned: "They are all emptiness and chasing the wind" (Eccles. 1:14). The Bible does not lack for clowns and jesters.[23]

THE ANALYSIS OF JOY

Analyzing joy may be as futile as explaining a joke. The fragility of joy in a tragic world, however, requires what strength the mind can muster. If joy would have its due, we need to test its claims before the court of reasonableness or the joke may be on the joyful.

The Bible does not give a philosophical theory of joy and laughter. Such is not the way of great and poetic literature. But the biblical writers do offer some teasing hints as to what these human phenomena entail and promise and show us why joy is part of the biblical moral creed. They direct our attention to: (1) the goodness of the earth, (2) the primacy of children, (3) the perils of slight expectations, and (4) the priority of ecstasy over efficiency.

In all of this, the Bible teaches a salubrious lesson: no theory of morality should lack a theory of joy.[24]

1. The "Very Good" Earth

The pages of the Bible contain a biological dictionary full of references to the fauna and flora of the Earth its writers knew. There is also a bursting interest in the origins, history, and future of our world. The wisdom found in these emphases can ground hope and joy in theists and nontheists alike.

If we are not stunned at the marvels of life, we are the children of the demon Blasé, that ugly enemy of joy. To some degree we are, one and all, tainted by the original sin of blunted wonder. *Consueta vilescunt*—the things to which we are accustomed become banal.

Inured to the wonder that is our setting, we lose the capacity for joy and its consort, hope. That leaves us intellectually wizened. But joy is expansive. The glad mind sees far.

The song of joy is a history of the Earth. To know the grounds of joy, recall and rehearse our planetary genesis. It is a necessary joy-sustaining and reverence-producing exercise that should be repeated frequently. At every point the story is amazing. But, like tragically depressed persons who cannot even bring themselves to look out a window, we ignore the feats with which biology surrounds us.[25]

We began billions of years ago when a huge, cosmic explosion produced a massive "cloud" of materials. Most of it condensed into a large central body that is the sun. As the sun reached the ignition level of several hundred million degrees centigrade, the hydrogen in its core ignited in explosions that continue to this day. Some of the material was cast away from the sun, and gradually formed into the planets. At first, even the earth, which found the best orbit, was a hopeless looking mass of chaos and erosion. Some of the heat of the original explosion was retained in the earth and pours out still in marvelous displays of molten lava or in gentle hot springs.

Only the earth, in this small family of planets, was the right distance from the sun to allow released steam to condense as rain.

We became the water planet. Events moved slowly. The universe
has plenty of time. Ongoing chemical reactions on the chaotic wet
earth gradually produced the compounds basic to life. *Somehow*—
and that is the word even the wisest of experts must use—somehow
these elements formed into minute cellular organisms. It seems that
the matter is geared to life, and given the right conditions it will
generate that life. That seems to be the working assumption of as-
trophysics. The conditions were not there on Venus or other in-
felicitously located bodies. But the conditions were here and life
began. Not only did it begin, but it evinced an inner urgency to
reproduce. And yet, there was more. It did not just reproduce in
kind, or the oceans would simply be pools of bacteria, encircling
jejune continental wastelands. Life had an incorrigible need for
diversity. New species proliferated. After repeated failures, life took
hold on this inhospitable land, and displayed yet another talent: ad-
aptation. When necessary, it fashioned new methods of locomotion
and learned to breathe. Some of life even took flight, and soared
triumphantly over the whole scene with a newfound grace.

We start with an interstellar explosion and now we have bees
that communicate with one another, drawing maps by their movements to the latest find and setting up passwords to their separate
hives. There are "flashlight fish" who store cooperative luminescent
bacteria in pockets under their eyes to produce a light so bright
that a newspaper could be read in an aquarium lit by a single fish.
Thus equipped, the fish pursue small crustaceans in dark waters
and trick pursuers by flashing the light off and on. The ungainly
sand wasp produces a litter of larvae and then paralyzes the motor
nerve centers of a hapless worm, not killing it, but—with parental
foresight—leaving it incorrupt as food for the little ones when they
reach a hungry maturity. The female cardinal develops a suitable
treelike camouflage that keeps her safe for nesting, whereas her
carefree mate indulges in colors that reflect his greater freedom.

Pregnancy encapsulates repeatedly the whole evolutionary
drama. The eye forms in all its subtlety in a womb where the eye
has never seen. The fetus, in its final weeks before birth, begins to
practice sucking and smiling. And when it is born and its little eyes
clear, it smiles at faces, not at elbows. The neonate eyes seek out

"the windows of the soul" and smile at what they see. Meanwhile, the maternal breasts, which helped to stimulate the pre-conceptual sexual festivities, prepare to welcome the newborn, first with a mild serum and then, within days, with a suitably enriching and protective milk.

Even when humans interfere, life can respond with versatility. For example, as a result of an experiment, a dolphin in captivity became so chilled that it could not swim. Placed back in the main tank with two other dolphins, it sank to the bottom, where it was bound to suffocate unless it could reach the surface to breathe. However, it gave the distress call and the other two immediately lifted its head until the blowhole was out of water, so that it could take a deep breath. It then sank and a great deal of whistling and twittering took place among the three animals. The two active ones then began swimming past the other so that their dorsal fins swept over its ano-genital region in a manner that caused a reflex contraction of the fluke muscles, much as one can make a dog scratch itself by rubbing the right spot on its flank. The resultant action of the flukes lifted the animal to the surface. The dolphins repeated the procedure for several hours until the ailing dolphin had recovered.[26]

The appropriate music for the biological scene within us and around us is Ludwig von Beethoven's "Song of Joy." There are, of course, discordances in nature, and violence—life in its ebullience is not as consistent as Beethoven's great symphony. But that great work is also part of the miracle that began with a chaotic interstellar explosion. Gifted though we are with intellectual consciousness, and given the biological drama in which we are cast, our spirits rejoice and applaud too little. Our unique talent for appreciation is little realized. And so, for the want of joyful awe, we devastate the earth and one another.

Both theist and nontheist can share in that joy and live out that awe. Whether the processes of this universe are self-generating or the product of some holy and artistic mystery, no one can definitively say. What we can do is bond in solidarity and appreciation for the gift that it is to be on so fair an Earth.

2. The Primacy of Children

How we see children tells much of our tale. Every society assumes a moral and political attitude on children. The attitudes range on a scale from treating them as property to seeing them as coequal persons with full human rights. Part of the moral revolution in early Israel and early Christianity was a transformation in the status of children. Children came to be seen as precious gifts from the creator but also as norms for human behavior and thinking.

Children were seen as having a better sense of the values that make life flourish. The childlike frame of reference was seen as wiser than the pomposities of adults. Psalm 8 sets the tone: "Out of the mouths of babes, of infants at the breast, thou has rebuked the mighty, silencing enmity and vengeance to teach thy foes a lesson" (v. 2). In one of the visionary texts of Isaiah God's future reign will be one in which "a little child shall lead them" (11:6). These ideas develop into a dominant theme in the Christian Scriptures. Here, becoming childlike licenses you to enter the reign of God: "Whoever does not enter the kingdom of God like a child will never enter it" (Luke 18:17). "Let the children come to me . . . for the kingdom of God belongs to such as these" (Mark 10:14). Those who seek authoritarian power are told that "the highest among you must bear himself like the youngest" (Luke 22:26). Special insights are credited to little children. Rabbi Jesus prays: "I thank you, Father, Lord of heaven and earth, for hiding these things from the learned and wise," and revealing them to toddlers (Luke 10:21; Matt. 11:25).[27] Jesus invoked Psalm 8 ("Out of the mouths of babes . . .") to defend the children who seemed to understand him better than their parents (Matt. 21:16). Indeed, in alternate readings of Luke 23:1 and what follows, Jesus was accused of having a subversive influence on "women and children" who understood him better, and men complained that "he has turned our children and wives away from us."[28]

Being "Childed" Even some of those who should know better belittle the notion of being "childed."[29] It was no small error for psychologists Lawrence Kohlberg and Jean Piaget to classify small children as "premoral." As Gabriel Moran says: "Their blindness on

this point is not an error in calculation but a revelation of fundamental deficiency in their image of development and their meaning of morality."[30] Educational theorist Kieran Egan does get at the
point when he says that what children know best are "the most
profound human emotions and the bases of morality."[31] In several
ways, children are moral norms. Only a very rationalistic model of
morality could restrict it to adult experience.

The "moral" is that which befits persons, and children instinctively know what is best for human flourishing. The moral rhythms
that pulse through the veins of our children are what will save this
confused species, if saved it will be. Children know the normativeness of joy and the primacy of trust and hope and love, and they
shy from that which is violent and harsh. Little white hands reach
spontaneously for little hands of any other color, all of which reach
naturally for old and wrinkled hands—until messages from the adult
community bring alienation into their malleable souls. Children are
not born with the gloom of any "original sin"; they inherit it from
us. We teach them racism, sexism, age-ism, heterosexism.

The ideal, of course, is not to shed the experience and technical knowledge of an adult, but to resurrect the wholesome instincts
and suppressed hopes of childhood—hopes for peace and trust and
celebration—all of which have the priority of goals standing above
our every scheme. In this sense, "a little child shall lead you."

There is another sense in which we must not kill the joyful
child that is in us. The scientist-philosopher Michael Polanyi saw in
the biblical instruction to "become like little children" an expression of the need to "break out of our normal conceptual framework."[32] Our knowledge is broader than our words and concepts,
and those words or concepts cannot package it as tidily as the adult
rationalist in us would wish. Still, we have a go at it and eventually
come to settle for our mental photographs and models. Cognitively,
we shrink. We lose contact with "our pre-conceptual capacities of
contemplative vision."[33] We need to be restored to fuller and more
sentient consciousness. Poetry tries to do that. Children do it naturally. It is part of their charm that they do not share our universe of
discourse. To borrow Shelley's words on poetry and apply them to
children, they "purge from our inward sight the film of familiarity

which obscures from us the wonder of our being," and they bring us back into "a world to which the familiar is chaos."[34] The child has been very alive in all persons of genius I have met. The well-childed genius is no prisoner of the familiar constructs that we conspire to let pass for truth.

Finally, children are moral norms because they are the clearest reminders of the pricelessness of human life and they are the fairest product of this fruit-filled Earth. Indeed, if one were pressed to give a single statement to sum up morality, I would return to: what is good for children is good and what is bad for children is ungodly. With that principle alone, our politics, economics, and religions could all be brought under searing moral scrutiny. Foreign policy can be assessed by this elementary principle. For example, on December 9, 2004, the United Nations Children's Fund announced that more than a billion children, more than half of the children in the world, suffer extreme deprivation because of war, HIV/AIDS, or poverty. War we support with our policies and pocketbooks; children we do not. If, for example, after hundreds of millions of dollars were poured into military aid to El Salvador, 80 percent of the Salvadoran children were hungry, that policy was a scandalous failure.[35] It is bad for children, and that is enough. What moral reasons or political reasons could outweigh that? Wars, invasions, and grossly inflated military budgets kill children, the true treasures of the species. Were we not so morally frozen in our collective consciousness, the arguments for a "just war" would melt before the prospect of shedding children's blood.

3. Paltry Expectations

Biblical laughter is directed at our feeble sense of what is possible. From Hannah to Mary, from Isaac to Zechariah, the Bible taunts our wilted sense of what could be. Paradoxical parables dash against our responsible expectations. The first are last and the last are first. Virgins and old women conceive the most remarkable offspring. Workers who come at the last hour are paid like those who worked all day. The parable of the Prodigal Son is a typical example of the Bible's comic collision with our expectations. In this story of two sons it's clear which son a parent would wish for. The older son stayed home where he was needed and "slaved" on the farm for years. He never disobeyed orders and required no special treatment in return. We might say he was a paragon of the "Protestant work ethic."

The younger son grabbed his share of the family money and "left home for a distant country, where he squandered it in reckless living . . . running through [the] money with his women." Upon his return home, this rascal becomes the unlikely hero of the story. The father orders: "Quick! Fetch a robe, my best one, and put it on him; put a ring on his finger and shoes on his feet. Bring the fatted calf and kill it, and let us have a feast to celebrate the day" (Luke 15:11-32).

According to this parable, it hardly pays to be sensible. The disciplined son is reduced to a sideline complainant in the story. The ironic turn here is that the hero is the one who wildly "dared to hope for the humanly impossible and was reckless and unlimited even in his image of God."[36] The "ideal son" played it safe, staying in the established ridges of orthodoxy. He did not test the waters of other possibilities. The other son could be forgiven much because he loved and trusted much. He was as reckless in his hope for new beginnings as he had been in his life abroad. And so the parable says, "Let us have a feast to celebrate" the likes of him.

4. Ecstasy over Efficiency

If it is mercy that seasons justice, it is joy that seasons reason. Beware the mind that forgets that ecstasy is our destiny. In the joyless mind, efficiency declares itself god and persons are lost in equations. The stress on joy functions as a morality monitor. If the most efficient way to package chicken, attach bolts, or make clothing takes no account of the human need to rejoice even in work, it is immoral and will eventually be undone. Even efficiency becomes inefficient if it ignores the primacy of joy. Human beings will not thrive, or produce, if treated as automatons without joy for long.

The greatest evil, as Jean-Paul Sartre said, is to treat as abstract that which is concrete. The most important concrete reality is life on Earth. If intelligence becomes beguiled with abstractions like "efficiency," "national security," "nuclear superiority," "bottom-line thinking," and "lifeboat ethics," intelligence becomes disembodied.[37] We lose contact with reality. We move closer to the colonel who stood in the smoking ashes of the totally devastated village of Ben Tre, Vietnam, and told the press corps: "We had to destroy this village in order to save it." What abstractions reigned in the colonel's mind if *devastation* and *saving* could be equated? His mental malady is not a rarity, but an epidemic. Plans have been active in just the last decade to destroy Ethiopia, Afghanistan, the Middle East, the Balkans, and even the planet, all in order to "save" them. How would we explain such plans to children who know that joy is the crown of our being and that we are not "saved" without it?

Joy keeps us in touch with our bodies, and our bodies connect us to the world. You cannot rejoice without bodily participation. A polygraph would detect every moment of joy. There is no such thing as purely spiritual joy. The phenomenon of joy is our sweet link to the earth. Joy has, of course, an intellectual component. We speak of animals as having pleasure or delight, but not as having joy. Joy implies a sense of fulfilled purpose and achieved destiny that seems most properly attributed to intellectual beings. But our intellectuality is embodied, and we become dangerous when affectivity is uncoupled from our material matrix.

Joy has a natural supremacy in the moral order. Justice is good because it is a precondition for joy. Peace is good because it is the fulfillment of joy. Work is noble because it expresses, causes, and facilitates joy. If efficiency is good, it is because it serves joy, and does not subvert it. Joy, which seems such a frail, monosyllabic abstraction, is actually the pinnacle of practicality. When its normative status is slighted, our brightest plans go awry. When its claims are honored, we are pointed inexorably toward peace . . . and also productivity!

IN DEFENSE OF FUN

Laughter is essential or our prophecy will simply burn out. According to G. K. Chesterton, the English writer, if you want to be serious, be serious about your necktie. But in really important matters, like death, sex, and religion, there will be mirth or there will be madness.

Next I will quote my mother, whom we all called Cassie. (What kind of an Irishman would I be if I didn't quote my mother in this entire book!) Cassie had four years of schooling and a life full of learning. One of her philosophies was this: in any human endeavor—whether it's a parish or a school, a business or professional office, a White House or a Pentagon—where there is no fun the situation corrodes—it deteriorates; it dehumanizes. Once, when she was in her nineties, I came to relieve her main caretaker, my priest brother, Joe. I had just come from a theological conference and I was excited. I began telling Joe about the impressive speakers who were there, what this one said, what that one said, et cetera. Cassie sat there on the couch listening to the two of us emoting about the conference. After ten minutes, an indicting question came from the couch, "Was there *fun* at that conference?" In Cassie's view if there was no fun it was hopeless. And here I am twenty-five years later—I haven't the slightest idea what the conference was about but I'm still quoting Cassie and commending her wisdom to you.

And finally I turn to my favorite poem (with commentary), which makes the same point Chesterton and Cassie were making. The poem is "The Fiddler of Dooney," by W. B. Yeats. The fiddler speaks:

When I play on my fiddle in Dooney,
Folk dance like a wave of the sea;
My cousin is priest in Kilvarnet,
My brother in Moharabuiee.

(*The poem's a little strange here: he had a dance going but now he's dragging in the clergy relatives . . .*)

I passed my brother and cousin:
They read in their book of prayer;
I read in my book of songs
I bought at the Sligo fair.

When we come at the end of time,
To Peter sitting in state,
He will smile on the three old spirits,
(*The two clergymen were pious but a bit on the dour side so Peter will call*
them in and cheer them up . . .)
But call me first through the gate;

For the good are always the merry,
Save by an evil chance,
And the merry love the fiddle
And the merry love to dance:

And when the folk there spy me,
They will all come up to me,
With "Here is the fiddler of Dooney!"
And they'll dance like a wave of the sea.[38]

CONCLUSION

From the beginning, there has never been just one Christianity. Christians have always shown an ability to distort the message, or to emphasize different aspects of their faith, while neglecting other—often more basic—challenges of that faith. One revealing manifestation of one form of Christianity seen today appears in the biblical texts held up on signs behind the goal posts at football games. These texts are invariably dogmatic assertions, not moral challenges. These signs never direct us to the Sermon on the Mount or the Prophets of Israel. Never do these held-high signs proclaim that "blessed are the poor" (Luke 6:20) or "blessed are the peacemakers" (Matt. 5:9). They do not direct us to "beat [our] swords into plowshares" (Isa. 2:4) or to take seriously the biblical command to eliminate all poverty (Deut. 15:4). They do not urge us to accuse corrupt political and religious leaders of being "hypocrites, blind guides, blind fools, snakes, tombs covered with whitewash, or vipers" guilty of spilling "innocent blood" as Jesus did (Matt. 23).

You would never know from these signs—and the interpretation of Christianity they represent—that there is an exciting, demanding moral creed in the biblical tradition. The religion we call Christianity is a moral classic. At times it has turned civilization dramatically in a humanizing direction. At other times, it has decayed and become little more than comfort food.

Theology's role is to call us back to this moral creed that is the heart and center of biblical religion where there is good news for the poor and praise for the peacemakers and doers of justice. Responding to that vocation has been the work and purpose of this book. If the mainline Christian churches have been emptying, it may be because this vision and the excitement it can produce have been lost.

Past achievements of the Christian movement shame our impotent timidity, our defection from prophecy. A remarkable diversity of scholars have testified to prophetic religion's effective and beneficent economic and political power. Hannah Arendt observes that Christianity enhanced respect for physical labor and for those who do it, and was a major stimulus for the development of science. The modern world, she said, "never even thought of challenging this fundamental reversal which Christianity had brought into the dying ancient world."[1] Friedrich Engels marveled at the extraordinary political power of early Christianity, a power that, at the time, startled Diocletian and a number of emperors into harsh, repressive reaction. Engels speaks admiringly of Christianity as "the party of overthrow." It "flatly denied that Caesar's will was the supreme law" and thus undermined "all the foundations" of Caesar's brutal empire. Christian symbols were forbidden, he observes, and efforts were made to ban Christians from public life because they were so dangerously anti-empire. This influence endured until Christianity became the state religion and lost its subversive power.[2] Lenin also saw early Christianity as a beacon of hope to oppressed peoples, but, he lamented, when it became the state religion it "forgot" its "democratic-revolutionary spirit."[3]

According to Elaine Pagels, the early Christians courageously defied Roman totalitarianism, and in the face of often brutal violence, they "forged the basis for what would become, centuries later, the western ideas of freedom and of the infinite value of each human life."[4] Henri Bergson, a Jewish scholar, said the "teachings of the Gospels" laid the ground work for modern proclamations of human rights.[5] Mahatma Gandhi, a Hindu, noted the influence of the Sermon on the Mount on non-Christian cultures. In early U.S. history African slaves received from their white masters a corrupted and authoritarian form of Christianity, but with striking genius they saw through this distortion. They discovered that the biblical stories taught freedom from oppression; that everyone, even slaves, were made in the image of God and that humanity is a shared grandeur; that their children were on par with the master's children. They were the unlettered but brilliant forerunners to the modern liberation theology movement.[6]

So Christianity has a track record, reaching in some instances into modern times. It keeps showing that it has the potential to be "the party of overthrow," a counterforce to the varied forms of empire that crush human life. Most of the revolutionary movements that transformed, shaped, and reshaped the American nation, "abolitionism, women's suffrage, the union movement, the civil rights movement . . . grew out of religious circles."[7] But the moral revolution of the early Jesus movement is unrecognizable in today's many analgesic, trivialized, and made-for-TV forms.

The permanent challenge of theology and of sound preaching is to recover the moral energies that gave Christianity birth and enflesh them in contemporary life. The experts at this were the prophets of Israel and they are as relevant today as they have ever been. Sensitive citizens of the United States should squirm while reading Norman Gottwald's description of Israel's prophets: "These prophets were troubled by the chauvinist and elitist assumptions about Israelite superiority to other peoples and about the virtues and wisdom of established rulers. They exposed smug self-righteousness and narrow self-interest in the politically and socially powerful who claimed to be serving Israel. . . . They turned a pitiless eye on the inhuman effects of national leadership on the majority of ordinary Israelites. They foresaw the ruin of the nation through internal spoliation [in modern times, tax breaks for the rich] and external conquest."[8] We cannot avoid seeing ourselves as the object of those prophets' laments.

Jesus joined the two disciples on the road to Emmaus. Their comment after he left them was: "Did we not feel our hearts on fire as he talked with us on the road and explained the scriptures to us?" (Luke 24:32). If theologians, preachers, teachers, and parents cannot set hearts ablaze with the moral creed that has been willed to us, the fault is ours and we are "unprofitable servants" (Luke 17:10).

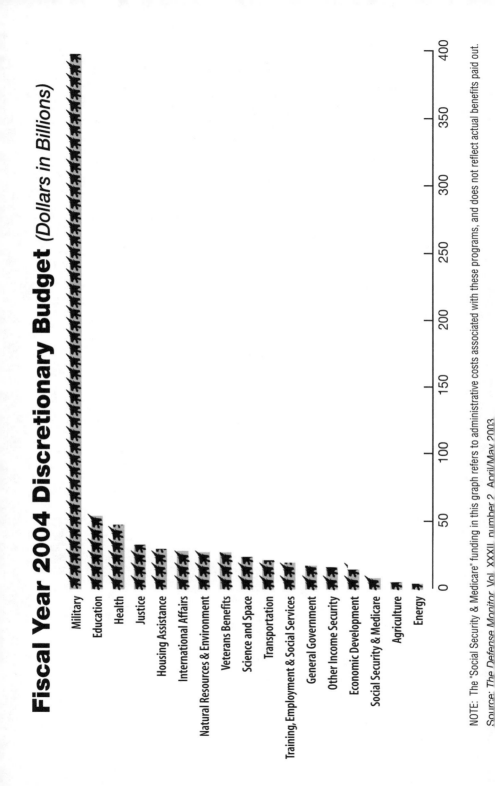

Fiscal Year 2004 Discretionary Budget *(Dollars in Billions)*

NOTE: The "Social Security & Medicare" funding in this graph refers to administrative costs associated with these programs, and does not reflect actual benefits paid out.

Source: *The Defense Monitor*, Vol. XXXII, number 2, April/May 2003

NOTES

CHAPTER ONE

1. Quoted in Goran Moller, *Ethics and the Life of Faith: A Christian Moral Perspective* (Leuven, Belgium: Peeters, 1998), 35.
2. Gerd Theissen, *Biblical Faith: An Evolutionary Approach* (Minneapolis: Fortress Press, 1985), 122.
3. Loren Eisely, *The Firmament of Time* (New York: Athenaeum, 1960), 123–24.
4. Edward O. Wilson, *The Future of Life* (New York: Knopf, 2002), 94. Wilson points out that if everyone were to consume as we in the American empire consume, it "would require four more planet Earths" (150).
5. See David W. Orr, *Ecological Literacy: Education and the Transition to a Postmodern World* (Albany: SUNY Press, 1992), 3–5, and *Earth in Mind: On Education, Environment and the Human Prospect* (Washington, D.C.: Island, 1994), 1–3.
6. H. Govind, "Recent Developments in Environmental Protection in India: Pollution Control," *Ambio* 18, no. 8 (1989): 429, quoted in Paul M. Kennedy, *Preparing for the Twenty-First Century* (New York: Vintage, 1994), 191. Kennedy notes that this use of the term "environmental pollution" is broad and looks to more than respiratory effects.
7. See Daniel C. Maguire and Larry L. Rasmussen, *Ethics for a Small Planet: New Horizons on Population, Consumption, and Ecology* (Albany: SUNY Press, 1998), 23–25. In this book, I go on to discuss the cognitive status of God and the theistic and non-theistic understandings of the sacred.
8. The macabre execution of Jesus presented problems to the early mem-

bers of the Jesus movement. Their first instinct was not to make crucifixes and put them around their necks or above their altars any more than they would have made amulets or statues of electric chairs if that were the way Jesus had been killed. Instead they reached into their religious tradition of sacrifice in which you took something precious, a lamb, and killed it and burned it, in effect returning it to God as a gift. Making Jesus the "Lamb of God" made some strategic interpretative sense but introduced a heavy dose of sadomasochistic poison into the Christian tradition. Salvation by way of the incarnation, as favored by many in the Eastern Christian tradition, avoids the expiation-by-blood-and-gore interpretations of Jesus's death.

In his *The Cross in Our Context: Jesus and the Suffering World,* Douglas John Hall speaks of "the astonishing persistence of the Latin or Anselmic/Calvinistic theory of atonement. . . . Much of the West got stuck in this theory—and it still is. This is partly because the Latin theory of substitutionary atonement is indeed a powerful one, which found its way into every nook and cranny of ecclesiastical life in the western hemisphere—into prayers and liturgies, into deeply emotional hymns, in art, into scriptural interpretation, and so forth" (Minneapolis: Fortress Press, 2003), 130.

Bruce J. Malina argues that with the original "take up my yoke" the "yoke falls out and the cross is put in" in the "process of traditioning" (*The Social Gospel of Jesus: The Kingdom of God in Mediterranean Perspective* [Minneapolis: Fortress Press, 2001], 117–18).

The first followers in the Jesus movement were perplexed about how to explain the ignominy of Jesus' execution. The *Apocalypse of Peter,* one of the so-called Gnostic gospels, presents Jesus as "glad and laughing on the cross" (*Apocalypse of Peter,* 81:10–11).

9.   Quoted in J. Mark Thomas and Vernon Visick, eds., *God and Capitalism: A Prophetic Critique of Market Economy* (Madison: A-R Editions, 1991), 18.

10. Richard A. Horsley, *Jesus and Empire: The Kingdom of God and the New World Disorder* (Minneapolis: Fortress Press, 2000), 28.

11. Walter Wink, *Naming the Powers: The Language of Power in the New Testament* (Minneapolis: Fortress Press, 1986), 109.

12. John Hughes, "Unspeakable Utopia: Art and the Return to the Theological in the Marxism of Adorno and Horkheimer," *Cross Currents* (Winter 2004): 486.

13. Theodor W. Adorno and Max Horkheimer, *Dialectic of Enlightenment* (London: Verso, 1997), 178.

14. Horsley, *Jesus and Empire,* 126.

15. Ibid., 121–28.

16. Religion, politics, and economics were only distinguished and separated as concepts in modern times. In Jesus' time they were of a piece and he was in the thick of it. Economics and politics were his religious business.

17. Horsley, *Jesus and Empire,* 122. Keep in mind that the sentimentalized idea of modern affluent "childhood" did not exist in Jesus' time.

18. Regarding the current U.S. government's rhetorical mask, Gore Vidal commented that a "war on terrorism [is] a nonsensical notion like a war on dandruff" (*Imperial America: Reflections on the United States of Amnesia* [New York: Nation, 2004], 15).

19. Laurie Zoloth, "The Promises of Exiles: A Jewish Theology of Responsibility," in *Visions of a New Earth: Religious Perspectives on Population, Consumption, and Ecology,* ed. Harold Coward and Daniel C. Maguire (Albany: SUNY Press, 2000), 98.

20. Ibid.

21. Walter Wink, *Jesus and Non Violence: A Third Way,* Facets (Minneapolis: Fortress Press, 2003), 87.

22. See Bernard Bailyn, *The Ideological Origins of the American Revolution* (Birmingham, Ala.: Palladium, 2002); Forrest McDonald, *Novus Ordo Seclorum: The Intellectual Origins of the Constitution* (Lawrence: University of Kansas Press, 1985); and Anders Stephanson, *Manifest Destiny: American Expansion and the Empire of Right* (New York: Hill and Wang, 1995).

23. Chalmers Johnson, *The Sorrows of Empire: Militarism, Secrecy, and the End of the Republic* (New York: Holt, 2004), 28.

24. See William Blum, *Rogue State: A Guide to the World's Only Superpower* (Monroe, Me.: Common Courage Press, 2000); and Chalmers Johnson, *Blowback: The Costs and Consequences of American Empire* (New York: Holt, 2000). Johnson's book, written two years before September 11, 2001, predicted "blowback" (a CIA term) from Osama bin Laden due to U.S. Middle East presence and policies.

25. Chandra Muzaffar, Editorial, *Just Commentary* 4, no. 11 (November 2004): 2.

26. Nathaniel W. Taylor, *Concio ad Clerum: A Sermon Delivered in the Chapel of Yale College, September 10, 1828,* quoted in William A. Clebsch, *From Sacred to Profane America* (New York: Harper & Row, 1968), 32.

27. George S. Phillips, *The American Republic and Human Liberty Foreshadowed in Scripture* (Cincinnati: Poe & Hitchcock, 1864), quoted in William A. Clebsch, *From Sacred to Profane America* (New York: Harper & Row, 1968), 189–91.

28. Wink, *Naming the Powers,* 140.

29. Garry Wills, "With God on His Side," *New York Times Magazine* (March 30, 2003): 26–28.

30. Horsley, *Jesus and Empire,* 22.

31. Henry Parks Wright, ed., *Juvenal* (Boston: Ginn & Company, 1901) 77–89. *"Duas tantum res anxius optat, panem et circenses."* As editor, Wright comments this "well characterizes the desires of the Roman people under the empire" (118).

32. Norman K. Gottwald, *The Tribes of Yahweh: A Sociology of the Religion of Liberated Israel, 1250–1050 B.C.E.* (Maryknoll, N.Y.: Orbis, 1979), 640.

33. Quoted in ibid., 23.

34. Arnold Toynbee, *Change and Habit: The Challenge of Our Time* (New York: Oxford University Press, 1966), 112.

35. Ibid., 107.

36. On the tendency of the privileged to maintain a studied ignorance about the exploitation that supports them, see Mary Elizabeth Hobgood, *Dismantling Privilege: An Ethics of Accountability* (Cleveland: Pilgrim, 2000). She writes that "none of the official churches assists people in analyzing the roots of poverty or other forms of economic injustice. Knowledge about how the class structure impacts groups differently is largely unknown to First World Christians" (70).

37. Bruce Murphy, *Milwaukee Journal Sentinel,* posted on JSONLINE on October 9, 2004. This is part of an excellent four-part series on excessive managerial pay.

38. Walter Ullmann, *The Growth of Papal Government in the Middle Ages* (London: Methuen, 1955), 7; Walter Ullmann, *A Short History of the Papacy in the Middle Ages* (London: Methuen, 1972), 22. Bishop Leo did not even try to justify his pompous imperial claims by referring to the text in Matthew's Gospel, "Thou art Peter," etc. (16:18 KJV). That argument was added later. Leo had his eyes on the church in Constantinople, which was making power claims that Leo didn't appreciate. As one theological wag put it, Jesus no more planned the current form of papacy than did Sitting Bull plan the Bureau of Indian Affairs.

CHAPTER 2

1. See Daniel C. Maguire, *The Moral Core of Judaism and Christianity* (Minneapolis: Fortress Press, 1993), 67–84.

2. Pierre Teilhard de Chardin, *The Vision of the Past* (New York: Harper & Row, 1966), 227.

3. Ibid. See also Pierre Teilhard de Chardin, *Christianity and Evolution* (New York: Harcourt Brace Jovanovich, 1969), 154, and his *Human Energy* (London: Collins, 1969), 54, 94.

4. Gerd Theissen, *Biblical Faith: An Evolutionary Approach* (Philadelphia: Fortress Press, 1985), 167–68.

CHAPTER 3

1. Bruce J. Malina, *The Social Gospel of Jesus: The Kingdom of God in Mediterranean Perspective* (Minneapolis: Fortress Press, 2001), 1, 144.
2. Ibid., 10.
3. See Garry Wills, "Faith and the Race for God and Country," *Sojourners* 15 (March 14, 1998): 4–5.
4. Ibid., 71.
5. Morton Smith, "Palestinian Judaism in the First Century," in *Israel: Its Role in Civilization*, ed. Moshe David (New York: Jewish Theological Seminary of America, 1956), 67–81.
6. Ibid., 81.
7. Mary Elizabeth Hobgood, *Dismantling Privilege: An Ethics of Accountability* (Cleveland: Pilgrim, 2000), 27.
8. Ibid.
9. Gerd Theissen, *Biblical Faith: An Evolutionary Approach* (Philadelphia: Fortress Press, 1985), 122.
10. Allan W. Watts, *Myth and Ritual in Christianity* (New York: Vanguard, 1953), 7, quoted in Norman Perrin, "Jesus and the Language of the Kingdom," in *The Kingdom of God in the Teaching of Jesus,* ed. Bruce Chilton (Philadelphia: Fortress Press, 1984), 93. Myths and symbols overlap in meaning. A symbol may house myths and a myth may use many symbols. On myth, see Daniel C. Maguire, *The Moral Choice* (Garden City, N.Y.: Doubleday, 1978), 338, 354, 409–32.
11. Perrin, "Jesus and the Language of the Kingdom," 92.
12. E. P. Sanders, *Jesus and Judaism* (Philadelphia: Fortress Press, 1985), 126.
13. Alan Richardson, "Kingdom of God," in *A Theological Wordbook of the Bible,* ed. Alan Richardson (New York: Macmillan, 1962), 119.
14. Richardson, "Kingdom of God," 119.
15. Rudolph Schnackenburg, *The Moral Teaching of the New Testament* (New York: Herder & Herder, 1965), 145.
16. Stephen Charles Mott, *Biblical Ethics and Social Change* (New York: Oxford University Press, 1982), 82.
17. Richard A. Horsley, *Jesus and Empire: The Kingdom of God and the New World Disorder* (Minneapolis: Fortress Press, 2003), 75.
18. Jorge V. Pixley, *God's Kingdom: A Guide for Biblical Study* (Maryknoll, N.Y.: Orbis, 1981), 3.
19. Mott, *Biblical Ethics and Social Change,* 84.
20. T. W. Manson, *Ethics and the Gospel* (New York: Scribner, 1960), 65. The actual phrase "kingdom of God" does not appear in the Hebrew Bible, except for the phrase "kingdom of the Lord" in 1 Chron. 28:5. The word *kingdom,* however, is frequently used in connection with God, and the

overall meaning of the expression is "deeply rooted in the thought of the Old Testament" and is "everywhere present." See *Interpreter's Dictionary of the Bible* (1962), s.v. "Kingdom of God, of Heaven."

21. Pixley, *God's Kingdom,* 14–15.

22. This term is used by Gerhard Lohfink, *Jesus and Community: The Social Dimension of Christian Faith,* trans. John P. Galvin (Philadelphia: Fortress Press, 1984), 66.

23. Pixley, *God's Kingdom,* 30.

24. *Interpreter's Dictionary of the Bible* (1962), s.v. "Kingdom of God, of Heaven."

25. See Allen Verhey, *The Great Reversal: Ethics and the New Testament* (Grand Rapids, Mich.: Eerdmans, 1984).

26. Theissen, *Biblical Faith,* 105.

27. George Wolfgang Forell, *History of Christian Ethics* (Minneapolis: Augsburg Publishing House, 1979), 1:20.

28. Albert Nolan, *Jesus before Christianity* (Maryknoll, N.Y.: Orbis, 1978), 48.

29. The effort to restore creativity to its natural place in ethics has already begun. See Philip S. Keane, *Christian Ethics and Imagination: A Theological Inquiry* (New York: Paulist, 1984). See also Daniel C. Maguire, *The Moral Choice* (Garden City, N.Y.: Doubleday, 1978) (San Francisco: Harper & Row, 1979), chap. 6; and Daniel C. Maguire and A. Nicholas Fargnoli, *On Moral Grounds: The Art/Science of Ethics* (New York: Crossroad, 1991).

30. Some scholars say that the reign of God refers not to human activity, but to divine action that alone can save us. This kind of quietism would never explain the scorching blasts of the prophets or the urgent moral imperatives that are central to Hebrew religion. The morality of the Bible is not a precondition for the release of a miracle. We touch the sacred by doing justice. God is not the only agent who counts in this perspective.

31. Norman K. Gottwald, *The Tribes of Yahweh: A Sociology of the Religion of Liberated Israel, 1250–1050 B.C.E.* (Maryknoll, N.Y.: Orbis, 1979), 598.

32. Franciscus Zorell, *Lexicon Graecum Novi Testamenti* (Paris: Lethielleux, 1931), s.v. "metanoia" and "metanoew."

33. Herbert Marcuse, *One-Dimensional Man: Studies in the Ideology of Advanced Industrial Society* (Boston: Beacon, 1964), 123.

34. The Hebrew word *ruach* is not a univocal word. It can mean "wind," "breath," "soul," or "principle of life," or it can refer to the creative, ruling power of God. In Ezekiel 36, it has multiple meanings; clearly, one of these meanings is the notion of the people of Yahweh sharing in Yahweh's power to the extent that the divine holiness will be manifested in them and they will show the nations of the world how to live. This notion indicates the people's power to share in Yahweh's providence. In this sense,

spirit theology is a theology of hope, giving us confidence that we can help to remake the earth.

35. Gerhard von Rad, *The Problem of the Hexateuch and Other Essays* (New York: McGraw-Hill, 1966), 139.

36. Joachim Jeremias, *New Testament Theology,* trans. John Bowden (New York: Scribner, 1971), 198.

37. See Rosemary Radford Ruether, *The Radical Kingdom: The Western Experience of Messianic Hope* (New York: Paulist, 1970).

38. Eric Voegelin, *The New Science of Politics, an Introduction* (Chicago: University of Chicago Press, 1952), 100.

39. This report comes from the Christian Cyprian, *Ep.* 55. See Karl Baus, *Handbook of Church History,* ed. Hubert Jedin and John Dolan (New York: Herder & Herder, 1965), 1:380. See also Malina, *The Social Gospel of Jesus,* 94–95. Says Malina, all of Jesus' preaching about the reign of God was "political language for a first-century person. Jesus taught in public, the arena of politics, and came to Jerusalem to proclaim his prophetic message at the very center of political religion, the temple" (94–95). For that reason, the political leaders had him killed.

CHAPTER 4

1. Aristotle, *Nichomachean Ethics* 1132b. Aristotle speaks of "proportional requital" holding the city together, but he does so as an explanation of the proportional requisites of justice. On cultural variants in the notion of justice, see Max L. Stackhouse, *Creeds, Society, and Human Rights: A Study in Three Cultures* (Grand Rapids, Mich.: Eerdmans, 1984). See also Douglas Sturm, *Community and Alienation: Essays on Process Thought and Public Life* (Notre Dame, Ind.: University of Notre Dame Press, 1988); and David J. O'Brien and Thomas A. Shannon, eds., *Renewing the Earth: Catholic Documents on Peace, Justice, and Liberation* (Garden City, N.Y.: Image, 1977).

2. Aristotle, *Nichomachean Ethics* 1131a. See Paul Ramsey, *Basic Christian Ethics* (New York: Scribner, 1950), 13–14.

3. Stephen Charles Mott, *Biblical Ethics and Social Change* (New York: Oxford University Press, 1982), 65.

4. Stephen Charles Mott, "Egalitarian Aspects of the Biblical Theory of Justice," in *Selected Papers from the Nineteenth Annual Meeting of the American Society of Christian Ethics, 1978,* ed. Max L. Stackhouse (Waterloo, Canada: Council on the Study of Religion, 1978), 8. See also John R. Donahue, "Biblical Perspectives on Justice," in *The Faith That Does Justice,* ed. J. Haughey (New York: Paulist, 1977), 68–112.

5. C. H. Dodd, *The Founder of Christianity* (New York: Macmillan, 1970),
    64.
6. Abraham J. Heschel, *The Prophets* (Philadelphia: Jewish Publication
    Society of America, 1962), 198.
7. Martin Buber, *The Prophetic Faith* (San Francisco: Harper Torchbooks,
    1960), 102.
8. Quoted in Heschel, *The Prophets*, 215n27.
9. On this text, see Jose Porfirio Miranda, *Marx and the Bible: A Critique of
    the Philosophy of Oppression* (Maryknoll, N.Y.: Orbis, 1974), 78.
10. Quoted in ibid., 46.
11. Obviously, one must paint with careful but necessarily broad strokes in
    doing cross-cultural comparisons. Distinctive features and lineaments of
    cultures can be isolated that differentiate the real differences in moral
    climate. A fine example of a study of the American moral climate that
    offers more than its title suggests is Yehoshua Arieli, *Individualism and
    Nationalism in American Ideology* (Cambridge: Harvard University Press,
    1964).
12. Aristotle, *Nichomachean Ethics* 1132a.
13. Norman H. Snaith, *The Distinctive Ideas of the Old Testament* (London:
    Epworth, 1962), 70.
14. Ibid. Some suggest that texts requiring fairness for all undermine the
    powerful biblical bias in favor of the poor. Leviticus 19:15 is used in this
    way: "You are not to pervert justice, either by favoring the poor or by
    subservience to the great. You are to administer justice to your fellow-
    citizen with strict fairness." This rule, common to all ethics, of not cheat-
    ing anyone does not silence the thundering and incessant *leitmotiv* of the
    biblical symphony, concern for the exploited poor of the earth.
15. Mott, "Egalitarian Aspects of the Biblical Theory of Justice," 12.
16. Compassion also has a centrality in other major religions. See, for exam-
    ple, the texts of Confucianism, which say that compassion is the soul of
    successful statecraft. See Ninian Smart and Richard D. Hecht, eds., *Sacred
    Texts of the World: A Universal Anthology* (New York: Crossroad, 1982),
    316.
17. Augustine, *The Trinity (De Trinitate),* in *Patrologia Latina* 42:1046.
18. See Willy Schottroff and Wolfgang Stegemann, eds., *God of the Lowly:
    Socio-Historical Interpretations of the Bible* (Maryknoll, N.Y.: Orbis, 1984).
    Justice takes on many enriching modalities in the experience of differ-
    ent races and genders. See Katie Cannon, *Black Womanist Ethics* (Atlanta:
    Scholars, 1988); Barbara Hilkert Andolsen, Christine E. Gudorf, and Mary
    D. Pellauer, *Women's Consciousness, Women's Conscience: A Reader in Feminist
    Ethics* (San Francisco: Harper & Row, 1985); and June O'Connor, *The

Moral Vision of Dorothy Day: A Feminist Perspective (New York: Crossroad, 1991).

19. See Marvin Fox, "Reflections on the Foundations of Jewish Ethics and Their Relation to Public Policy," in *Selected Papers from the Twenty-First Annual Meeting of the Society of Christian Ethics, 1980,* ed. Joseph L. Allen (Waterloo, Canada: Council on the Study of Religion, 1980), 47–48.

20. Jesus is said to have used this expression in complimenting Nathaniel. See John 1:47.

21. See Luke Timothy Johnson, *Sharing Possessions: Mandate and Symbol of Faith* (Philadelphia: Fortress Press, 1981), 21–22.

22. See Robert Gnuse, *You Shall Not Steal: Community and Property in the Biblical Tradition* (Maryknoll, N.Y.: Orbis, 1985).

23. For this reading, see Miranda, *Marx and the Bible,* 17. *The New English Bible* (New York: Cambridge University Press, 1971) puts it: "A money-grubber will always turn a blind eye. As a peg is held fast in the joint between stones, so dishonesty squeezes in between selling and buying."

24. See Jacob Neusner, *Judaism in the Beginnings of Christianity* (Philadelphia: Fortress Press, 1984), 68.

25. See also Amos 6:1, 4; Mic. 2:1-2; Isa. 3:16; 5:8; and Jer. 22:13. Also, the wicked were seen as punished by a destruction of their wealth, suggesting complicity between wealth and injustice. See Hos. 9:6; Joel 3:5; Nah. 2:9; Zeph. 1:12-13; Zech. 9:3-4; Isa. 3:18-24; 5:9; 14:11; 42:22; Jer. 5:16-17; 6:12; 15:13; 17:3; 20:5; and Ezek. 7:19-21; 23:25.

26. H. Hendricks, *The Infancy Narratives* (London: Chapman, 1984), 84.

27. Quoted in Reinhold Niebuhr, *Moral Man and Immoral Society: A Study in Ethics and Politics* (New York: Scribner, 1960), 125.

28. Quoted in Arieli, *Individualism and Nationalism in American Ideology,* 334.

29. Quoted in Walter L. Owensby, *Economics for Prophets: A Primer on Concepts, Realities, and Values in Our Economic System* (Grand Rapids, Mich.: Eerdmans, 1988), 19.

30. Robert Nozick, *Anarchy, State, and Utopia* (New York: Basic, 1974), ix.

31. Ibid., 169.

32. As an antidote to the simplistic notion of poverty as a self-inflicted absence of wealth, see John D. Jones, *Poverty and the Human Condition: A Philosophical Inquiry* (Lewiston, N.Y.: Mellen, 1990).

33. Aristotle, *Politics* 1267a.

34. Ibid.

35. Heschel, *The Prophets,* 359.

36. See John Howard Yoder, *The Politics of Jesus: Vicit Agnus Noster* (Grand Rapids, Mich.: Eerdmans, 1972), 68–72.

37. Ibid., 66

38. Owensby, *Economics for Prophets*, 35.

39. Buber, *The Prophetic Faith*, 99.

40. Bruce J. Malina, *The Social Gospel of Jesus: The Kingdom of God in Mediterranean Perspective* (Minneapolis: Fortress Press, 2000), 110.

41. See chap. 3, above.

42. Trude Weiss-Rosmarin, "The Editor's Quarter," *Jewish Spectator* 43 (Spring 1978): 3.

43. Snaith, *The Distinctive Ideas of the Old Testament*, 72.

44. One proud exception to the trusting blindfolded lady is on the ceiling of the Capitol dome in Madison, Wisconsin. There, a sturdy woman sits majestically with the scales in her strong hands, with no blindfold and a look of command on her face. Jesus and Isaiah would commend that as more realistic.

45. Benjamin N. Cardozo, *The Growth of the Law* (New Haven, Conn.: Yale University Press, 1934), 23–26.

46. See Gregory Baum, *The Priority of Labor: A Commentary on Laborem Exercens: Encyclical Letter of Pope John Paul II* (New York: Paulist, 1982). This book includes the full text of the papal encyclical.

47. Alan Watson, *The Law of the Ancient Romans* (Dallas: Southern Methodist University Press, 1970), 3.

48. See Owensby, *Economics for Prophets*, 24–25.

49. Charles Avila, *Ownership: Early Christian Teaching* (London: Sheed & Ward, 1983), 7.

50. W. W. Buckland and Peter Stein, *A Textbook of Roman Law from Augustus to Justinian* (Cambridge: Cambridge University Press, 1966), 188.

51. Quoted in Avila, *Ownership*, 14.

52. Robert Drinan, "Will History Condemn Us for Third World Debt?" *National Catholic Reporter* 28 (January 12, 1990): 19.

53. *Economic Justice for All: Pastoral Letter on Catholic Social Teaching and the U.S. Economy* (Washington, D.C.: U.S. Catholic Conference, 1986), 133, # 274. See www.osjspm.org/cst/eja.htm for the text of this letter.

54. See Graef S. Crystal, "At the Top: An Explosion of Pay Packages," *New York Times Magazine* (December 3, 1989): 25.

55. See James. O. Grunebaum, *Private Ownership* (New York: Routledge & Kegan Paul, 1987), 20–24.

56. Thomas Jefferson, to the Rev. James Madison, October 28, 1785, quoted in Arieli, *Individualism and Nationalism in American Ideology*, 159.

57. Augustine pointed out the implications of calling one's own property "private": "It connotes more a loss than an increase. For all privation is diminution" (*De Gen.* 11.15, in *Patrologia Latina* 34:436).

58. Plato, *Timaeus* 28c.

59. M. Douglas Meeks, "God as Economist and the Problem of Property," *Occasional Papers* 21 (Collegeville, Minn.: Institute for Ecumenical and Cultural Research, 1984), 2. See M. Douglas Meeks, *God the Economist: The Doctrine of God and Political Economy* (Minneapolis: Fortress Press, 1989). See also Lawrence Becker, *Property Rights: Philosophic Foundations* (Boston: Routledge & Kegan Paul, 1977); and Virginia Held, ed., *Property, Profits and Economic Justice* (Belmont, Calif.: Wadsworth, 1980).

60. C. B. MacPherson, *The Political Theory of Possessive Individualism: Hobbes to Locke* (Oxford: Clarendon, 1962), 1.

61. Maggie Thatcher, quoted in Richard Hoggart, *The Way We Live Now* (London: Chatto and Windis, 1995), 1

62. MacPherson, *The Political Theory of Possessive Individualism,* 3.

63. Ibid. See also 263–77.

64. C. B. MacPherson, "Property as Means or End," in *Theories of Property: Aristotle to the Present,* ed. Anthony Parel and Thomas Flanagan, (Calgary: Wilfred Laurier University Press, 1979), 3.

65. Ibid., 8. In the western tradition, from ancient to medieval times, from Aristotle to Augustine to Aquinas, property was justified as a means to some ethical end.

66. For a discussion of the relationship of rights and needs in the context of a theory of social justice, see David Hollenbach, *Claims in Conflict: Retrieving and Renewing the Catholic Human Rights Tradition* (New York: Paulist, 1979). See also Joe Holland and Peter Henriot, *Social Analysis: Linking Faith and Justice* (Maryknoll, N.Y.: Orbis, 1983).

67. Owensby, *Economics for Prophets,* 3.

68. See Daniel C. Maguire, *A Case for Affirmative Action* (Dubuque, Iowa: Shepherd, 1992). On a significant development of justice theory, see Norman J. Paulhus, *The Theological and Political Ideals of the Fribourg Union* (Ann Arbor, Mich.: University Microfilms, 1985).

69. John Chrysostom, *Oportet Haereses,* in *Patrologia Graeca* 51:255.

70. Avila, *Ownership,* 3.

71. Richard Hofstadter's phrase in *The American Political Tradition and the Men Who Made It* (New York: Vintage, 1954), vii.

72. Paul Samuelson, *Economics,* 8th ed. (New York: McGraw-Hill, 1970), 250.

73. Johnson, *Sharing Possessions,* 89.

74. Abraham Heschel, *A Passion for Truth* (New York: Farrar, Straus and Giroux, 1973), 259.

75. Ibid., 175.

76. Johnson, *Sharing Possessions,* 21–23.

77. John Chrysostom, *In Act. Apost.* 11.3.

78. Justin, *Apologetics (Apologia)* 1.14.

79. R. H. Charles, ed., *Apocrypha and Pseudepigrapha of the Old Testament* (Oxford: Clarendon, 1913), 3:767, 883–84.

80. Heschel, *Passion for Truth,* 175.

81. Ibid., 177.

82. See 1 QSX and *Damascus Rule* 6.15.

83. John Chrysostom, *In Inscrip.* 1.2.

84. Augustine, *De Nab. Jes.* 14–15.

85. Johnson, *Sharing Possessions,* 46.

86. William Greider, *Secrets of the Temple: How the Federal Reserve Runs the Country* (New York: Simon & Schuster, 1987), 230.

87. David Loy, "The Religion of the Market," in *Visions of a New Earth: Religious Perspectives on Population, Consumption, and Ecology,* ed. Harold Coward and Daniel C. Maguire (Albany: SUNY Press, 2000), 15–16.

88. Ibid.

89. Thomas Settle, "The Ground of Morals and the Propriety of Property," in *Theories of Property: Aristotle to the Present,* ed. Anthony Parel and Thomas Flanagan (Calgary: Wilfred Laurier University Press, 1979), 331.

90. Meeks, "God as Economist," 3.

91. I am grateful to Walter Owensby for this; see *Economics for Prophets,* xvii.

92. Reuters, "Relief Agency Criticizes Rich Lands," *New York Times,* A12, December 6, 2004. Sweden, Norway, Denmark, the Netherlands, and Luxembourg have reached the U.N. proposal of 0.7 %. As of this writing, the United States, "the stingiest of all" the G-7 wealthy nations, is locked at 1.8% with no announced plans to change that. *New York Times,* April 14, 2005, A30, editorial. The Oxfam report is called "Paying the Price: Why Rich Countries Must Invest Now in a War on Poverty." The Oxfam press release at http://www.oxfam.org/eng/pr041206_MDG.htm includes a link to a PDF version of the report. On children's deaths due to poverty-related causes, see Clive Ponting, *A Green History of the World* (New York: Penguin Books, 1995), 254.

93. "Today children are the largest single group among the poor" (*Economic Justice for All,* 8). See Jonathan Kozol, *Rachel and Her Children: Homeless Families in America* (New York: Crown, 1988).

94. See Leonard Goodwin, *Causes and Cures of Welfare: New Evidence on the Social Psychology of the Poor* (Lexington, Mass.: Lexington, 1983), chap. 1. See also Leonard Goodwin, "Can Workfare Work?" *Public Welfare* 39 (Fall 1981): 19–25.

95. George Gilder, *Wealth and Poverty* (New York: Basic, 1981), 313.

96. Elisabeth Schüssler Fiorenza, *In Memory of Her: A Feminist Theological Reconstruction of Christian Origins* (New York: Crossroad, 1983), 123.

97. The hope for a "new temple" in Jewish literature was never just a hope for a prettier building and cultic reforms. It was tied to hopes for "new heavens and the new earth" (Isa. 66:22) that the victory of *tsedaqah* would bring about. See E. P. Sanders, *Jesus and Judaism* (Philadelphia: Fortress Press, 1985), 77–90.

98. Mott, *Biblical Ethics and Social Change,* 98.

99. Sanders, *Jesus and Judaism,* 294–318.

100. See Mott, *Biblical Ethics and Social Change,* 4–6, 98–100.

101. C. H. Dodd, *The Johannine Epistles* (London: Hodder & Stoughton, 1946), 42–44.

102. See Paul Savoy, "Time for a Second Bill of Rights," *The Nation* 252, no. 23 (June 17, 1991): 797, 814–16.

103. Quoted in Owensby, *Economics for Prophets,* 77.

104. Aristotle, *Politics* 1265b.

105. On this, the biblical view squares with the Buddhist view, which sees full employment as a basic postulate of humane economics. See E. F. Schumacher, *Small Is Beautiful* (San Francisco: Harper & Row, 1973), 53–61.

106. See Leonard Goodwin, *Do the Poor Want to Work? A Social-Psychological Study of Work Orientations* (Washington, D.C.: Brookings Institution, 1972), ix, 7–8, 81, 112, 117; and Goodwin's *Causes and Cures of Welfare.* Goodwin attacks the unsupported myth that the poor do not want to work: "The data that do exist indicate the [Aid to Families with Dependent Children] recipients are as committed to supporting their families through work as are regularly employed persons" (*Causes and Cures of Welfare,* 7). See also Daniel C. Maguire, *A New American Justice: Ending the White Male Monopolies* (New York: Doubleday, 1980).

107. Joint Economics Committee, *Thirtieth Anniversary of the Employment Act of 1946—A National Conference on Full Employment* (Washington, D.C.: Government Printing Office, 1976), 276. See also Gar Alperovitz, "Planning for Sustained Community," in *Catholic Social Teaching and the United States Economy,* ed. John W. Houck and Oliver F. Williams (Washington, D.C.: University Press of America, 1984), 331–58.

CHAPTER FIVE

1. J. Glenn Gray, *The Warriors: Reflections on Men in Battle* (New York: Harper & Row, 1959), 204.

2. Gustavo Gutiérrez, *A Theology of Liberation* (Maryknoll, N.Y.: Orbis, 1973), 32.

3. Walter Brueggemann, *The Prophetic Imagination* (Minneapolis: Fortress Press, 1989), 13.

4. Speaking of the Gospels as prophetic documents, in *Naming the Powers: The Language of Power in the New Testament,* Walter Wink says: "Fidelity to the gospel lies not in repeating its slogans, but in plunging the prevailing idolatries into its corrosive acids" (Minneapolis: Fortress Press, 1984), 111.

5. Martin Buber, *The Prophetic Faith* (San Francisco: Harper & Row, 1960), 110.

6. S. Ranulf, *The Jealousy of the Gods and the Criminal Law at Athens* (London: Williams & Norgate, 1934), 1:20.

7. Ralph Linton, "The Problem of Universal Values," in *Method and Perspective in Anthropology: Papers in Honor of Wilson D. Wallis,* ed. Robert F. Spencer (Minneapolis: University of Minnesota Press, 1954), 157.

8. Robert J. Bonner and Gertrude Smith, *The Administration of Justice from Homer to Aristotle* (Chicago: University of Chicago Press, 1930), 16.

9. Robert L. Heilbroner, *An Inquiry into the Human Prospect* (New York: Norton, 1975), 15.

10. Ibid., 112.

11. Abraham J. Heschel, *The Prophets* (Philadelphia: Jewish Publication Society of America, 1962), 314.

12. Buber, *The Prophetic Faith,* 106.

13. George Arthur Buttrick, ed., *Interpreter's Dictionary of the Bible* (New York: Abingdon, 1962), 3:896.

14. Bruce J. Malina, *The Social Gospel of Jesus: The Kingdom of God in Mediterranean Perspective* (Minneapolis: Fortress Press, 2000), 149.

15. See ibid. The term *prophet* had a complex history in Israel, and often was extended to include eccentrics and charlatans. In the midst of this confusion, however, there emerged a rich development of this form of social criticism.

16. Heschel, *The Prophets,* xiii.

17. Ibid., 9.

18. Heilbroner, *An Inquiry into the Human Prospect,* 170.

19. Heschel, *The Prophets,* 57–58. See also Buber, *The Prophetic Faith,* 115: "'To know' here does not signify the perception of an object by a subject, but the intimate contact of the two partners of a two-sided occurrence."

20. Henri Bergson, *The Two Sources of Morality and Religion* (Garden City, N.Y.: Doubleday, 1956), 58.

21. This translation is that of Heschel, *The Prophets,* 113. The Revised Standard Version says: "Thou has deceived me . . .; thou art stronger than I." The New English Bible says: "Thou hast duped me . . . thou has outwitted me." Heschel finds the RSV's rendering a "pitiful platitude" and a misunderstanding of the two verbs *patah* and *hazak.*

22. Dag Hammarskjøld, *Markings* (New York: Knopf, 1966), 154.

23. On the power of fear, profit, ideals, and healthy guilt to promote social change, see Daniel C. Maguire, *A New American Justice: Ending the White Male Monopolies* (San Francisco: Harper & Row, 1981), 103–17.

24. Wink, *Naming the Powers,* 111.

25. Thomas Aquinas, *Summa Theologiae* 2-2, q. 158, a. 8, c. The citation is from John Chrysostom, *(Super Mt.)* 1c, n. 7.

26. Thomas Aquinas, *Summa Theologiae* 2-2, q. 158, a. 8, c.

27. Ibid., 2-2, q. 157, a. 2, ad 2.

28. Elisabeth Schüssler Fiorenza, *In Memory of Her: A Feminist Theological Reconstruction of Christian Origins* (New York: Crossroad, 1983), 295–96, 307.

29. Robert Bellah et al., *Habits of the Heart: Individualism and Commitment in American Life* (San Francisco: Harper & Row, 1985), 56.

30. Ralph Waldo Emerson, *Essays and Lectures* (New York: Library of America, 1983), 261–62.

31. To see how all this comes to roost and to see the power of a self-serving bad idea, see Loretta Schwartz-Nobel, *Growing Up Empty: The Hunger Epidemic in America* (New York: Harper Collins, 2002); Herbert J. Gans, *The War Against the Poor: The Underclass and Antipoverty Policy* (New York: Harper Collins, 1995); David K. Shipler, *The Working Poor: Invisible in America* (New York: Knopf, 2004); Barbara Hilkert Andolsen, *The New Job Contract: Economic Justice in an Age of Insecurity* (Cleveland: Pilgrim, 1998); Gloria H. Albrecht, *Hitting Home: Feminist Ethics, Women's Work, and the Betrayal of "Family Values"* (New York: Continuum, 2002); and Jonathan Kozol, *Rachel and Her Children: Homeless Families in America* (New York: Crown, 1988).

32. The words are those of Buber, *The Prophetic Faith,* 3.

33. Norman Gottwald et al., *God and Capitalism: A Prophetic Critique of Market Economy,* ed. J. Mark Thomas and Vernon Visick (Madison, Wisc.: A-R Editions, 1991), 15.

34. Ibid, 14–15.

35. See Buttrick, *Interpreter's Dictionary of the Bible,* 3:909.

36. See David C. Korten, *When Corporations Rule the World* (West Hartford, Conn.: Kumarian, 1995), 321.

37. Quoted in Martin Buber, *Moses: The Revelation and the Covenant* (San Francisco: Harper Torchbooks, 1958), 87.

38. Roland de Vaux, *Ancient Israel* (New York: McGraw-Hill, 1965), 1:113.

39. Buber, *The Prophetic Faith,* 174.

40. See Stephen Charles Mott, *Biblical Ethics and Social Change* (New York: Oxford University Press, 1982), 151. Mott refers to Matt. 22:21.

41. Darryl Schmidt, "Luke's 'Innocent' Jesus: A Scriptural Apologetic," in *Political Issues in Luke-Acts,* ed. Richard Cassidy and Philip Scharper (Maryknoll, N.Y.: Orbis, 1983), 119.

42. Mott, *Biblical Ethics and Social Change,* 151; see Alice Laffey, "Biblical Power and Justice: An Interpretative Experiment," in *Interpreting Tradition,* ed. Jane Kopas (Chico, Calif.: Scholars, 1983), 55–71.

43. Gray, *The Warriors,* 212.

44. Frances Moore Lappé, "The World Food Problem," *Hastings Center Report* 3, no. 5 (November 1973): 11.

45. See Garrett Hardin, "Living on a Lifeboat," *BioScience* 24, no. 10 (October 1974): 565.

46. Paul Harvey, syndicated column, April 1, 1975, quoted in *Worldview* 18, nos. 7–8 (July–August 1975): 8.

47. See Duane Elgin, *Promise Ahead* (New York: William Morrow, 2000), 127.

48. The New English Bible notes: "The prophet probably acted out this verse."

49. Brueggemann, *The Prophetic Imagination,* 102.

50. E. P. Sanders, *Jesus and Judaism* (Philadelphia: Fortress Press, 1985), 289, 293, 317.

51. See Douglas N. Walton, *Courage: A Philosophical Investigation* (Berkeley: University of California Press, 1985). Walton concedes: "Generally, the subject appears to have been neglected in moral philosophy."

52. See Rosemary Radford Ruether, "Courage as a Christian Virtue," *Cross Currents* 33 (Spring 1983): 8–16.

53. Plato, *Laws (Laches)* 190e ff.

54. Thomas Aquinas, *Summa Theologiae* 2-2, q. 123, a. 2. Thomas says that courage (*fortitudo*) is in a sense the precondition of any virtue because it implies the commitment of will that is identical with moral goodness. His *"fortitudo"* is not the perfect equivalent of our "courage," but the main elements of our "courage" are there.

55. Oscar Wilde, "The Critic as Artist," in *Complete Works of Oscar Wilde* (Glasgow: Collins, 1973), 1058.

56. Michel Foucault, *Power/Knowledge: Selected Interviews and Other Writings, 1972–1977,* ed. Colin Gordon, trans. Colin Gordon et al. (New York: Pantheon, 1980), 81.

57. Abraham Heschel, *A Passion for Truth* (New York: Farrar, Straus and Giroux, 1973), 205.

58. Buber, *The Prophetic Faith,* 171–72.

CHAPTER SIX

1. Pinchas Lapide, *The Sermon on the Mount: Utopia or Program for Action?* (Maryknoll, N.Y.: Orbis, 1986), 35. A brilliant and timely effort to put this biblical challenge into practice is contained in Glen Stassen, *Just Peacemaking: Ten Practices for Abolishing War* (Cleveland: Pilgrim, 1998).

2. Erich Fromm, *The Anatomy of Human Destructiveness* (New York: Holt, Rinehart and Winston, 1973), 105.

3. Ibid.

4. Abraham J. Heschel, *The Prophets* (Philadelphia: Jewish Publication Society of America, 1962), 166.

5. See Heschel, *The Prophets,* 173.

6. Walter Brueggemann, *Revelation and Violence: A Study in Contextualization* (Milwaukee: Marquette University Press, 1986), 25–26.

7. See Norman K. Gottwald, *The Tribes of Yahweh: A Sociology of the Religion of Liberated Israel, 1250–1050 B.C.E.* (Maryknoll, N.Y.: Orbis, 1979), 543. Gottwald observes that there is a different attitude in Israel regarding horses because they are war animals. It was considered reprehensible to kill other animals without just cause.

8. The United States Catholic bishops' pastoral letter on war and peace, *The Challenge of Peace: God's Promise and Our Response* (Washington, D.C.: U.S. Catholic Conference, 1983), gives a number of essential criteria for a just war. If a strict construction of just war is used, as it must be in such a mortal matter, all war, and certainly modern war, would seem excluded even by this imperfect tool. In view of that, it was astonishing to see Catholic theologians like Bryan Hehir and John Langan use just-war thinking to justify the first undeclared Gulf War. Given the existent alternatives to violence that were already in place (the international boy-cott of the single product of Iraq), given the indiscriminate slaughter of hundreds of thousands of troops and civilians that was foreseeable and did happen, given the destruction of the essential medical and nutrition-al infrastructure of the nation, given the huge displacement of peoples, and given the devastation of the ecology, one must wonder how Hehir could oxymoronically call the war after its conclusion "just but unwise," and Langan could confusingly dub it "an imperfectly just war" (*New York Times,* March 17, 1991, E4). Just-war theory, since it rests on the fateful assumption that war can be reasonable, easily becomes court theology, blessing the social killings of Caesar. In the second President Bush's war on Iraq and Afghanistan, Pope John Paul II called it "a defeat for human-ity." Too few Christians joined his protest.

9. Duane Elgin, *Promise Ahead: A Vision of Hope and Action for Humanity's Future* (New York: Harper Collins, 2000), 117.

10. Ibid.

11. See John Howard Yoder, *The Politics of Jesus: Vicit Agnus Noster,* 2nd ed. (Grand Rapids, Mich.: Eerdmans, 1994).

12. Elisabeth Schüssler Fiorenza, *In Memory of Her: A Feminist Theological Reconstruction of Christian Origins* (New York: Crossroad, 1983), 134.

13. Ibid., 135. The reference is to Matt. 11:12.

14. See John Helgeland, Robert J. Daly, and J. Patout Burns, *Christians and the Military: The Early Experience,* ed. Robert J. Daly (Philadelphia: Fortress Press, 1985), 1. The authors in this study are painstakingly concerned not to overstate the pacifistic case. Recent scholarship does not support the idea of finding a pure pacifism in the early Jesus movement or in the early Christian churches. See David G. Hunter, "A Decade of Research on Early Christians and Military Service," *Religious Studies Review* 18, no. 2 (April 1992): 87–94. There is an acknowledgment of the inevitable pluralism in thoughtful movements, and, in my language, there is general agreement on the rough birthing of the ideal.

15. See Gerd Theissen, *Biblical Faith: An Evolutionary Approach* (Philadelphia: Fortress Press, 1985), 99.

16. Walter Wink, *Jesus and Nonviolence: A Third Way,* Facets (Minneapolis: Fortress Press, 2003), 1–2.

17. Gene Sharp, *The Politics of Nonviolent Action,* editorial assistance by Marina Finkelstein (Boston: Sargent, 1973). See also Ronald J. Sider and Richard E. Taylor, *Nuclear Holocaust and Christian Hope: A Book for Christian Peacemakers* (Downers Grove, Ill.: InterVarsity, 1982).

18. Wink, *Jesus and Nonviolence,* 52.

19. Karen Armstrong, *The Battle for God: A History of Fundamentalism* (New York: Ballantine, 2001), vi.

20. Ziauddin Sardar and Merryl Wyn Davies, *Why Do People Hate America?* (New York: Disinformation, 2002). The press calls itself "disinformation" to mock the false consolations offered to us by our government and by our journalistic mainstream media.

21. Elgin, *Promise Ahead,* 110.

22. Walter Wink, *Engaging the Powers: Discernment and Resistance in a World of Domination* (Minneapolis: Fortress Press, 1992), 175.

23. Ibid., 175–77.

24. Mahatma Gandhi, in Harijan, March 10, 1946, quoted in Mark Juergensmeyer, *Fighting with Gandhi* (San Francisco: Harper & Row, 1984), 43.

25. Ibid., 178–79.

26. Ibid., 182.

CHAPTER SEVEN

1. Origen, *Against Celsum (Contra Celsus)*, 8, 74.

2. Tertullian, *Idolatry (De Idololatria)*, XIX.

3. Lactantius, *The Divine Institutes (Divinarum institutionum libri)*, VI, xx 15–16.

4. Quoted from the Ethiopian version of the canons by Stanley Windass, *Christianity Versus Violence* (London: Sheed and Ward, 1964), 12. A catechumen is a person who is in the process of being educated about Christianity in order to be baptized and become a Christian.

5. Arnobius, *Against Nations (Adversus nationes)*, I, 6.

6. Roland H. Bainton, *Christian Attitudes toward War and Peace; A Historical Survey and Critical Re-evaluation* (New York: Abingdon, 1960), 73.

7. Eusebius, *Life of Constantine (Vita Constantini)*, 1, 24.

8. Lactantius, *The Divine Institutes (Divinarum institutionum libri)*, VII, 26.

9. Theodoret, *Hist. Eccl.* II, 26.

10. Theodosian, *Code (De Caritate)*, XVI, X. 21.

11. Augustine, *Epist.*138 ii 14.

12. See *Dictionaire de Theologie Catholique*, vol. 6, col. 1920.

13. Quoted in Bainton, *Christian Attitudes Toward War and Peace,* 110.

14. Windass, *Christianity Versus Violence*, 43.

15. Calvini Opera, in *Corpus Reformatorum,* VIII, 476; XXIV, 360: XLIV, 346.

16. See Daniel C. Maguire, *The New Subversives: Anti-Americanism of the Religious Right* (New York: Continuum, 1982).

17. Clyde Prestowitz, *Rogue Nation: American Unilateralism and the Failure of Good Intentions* (New York: Basic, 2003), 26.

18. See www.dissentmagazine.org/archive/fa01/reed.shtml.

19. For ongoing information on the irrationally inflated military budget and its effects, see *The Defense Monitor: The Newsletter of the Center for Defense Information* (see www.cdi.org and look in the newsletter section).

20. See Daniel C. Maguire, ed., *Sacred Rights: The Case for Contraception and Abortion in World Religions* (New York: Oxford University Press, 2003).

21. See the prescient work of Seymour Melman, *The Defense Economy: Conversion of Industries and Occupations to Civilian Needs* (New York: Praeger, 1970). In a lifetime of publishing Melman has scored the American commitment to what could accurately be called military socialism. See also Alan F. Geyer, *The Idea of Disarmament: Rethinking the Unthinkable* (Elgin, Ill.: Brethren, 1982).

22. Howard Zinn, "Dying for the Government," *The Progressive* 67, no. 5 (June 2003): 17.

23. Justice William O. Douglas, quoted in Robert Previdi, "America's Path to

War," *The Long Term View* 6, no. 2 (2004): 92.

24. Previdi, "America's Path to War," 92.
25. James Madison, quoted in Previdi, "America's Path to War," 104.
26. Senator Sam J. Ervin, quoted in Previdi, "America's Path to War," 97.

CHAPTER EIGHT

1. Tertullian, *Apology (Apologeticus),* 14.
2. There is no one Hebrew or Greek word for *truth* that parallels our usage of the term. Many aspects of the truth are brought out as we work through the broad and intricate lexicon of truth.
3. Søren Kierkegaard, *The Sickness unto Death,* in *Fear and Trembling, and the Sickness unto Death,* trans. Walter Lowrie (New York: Doubleday, 1954), 175–76.
4. See George Arthur Buttrick et al., eds., *The Interpreter's Dictionary of the Bible* (New York: Abingdon, 1962), 4:715.
5. Buttrick, *The Interpreter's Dictionary of the Bible,* 4:716.
6. Reinhold Niebuhr, *The Nature and Destiny of Man* (New York: Scribner, 1949), 2:217.
7. Miguel de Unamuno, *The Tragic Sense of Life* (London: Dover, 1921), 90.
8. John Milton, *Milton: Areopagitica,* ed. John W. Hales (Oxford: Clarendon, 1904), 38–39.
9. Francis Bacon, *Novum Organum* 49.
10. Juan Luis Segundo, *The Liberation of Theology,* trans. John Drury (Maryknoll, N.Y.: Orbis, 1976), 8. This is one of the key insights of liberation theology.
11. To see how Orwell's imagining of controlling truth ministries is not fiction but realistic social psychology, see Ben H. Bagdikian, *The Media Monopoly,* 2nd ed. (Boston: Beacon, 1987). Bagdikian is the paramount critic of truth ministries that function in publishing and journalism.
12. Quoted in Arthur Koestler, *The Act of Creation* (New York: Dell, 1967), 142.
13. See Michael Polanyi, *Personal Knowledge: Towards a Post-Critical Philosophy* (Chicago: University of Chicago Press, 1962), 138, 274–75.
14. Rollo May, *Love and Will* (New York: Norton, 1969), 226.
15.. In chapter 13 of *The Moral Choice* (Garden City, N.Y.: Doubleday, 1978), I trace some of the principal "hazards of moral discourse," including myth, ideology, cognitive mood, false analogues, demonic abstractions, selective vision, role control, and banalization.
16. Leonard Goodwin, *Do the Poor Want to Work? A Social-Psychological Study of Work Orientations* (Washington, D.C.: Brookings Institution, 1972), 112.

17. See Daniel C. Maguire, *A New American Justice: Ending the White Male Monopolies* (San Francisco: Harper & Row, 1980), 137.

18. See Stephen G. Ray Jr., *Do No Harm: Social Sin and Christian Responsibility* (Minneapolis: Fortress Press, 2003).

19. J. Glenn Gray, *The Warriors: Reflections on Men in Battle* (New York: Harper Torchbooks, 1967), 20.

20. Jean Sulivan, *Eternity, My Beloved* (St. Paul, Minn: River Boat, 1998), 9.

21. Eibhear Walshe, "The Irish-American in Anglo-Irish Literature," *Studies* 77 (Summer 1988): 233.

22. Sulivan, *Eternity, My Beloved,* 92.

CHAPTER NINE

1. For references to Hegel's thought on this, see Walter Kasper, *The Christian Understanding of Freedom and the History of Freedom in the Modern Era: The Meeting and Confrontation between Christianity and the Modern Era in a Postmodern Situation* (Milwaukee: Marquette University Press, 1988), 5–6, 26, 52n10.

2. See Elaine Pagels, *Adam, Eve, and the Serpent* (New York: Random House, 1988).

3. Kasper, *The Christian Understanding,* 13.

4. M. Douglas Meeks, "God as Economist and the Problem of Property," *Occasional Papers,* no. 21 (Collegeville, Minn.: Institute for Ecumenical and Cultural Research, 1984), 5.

5. For a penetrating study of the relationship of freedom, justice, and love in the context of commitments, see Margaret A. Farley, *Personal Commitments: Making, Keeping, Breaking* (San Francisco: Harper & Row, 1986).

6. Norman K. Gottwald et al., *God and Capitalism: A Prophetic Critique of Market Economy,* ed. J. Mark Thomas and Vernon Visick (Madison, Wisc.: A-R Editions, 1991), 14.

7. Walter Brueggemann, *The Prophetic Imagination* (Philadelphia: Fortress Press, 1978), 97.

8. Luke Timothy Johnson, *Sharing Possessions: Mandate and Symbol of Faith* (Philadelphia: Fortress Press, 1981), 9.

9. This can also be translated as "human slaves" or "the slaves of men."

10. See Allen Verhey, *The Great Reversal: Ethics and the New Testament* (Grand Rapids, Mich.: Eerdmans, 1984), 114–15.

11. Martin Buber, *The Prophetic Faith* (San Francisco: Harper Torchbooks, 1960), 174.

12. Pagels, *Adam, Eve, and the Serpent,* 98.

13. Gregory of Nyssa, *(De Hominis Opificio)* 4.1; 16.11.

14. Quoted in H. Frankfort et al., eds., *The Intellectual Adventure of Ancient Man; An Essay on Speculative Thought in the Ancient Near East* (Chicago: University of Chicago Press, 1946), 203.

15. Quoted in Franklin La Van Baumer, *The Early Tudor Theory of Kingship* (New York: Russell & Russell, 1966), 86.

16. Ibid.

17. See Elaine Pagels, *Beyond Belief: The Secret Gospel of Thomas* (New York: Random House, 2003), 138.

18. Minucius Felix, *Octavius* 37.

19. Tertullian, *Apology (Apologeticus)* 28.1 (emphasis added).

20. John Chrysostom, *Homily on the Letter to the Ephesians (Homiliae in epistolam ad Ephesios)* 11.15-16.

21. To see how the notion of freedom prospered in the African American setting, see Peter J. Paris, *The Social Teaching of the Black Churches* (Philadelphia: Fortress Press, 1985).

22. For a sorry example of how this freedom was lost in much of the Roman Catholic academic world, see Charles E. Curran, *Catholic Higher Education, Theology, and Academic Freedom* (Notre Dame, Ind.: Notre Dame University Press, 1990). Curran, a well-respected scholar, was hounded out of his tenured professorship by the Vatican and then effectively shunned by the rest of the American Catholic academe. This occurred after the Vatican Council II paid verbal tribute to the ancient idea of religious liberty. For more hopeful prospects in the intellectually vigorous Irish church, see A. Alan Falconer, Enda McDonagh, and Sean MacReamoinn, eds., *Freedom to Hope? The Catholic Church in Ireland Twenty Years after Vatican II* (Dublin: Columba, 1985).

23. Mary Elizabeth Hobgood, *Dismantling Privilege: An Ethics of Accountablity* (Cleveland: Pilgrim, 2000), 82.

24. Ibid., 94.

25. Abraham Heschel, *"The Earth Is the Lord's; and "The Sabbath"* (New York: Harper & Row, 1962), 8, in *The Sabbath* (New York: Farrar, Straus, Giroux, 1975).

26. Israel may have transformed the Babylonian *sabbatu,* or evil day on which work was to be avoided since it was presumed foredoomed by evil. See Nel Noddings, *Women and Evil* (Berkeley: University of California Press, 1989), 38–39. See also Gloria Albrecht, *Hitting Home:*

27. See ibid., 13.

28. Aristotle, *Nichomachean Ethics* 10.6.1176b.

29. Mikilta de-Rabbi Shimeon ben Yohai, quoted in Heschel, *The Sabbath,* 28.

30. See Heschel, *The Sabbath,* 22-23.

31. For excellent insights into the value and changing meaning of work, see John C. Raines, "Capital, Community, and the Meaning of Work," in *The Public Vocation of Christian Ethics,* ed. Beverly W. Harrison, Robert L. Stivers,and Ronald H. Stone (New York: Pilgrim, 1986), 211–22.

CHAPTER TEN

1. Robin Morgan, "Peony," in *Depth Perception: New Poems and a Masque* (Garden City, N.Y.: Doubleday, 1982), 13–15.

2. Pinchas Lapide, *The Sermon on the Mount: Utopia or Program for Action?* (Maryknoll, N.Y.: Orbis, 1986), 7.

3. John Macquarrie, *Christian Hope* (New York: Crossroad, 1978), 31.

4. Sophocles, *Antigone* 1337.

5. E. P. Sanders, *Jesus and Judaism* (Philadelphia: Fortress Press, 1985), 267.

6. See Macquarrie, *Christian Hope,* 33, 35.

7. Ibid., 37.

8. Walter Brueggemann, *The Prophetic Imagination* (Philadelphia: Fortress Press, 1978), 45.

9. Erich Fromm, *The Revolution of Hope: Toward a Humanized Technology* (New York: Bantam, 1968), 19.

10. Ibid., 18.

11. Macquarrie, *Christian Hope,* 50.

12. Gregory of Nyssa, *(Vita Moysi)* 2.239.315.

13. Israel's major symbol of hope may be found in its myths of creation. The hope lies in the belief that creation is not an accident, but the primeval miracle that continues in history through the providence of a living God. Creation myths abounded in the religions of the Near East, but Israel's took a different tack. Gerhard von Rad says this consisted of its theological linkage of creation and salvation history (see Gerhard von Rad, *Old Testament Theology,* trans. D. M. G. Stalker [New York: Harper, 1962], 1:136).

14. Macquarrie, *Christian Hope,* 4.

15. Origen, *Against Celsus (Contra Celsum)* 4.68.

16. A. E.Taylor, *The Faith of a Moralist: Gifford Lectures Delivered in the University of St. Andrews, 1926–1928* (London: Macmillan, 1937), 1:68.

17. Ibid.

18. The term is *oikonomous,* meaning an administrator, literally someone who rules a household. See Franciscus Zorell, *Lexicon Graecum Novi Testamenti* (Paris: Lethielleux, 1931), col. 902.

19. Thomas Aquinas, *Summa Theologiae* 1–2, q. 91, a. 2. "The rational creature

is under divine providence in a certain more excellent way inasmuch as it is a participant of providence, providing both for itself and others" (translation mine).

20. Obviously, this can be abused. Reverence for the Earth can be diminished if the "take-charge" mentality forgets that it exists under the mandate to will what God wills, the flourishing of all terrestrial life. Lynn White rang out an indictment of biblical influence in "The Historical Roots of Our Ecologic Crisis," *Science* 155 (1967): 1203.

21. Elie Wiesel, *Night* (New York: Bantam, 1982), 31.

22. Gabriel Marcel, *The Philosophy of Existentialism* (New York: Citadel, 1964), 33.

23. I defend the morality of doing this in certain circumstances in my book *Death by Choice,* 2nd ed. (Garden City, N.Y.: Doubleday, 1984).

24. On the association of hope with youth, see Aquinas, *Summa Theologiae* 1–2, q. 40, a. 6.

25. Ibid.

26. Ibid., 2–2, q. 17, a. 1.

27. Macquarrie, *Christian Hope,* 6.

28. William F. Lynch, *Images of Hope: Imagination as Healer of the Hopeless* (New York: New American Library, 1965), 37.

29. Aquinas, *Summa Theologiae* 2–2, q. 129, a. 4, ad 3; Aristotle, *Nichomachean Ethics* 4.2. Aristotle describes the virtue more narrowly, relegating it to the decorous use of large sums of money. Aquinas does not limit the discussion to the pecuniary.

30. Aquinas, *Summa Theologiae* 2–2, q. 129, a.1.

31. Ibid., 2–2, q. 129, a.5.

32. Josef Pieper, *On Hope* (San Francisco: Ignatius, 1986), 28.

33. Jürgen Moltmann, *Hope and Planning,* trans. Margaret Clarkson (London: SCM, 1971), 178.

34. See Daniel C. Maguire, *The Moral Choice* (San Francisco: Harper & Row, 1979), 430–32.

35. Andre Dumas, "The Ideological Factor in the West," in *The Church amid Revolution,* ed. Harvey G. Cox (New York: Association, 1967), 208–9.

36. Maguire, *The Moral Choice,* 409–32. Myth, in this sense, is not an indulgence in unrealism, but may be the very highest form of reality contact. Myth helps us reach to the "not yet" which is out there awaiting us.

37. H. Richard Niebuhr, *The Responsible Self* (New York: Harper & Row, 1963), 165–66.

38. Rosemary Radford Ruether, *The Radical Kingdom: The Western Experience of Messianic Hope* (New York: Harper & Row, 1970), 141.

39. Thomas L. Friedman, *The Lexus and the Olive Tree* (New York: Anchor,

2000), 14.

40. David C. Korten, *When Corporations Rule the World* (West Hartford, Conn.: Kumarian, 1995), 303.

41. Ibid., 302.

42. Macquarrie, *Christian Hope,* 16.

43. Schubert M. Ogden, *The Reality of God, and Other Essays* (New York: Harper & Row, 1966), 34, 37.

44. Edward O. Wilson, *The Future of Life* (New York: Knopf, 2002), 189.

CHAPTER ELEVEN

1. Friedrich Nietzsche, *Gesammelte Werke* (Musarion edition), 16:373, quoted in Abraham J. Heschel, *The Prophets* (Philadelphia: Jewish Publication Society of America, 1962), 258.

2. Heschel, *The Prophets,* 191n 3.

3. See the attacks on "stubbornness of heart" and "hardness of heart" (Deut. 29:18; Lam. 3:65). There is a richness of terms to make the point: "brazen-faced and stiff-hearted" (Ezek. 2:4); "stubborn of heart" (Isa. 46:12); "uncircumcised in the heart" (Jer. 9:26). See also: Jer. 9:23; Ps. 119:70; Isa. 42:20; 48:8; Prov. 28:14; 29:1; and Ps. 106:7.

4. Robert L. Heilbroner, *An Inquiry into the Human Prospect* (New York: Norton, 1974), 22.

5. See Robert N. Bellah et al., *Habits of the Heart: Individualism and Commitment in American Life* (New York: Harper & Row, 1985).

6. Interview by Elizabeth Kolbert, "Annals of Science," *New Yorker*, May 9, 2005.

7. Henri Bergson, *The Two Sources of Morality and Religion,* trans. R. Ashley Audra and Cloudesly Brereton with the assistance of W. Horsfall Carter (Garden City, N.Y.: Doubleday, 1956), 40.

8. "You have learned that they were told, 'Love your neighbor, hate your enemy'" (Matt. 5:43). Significantly, this mandate to hate your enemy is actually in neither the Hebrew Bible nor Pharisaic or rabbinic Judaism. Indeed, openness to the alien, who was often presumed an enemy, is the clear position in all of this literature.

9. Stephen Charles Mott, *Biblical Ethics and Social Change* (New York: Oxford University Press, 1982), 44.

10. Gerd Theissen, *Biblical Faith: An Evolutionary Approach* (Philadelphia: Fortress Press, 1985), 154.

11. Ibid., 79. Obviously there is a loss when God loses Asherah, but our symbols cannot do everything at once.

12. Ibid., 80.

13. Ibid. For an excellent study of the family and its relationship to the great-er community, see Robert Shelton, *Loving Relationships: Self, Others, and God* (Elgin, Ill.: Brethren, 1987).

14. Elaine Pagels, *Adam, Eve, and the Serpent* (New York: Random House, 1988), 15.

15. See John Koenig, *New Testament Hospitality: Partnership with Strangers as Promise and Mission* (Philadelphia: Fortress Press, 1985).

16. On "entertains," see Albert Nolan, *Jesus before Christianity* (Maryknoll, N.Y.: Orbis, 1978), 144n3.

17. See Allen Verhey, *The Great Reversal: Ethics and the New Testament* (Grand Rapids, Mich.: Eerdmans, 1984), 24–25.

18. Pinchas Lapide, *The Sermon on the Mount: Utopia, or Program for Action* (Maryknoll, N.Y.: Orbis, 1986), 79–80.

19. Epictetus, *Diatribai (Dissertationes)* 3.22.54.

20. Quoted in Theissen, *Biblical Faith,* 183n31. See Karl Jaspers, "The Axial Period," in *The Origin and Goal of History,* trans. Michael Bullock (New Haven, Conn.: Yale University Press, 1953), chap. 1. The axial period, Jaspers says, is between 800 and 200 B.C.E. when the original "enlighten-ment" took place in various ways in China, India, Iran, Palestine, and Greece. The extraordinary events in understanding took place "almost simultaneously in China, India, and the West, without any one of these regions knowing of the others," (2).

21. Aristotle, *Politics* 1253.20.

22. Hannah Arendt, *The Human Condition* (Garden City, N.Y.: Doubleday, 1959), 287–88.

23. Quoted in Heschel, *The Prophets,* 14.

24. Martin Buber, *I and Thou* (New York: Scribner, 1958), 8.

25. As Bruce J. Malina says, "Even John the Baptist knew God could make children of Abraham from stones (Matt. 3:9; Luke 3:8)" (*The Social Gospel of Jesus: The Kingdom of God in Mediterranean Perspective* [Minneapolis: Fortress Press, 2000], 136). The universalist thrust moved outside ethnic limits.

26. Buber, *I and Thou,* Ibid., 11.

27. Richard Dawkins, *The Selfish Gene* (Oxford: Oxford University Press, 1976), 215.

28. The collectivistic biblical mind-set where group interests are keenly felt is hard to comprehend in an individualistic society like that of the modern United States. The estimate is that 70 to 80 percent of societies are collectivistic while only some 30 percent are, like the United States, individualistic. Thus, "what is most important in the United States—in-dividualism—is of the least importance to the rest of the cultures of the world" (Malina, *The Social Gospel of Jesus,* 124).

29. Immanuel Levinas points out how erotic love does not achieve this full-ness of sociality (see *Totality and Infinity; An Essay on Exteriority*, trans. Alphonso Lingis [Pittsburgh: Duquesne University Press, 1969]). Erotic love can, of course, be wholesome and can lead to a bonding that in-creases the confidence and social conscience of the loving couple. See Lisa Sowle Cahill, *Between the Sexes: Foundations for a Christian Ethics of Sexuality* (Philadelphia: Fortress Press, 1985).

30. C. E. B. Cranfield, "Love," in *A Theological Wordbook of the Bible,* ed. Alan Richardson (New York: Macmillan, 1962), 133.

31. Ibid., 134.

32. It is interesting, as Rudolph Schnackenburg writes, that "apart from the great commandment Jesus nowhere spoke explicitly about loving God" (*The Moral Teaching of the New Testament* [New York: Herder & Herder, 1968], 98).

33. See Jose Porfirio Miranda, *Marx and the Bible: A Critique of the Philosophy of Oppression* (Maryknoll, N.Y.: Orbis, 1974), 99–103.

34. See the section on "The Guilt of Apathy" in chapter 5 above.

35. On essential needs, see Daniel C. Maguire, *A New American Justice* (N.Y.: Doubleday, 1980), 60–66.

36. Quoted in Miranda, *Marx and the Bible,* 62.

37. Ibid.

38. Aristotle, *Nichomachean Ethics* 1155a.

39. Pierre Bigo, *La Doctrine Sociale de l'Eglise* (Paris: Presses Universitaires de France, 1965), 378.

40. Thomas W. Ogletree, *Hospitality to the Stranger: Dimensions of Moral Understanding* (Philadelphia: Fortress Press, 1985), 35.

41. Arendt, *Human Condition,* 214–15.

42. Ibid.

43. Ibid. 216.

44. J. Glenn Gray, *The Warriors: Reflections on Men in Battle* (New York: Harper Torchbooks, 1967), 184–85.

45. Levinas, *Totality and Infinity,* 47. See Plato, *Gorgias* 469c. See also the first two books of *The Republic.*

46. Albert Camus, *Resistance, Rebellion, and Death,* trans. Justin O'Brien (New York: Knopf, 1969), 114.

47. Gray, *The Warriors,* 186.

48. Vladimir Solovyev, *The Meaning of Love* (London: Geoffrey Bles, 1945), 59.

49. Gregory Baum, *The Priority of Labor: A Commentary on "Laborem exercens," Encyclical Letter of Pope John Paul II* (Ramsey, N.J.: Paulist, 1982), 40.

50. Aristotle, *Nichomachean Ethics* 1158b, 1159a.

51. Baum, *The Priority of Labor,* 38.

52. Mary E. Hunt enriches the theology of friendship with feminist experience and insight in her *Fierce Tenderness: A Feminist Theology of Friendship* (New York: Crossroad, 1991).

53. Michael Harrington, *The Politics at God's Funeral: The Spiritual Crisis of Western Civilization* (New York: Penguin, 1985), 10.

54. See Solovyev, *The Meaning of Love,* 5–12.

55. Erich Fromm, *The Art of Loving: An Enquiry into the Nature of Love* (New York: Harper Colophon, 1962), 27.

56. Ibid., 26.

57. Ibid., 27.

58. Thomas Aquinas, *Summa Theologiae* 1–2, q. 28, a. 2.

59. Ibid., 1–2, q. 28, a. 1, a. 5. Things that are frozen, says Thomas, remain "constricted in themselves" (*in seipsis constricta*). This freezing and hardness of the heart are repugnant to love (1–2, a. 5). In a. 1, Thomas insists that healthy love does not blur our identities, but enhances them.

CHAPTER TWELVE

1. *Qiddushin* 66d, quoted in William E. Phipps, *Was Jesus Married? The Distortion of Sexuality in the Christian Tradition* (New York: Harper & Row, 1970), 16.

2. Erich Fromm, *Psychoanalysis and Religion* (New Haven, Conn.: Yale University Press, 1950), 37.

3. Ibid.

4. Rudolph Schnackenburg, *The Moral Teaching of the New Testament* (New York: Herder & Herder, 1968), 32.

5. Abraham Heschel, *A Passion for Truth* (New York: Farrar, Straus and Giroux, 1986), 51–52.

6. Michael Landmann, "Melancholies of Fulfillment," in *Concilium* 95: *The Theology of Joy,* ed. J. B. Metz and J. Jossua (New York: Herder & Herder, 1974), 32.

7. Ministers, as Edward Schillebeeckx writes, "are those who bring joy" (*Ministry: Leadership in the Community of Jesus Christ* [New York: Crossroad, 1984], 33).

8. The compatibility of suffering and joy was much developed in Christianity following the early Christians' reconciliation of the suffering death of Jesus with the joy of the reign. See Acts 5:41; Rom. 5:3; 2 Cor. 12:9; and Phil. 1:29.

9. Heschel, *A Passion for Truth,* 284.

10. See Phipps, *Was Jesus Married?,* 23–24.

11. E. P. Sanders, *Jesus and Judaism* (Philadelphia: Fortress Press, 1985), 208.

12. See Albert Nolan, *Jesus before Christianity* (Maryknoll, N.Y.: Orbis, 1978), 38.

13. Ibid.

14. Joseph A. Grassi, *God Makes Me Laugh: A New Approach to Luke* (Wilmington, Del.: Michael Glazier, 1986), 35.

15. In the kingdom of God, people will feast at table with their forebears, eating and drinking with Abraham, Isaac, and Jacob. See Matt. 8:11-12 and Luke 13:28-29. See Richard H. Hiers, *Jesus and the Future: Unresolved Questions for Understanding and Faith* (Atlanta: John Knox, 1981), 72–86.

16. See Grassi, *God Makes Me Laugh*, 20.

17. "Round Dance of the Cross" in *Acts of John* 94.1-4, quoted in Elaine Pagels, *Beyond Belief: The Secret Gospel of Thomas* (New York: Random House, 2003), 122–23.

18. *Apocalypse of Peter* 81.10—82.15.

19. Ibid., 133. Luke presents a small group of disciples putting on this event. If, as Matthew has it, "the whole city went wild" on the occasion, one would expect, as Grassi says, some Roman reaction.

20. See chapter 5 above.

21. See Harvey Cox, *Feast of Fools: A Theological Essay on Festivity and Fantasy* (New York: Harper & Row, 1969), 169. Cox entitles this chapter "Christ the Harlequin."

22. Grassi, *God Makes Me Laugh*, 8.

23. As Ivan Illich says, "Poets and clowns have always risen up against the oppression of creative thought by dogma. They expose literal-mindedness with metaphor" (*Tools for Conviviality* [San Francisco: Harper & Row, 1973], 60–61).

24. On the role of comedy in ethics, see Daniel C. Maguire, "The Comic and the Tragic in Ethics," in *The Moral Choice* (San Francisco: Harper & Row, 1979), chap. 11. I also discuss there the strange, intimate relationship of the comic and the tragic.

25. For a theologian's example of appreciating nature, see Ian G. Barbour, ed., *Earth Might Be Fair: Reflections on Ethics, Religion, and Ecology* (Englewood Cliffs, N.J.: Prentice-Hall, 1972); see especially the chapter by William G. Pollard, "The Uniqueness of the Earth," 82–99.

26. Walter Sullivan, *We Are Not Alone: The Search for Intelligent Life on Other Worlds* (New York: New American Library, 1966), 245.

27. The New English Bible translates *nepiois* as "the simple." The word, which comes from the root *epos*, "infant," means a very small child: "an infant and a child of very young age" *(infans et parvulus tenerae aetatis)*. See Franciscus Zorell, *Lexicon Graecum Novi Testamenti* (Paris: Lethielleux,

1931), col. 870. Albert Nolan notes the possibility that if the Aramaic word behind this is *sabra*, it might even refer to children with developmental disabilities (*Jesus before Christianity*, 145n10).

28. See Elisabeth Schüssler Fiorenza, *In Memory of Her: A Feminist Theological Reconstruction of Christian Origins* (New York: Crossroad, 1983), 265. For an overview of the transformation of perceptions of children in early Christianity see O. M. Bakke, *When Children Became People: The Birth of Childhood in Early Christianity* (Minneapolis: Fortress Press, 2005).

29. On the idea of being "childed" alongside the idea of being "parented," see Maureen Green, *Fathering* (New York: McGraw-Hill, 1976), 159; and Gabriel Moran, *Religious Education Development: Images for the Future* (San Francisco: Harper & Row, 1983), 180.

30. Moran, *Religious Education Development,* 177.

31. Kieran Egan, *Educational Development* (New York: Oxford University Press, 1979), 159.

32. Michael Polanyi, *Personal Knowledge: Towards a Post-Critical Philosophy* (Chicago: University of Chicago Press, 1962), 198.

33. Ibid., 199.

34. Quoted in ibid.

35. See Penny Lernoux, *Cry of the People: The Struggle for Human Rights in Latin America* (New York: Penguin, 1982), 62.

36. Grassi, *God Makes Me Laugh,* 126.

37. On abstractions as a hazard of moral discourse, see Maguire, *The Moral Choice,* 442–43.

38. A. Norman Jeffares, ed., *Yeats's Poems* (London: Gill and Macmillan, 1989) 109.

CONCLUSION

1. Hannah Arendt, *The Human Condition* (Garden City, N.Y.: Doubleday, 1959), 29.

2. Karl Marx and Friedrich Engels, *Marx and Engels: Selected Works in Two Volumes* (Moscow: Foreign Languages, 1958), 1:137–38.

3. V. I. Lenin, *State and Revolution* (New York: International, 1932), 38.

4. Elaine Pagels, *Adam, Eve, and the Serpent* (New York: Random House, 1988), xxiii–xxiv.

5. Henri Bergson, *The Two Sources of Morality and Religion* (Garden City, N.Y.: Doubleday, 1956), 78.

6. See Peter J. Paris, *The Social Teaching of the Black Churches* (Philadelphia: Fortress Press, 1985); and Eugene D. Genovese, *Roll, Jordan, Roll: The World the Slaves Made* (New York: Pantheon, 1974).

7. Garry Wills, "Faith and the Race of God and Country," *Sojourners* 15 (March 14, 1988): 4–5.

8. Norman Gottwald, "From Tribal Existence to Empire: The Socio-Historical Context for the Rise of the Hebrew Prophets," in *God and Capitalism: A Prophetic Critique of Market Economy,* ed. J. Mark Thomas and Vernon Visick (Madison, Wisc.: A-R Editions, 1991), 19.

INDEX OF NAMES AND SUBJECTS

INDEX OF SCRIPTURE